D0512757

xreet
uropean
xford Graduate
maker

YOUNG
&
INDECISIVE

219
WILL I
OU IN I

SIT

OMFORT ASSURED

I CAN GO ON ALL NIGHT

W

DISCIPLINE REQUIRED

WESTMINSTER TUBE,
2 MINUTES

THE
VILLAGE?

"LET ME SHOW YOU THE ROPES"

I WILL DO EVERYTHING
I'M TOLD

WILL YOU SUBMIT

07 219 5

PEN LATE

Usual Channel
*BIG BEN

YTHM METHO

ERY 15 MINS

V1)

X      X

# The Rebels:
## How Blair Mislaid His Majority

## Philip Cowley

POLITICO'S

First published in 2005
Politico's Publishing, an imprint of
Methuen Publishing Limited
11–12 Buckingham Gate
London
SW1E 6LB

10 9 8 7 6 5 4 3 2 1

Typeset by SX Composing DTP, Rayleigh, Essex
Printed and bound in Great Britain by Bookmarque Ltd, Croydon,
Surrey

Methuen Publishing Limited Reg. No. 3543167

A CIP catalogue record for this book is available from the British
Library.

ISBN 1 84275 127 1

Behold, how good and how pleasant it is for brethren to dwell together in unity! – Psalms 133:1

To Scoob

# Contents

# Preface

Think not those faithful who praise all thy words and actions, but those who kindly reprove thy faults. – Socrates

This book is (at least in part) a sequel to *Revolts and Rebellions* (Politico's, 2002), which examined the voting behaviour of MPs during Tony Blair's first term as Prime Minister. It is for readers and reviewers to decide whether it is a sequel in the mould of *The Godfather*, one that is better than the original, or whether perhaps it owes more to *Police Academy*, beginning badly and going downhill thereafter.

Shortly after that book came out, I hawked myself around TV and radio studios in an (ultimately futile) attempt to flog a few extra copies. I found that the thought that MPs voted the party line as a result of anything other than cowardice or self-interest was greeted with looks of sheer incredulity. The case for cohesion was simply ignored. The idea that MPs were getting concessions out of ministers behind the scenes was just dismissed. Prior to recording one interview on the subject, I spent an hour briefing a local TV station, hammering home the message that 'they' were not sheep. When I got to the TV studio, I found that they had prepared a graphic to accompany the interview filled with pictures of – you've guessed it – sheep. It was a moment that tested your moral courage. Do you walk out, refusing to be party to such a travesty? Or do you continue with the interview, hoping that you will sell a few extra copies of the book as a result?

Those who know me will be in no doubt as to what I did.

Halfway through its launch party, and amidst gallons of rotgut wine, one Conservative MP – himself no slave to the party whips – told me that it would 'never be possible to write a book like that again'. His complaint was the way that Parliament had been reformed ('modernised') since the election of the Blair government; Parliament was dead, he declared. Labour had killed it and as a result nobody cared how MPs voted. Another guest, a long-serving Labour MP, scolded me for being far too positive about the government whips. 'They like your book because it makes them look as if they have a difficult job to do. They don't. Their job's really easy.' Within a year, the Commons was voting on whether to go to war in Iraq, and both predictions looked somewhat ridiculous. Parliament clearly wasn't dead. People did care how MPs voted. And whatever else you said about the whips, no one was going round saying that they had an easy life. This book attempts to explain how we got from those sheep and the 'death of Parliament' to the point where Blair faced some of the most rebellious backbenchers of the postwar era.

This book draws on over a hundred interviews with Labour MPs. It is customary to accuse today's MPs of being shut off, cosseted and aloof. Yet one of the paradoxes of modern British politics is that we currently have the most accessible parliamentarians we've ever had – and probably the most professional and hard-working, too – and yet we hold them in lower esteem than ever before. Despite the ever-increasing demands on them, nearly all of the MPs I approached were incredibly generous with their time. They included rebels (a phrase many of them hate), loyalists (a phrase many of them hate), whips, special advisers, ministers, ex-ministers, would-be ministers, and ex-would-be ministers. Most of the interviews were conducted at Westminster (at one point I felt as if I had been in the Pugin Room more often than Pugin), with a handful carried out on the phone. A further 120

MPs responded to various queries by post, and there was also countless email correspondence. In one or two places, but especially in Chapter 3, I also draw on around 80 interviews with Labour MPs conducted during the 1997–2001 parliament. Interviewees were guaranteed anonymity (a condition I have broken only with their agreement) and so it's not possible to thank them all by name; some of their identities will be obvious in the following pages, and the rest know who they are. I hope they realise how very grateful I am for the help they gave during the writing of this book.

I'm also grateful to the various audiences on whom I've forced bits of this book in recent years, and who (in return) forced me to think about various issues afresh. They've included audiences of school pupils, journalists, MPs, peers, teachers, civil servants, academics, party activists, parliamentary clerks and researchers, and (just occasionally) interested members of the public. One thing these talks taught me: however prestigious the audience, it's always the rudest jokes that get the biggest laughs.

This book does not contain a full list of the 200-plus rebellions by Labour MPs that occurred during the 2001 parliament. The major revolts are listed in Appendix 3, and a full list is available for free from the website that accompanies this research – www.revolts.co.uk – as a report entitled 'Dissension amongst the Parliamentary Labour Party, 2001–2005'. That document lists every single revolt, every single rebel, and gives full breakdowns by subject, along with overall figures for every Labour MP who rebelled. Similar (albeit shorter) papers are also available from the website on Liberal Democrat and Conservative dissent.

So as not to clutter up the text, I've used as few footnotes as I think I can get away with. The majority of the unsourced quotations in the book come from interviews with MPs – and since they are anonymous, there's little point in providing footnotes which merely say 'Interview with MP'. Ditto for 'Private information', a vaguely meaningless phrase which usually just means 'something someone's told me'. All labels – 'a whip', 'a backbencher', 'a minister' – refer to an MP's status at the time of the interview. Some have since left the Commons; many others have changed jobs. Many of the whips that spoke to me, for example, are no longer whipping. A minority of the quotes come from media sources or Hansard, the official record of parliamentary debates. I've also eschewed footnotes here, except in specific circumstances. There's not much point in providing Hansard references (if you want to find the source of a quote, type it into the parliamentary website's search engine, and you'll have it in seconds). I've also only provided references to various media outlets (newspapers, websites, etc.) where a specific article is referred to. My last book had 87 footnotes in the first sixteen pages, and was criticised for being oversourced. This time the criticism will doubtless be that there are not enough references. That's life.

There is one other way in which this book is different from its predecessor. *Revolts and Rebellions* was lucky enough to win the Political Studies Association's award for the best political science book published in 2002. It was packed full of tables of statistics about legislative behaviour – statistics which meant that the Political Studies Association liked it but which gained it a couple of stinker reviews ('Dense statistics' – *Tribune*). This is a very different book, and so there are relatively few stats in what follows. Legislative anoraks need not despair: I have every intention of boring the pants off people with more dense statistics in the future – there are plenty of data still to be examined – but this is the not the place. With luck, what this book lacks in correlation coefficients it makes up for with accessibility and readability. That's the plan, anyway.

The book was completed with financial support from the Economic and Social Research Council, who enabled me to employ research assistance, and pay for travel and other associated expenses. It also benefited from initial support from the University of Nottingham's Research Strategy Fund. Most of the research was undertaken whilst I was based in the School of Politics at the University of Nottingham – as collegiate a place as exists anywhere in British academia – whilst much of the actual writing was done during a visiting spell at the London School of Economics. The former paid my salary, kept me in food and drink, and gave me time off to write; the latter gave me a desk and demanded nothing in return. Right at the end of the process, the Hansard Society also provided me with a desk and some company. I am grateful to them all.

The reader should be warned that there is – at least for a book on a subject like this – a relatively high swear count in what follows. Just like (almost) everybody else, MPs occasionally say rude words. Faced with a choice between leaving these words in any quotes, and thus running the risk of offending people, or instead bowdlerising them and making our parliamentarians sound like Mr Cholmondley-Warner, I've gone (with one exception) for the authenticity of the former.

The more back-breaking research for this book was carried out by Mark Stuart, in between moonlighting as the late John Smith's authorised biographer. As always, Mark was an exceptional researcher, who provided me with far more material than I could use or than his job entailed. I also draw briefly on two excellent pieces of student work which were sent to me: a dissertation on the 2001 intake from Ruth Greenwood, then at the University of Hull, and a dissertation on the 2001 parliament from Bronwen Noble, then at the University of York. For commenting on drafts, I'm grateful to Matthew Bailey, Sarah Childs, Mary Cowley, Clare Ettinghausen, Gemma Rosenblatt, Matthew Seward, Mark Stuart and Nathan Yeowell as well as many MPs who read parts of the manuscript but who would rather remain anonymous. Whilst I am hugely indebted to them for their help, the usual disclaimer applies: all errors of fact or interpretation are mine and mine alone.

The cover was designed with customary flair and imagination by

Andy Platt (andy@ilovefizzypop.co.uk). This was merely the latest in a series of projects where Andy's done all the work and I've merely ponced about issuing instructions. Long may that continue! Julian Glover suggested the subtitle, which was both better than my own idea ('How Labour MPs Stopped Worrying and Learnt to Ignore the Whip' – too smartypants for its own good) or the one initially suggested by the publishers ('When Labour MPs Go Bad' – far too ITV, darling). I'm grateful to John Schwartz (formerly at Politico's) for having the enthusiasm to commission a book on the 2001 parliament, and to Emma Musgrave (also formerly at Politico's) for forcing me (eventually) to deliver the manuscript in return for which I had taken the publisher's silver. Emma's steely mixture of barely concealed contempt and disappointment at yet another missed deadline can rouse you from your slumbers and get you to the keyboard like nothing else known to man.

For its author, this book has been a partial form of therapy, an antidote to all those occasions on which I've shouted at the radio or TV or thrown down the newspaper in disgust, in response to some ill-informed and submoronic comment about Parliament and MPs. It is only a partial refutation of the conventional wisdom – that MPs are hopeless, and that things are not half as good as they used to be – but it is, I hope, at least a first step.

# 1

# Fings ain't wot they used t'be

*Dispelling some myths – Why MPs still matter – The whips' initial goal*

> Honest differences of views and honest debate are not disunity. They are the vital process of policy-making among free men. – US President Herbert Hoover

The days of the independent-minded MPs who populated the House of Commons in the 1940s and 1950s are now, sadly, long gone. Back then we had politicians who were prepared to stand up to the government and to their whips, to tell them exactly what they could do with hastily made or poorly thought-through legislation. In their place we now have serried ranks of tame, compliant career politicians, who have precious little experience of the real world as it exists outside of the rarefied atmosphere of Westminster and Whitehall, and none of whom will speak their minds for fear of damaging their progress up what Disraeli called the greasy pole. The result has been a fearful tightening of party discipline. Gutless and feeble, today's politicians are too willing to do what their political masters tell them; terrified to follow their own consciences for fear of what might happen to them, they can be led by the nose to vote for almost anything put before them. It would be simpler and more economical to keep a flock of tame sheep and from time to time to drive them through the division lobbies in the appropriate numbers.

Whilst writing this book, I lost count of the number of times I saw letters published in the correspondence columns of supposedly serious newspapers arguing something like this. It is all received wisdom, trotted out whenever anyone wants to criticise the quality of British politicians or Westminster or British democracy in general. Yet like so much received wisdom, it is almost entirely wrong. Nearly every sentence in the above paragraph is incorrect. Indeed, it is not just that the sentences are incorrect. Nearly every sentence in the above paragraph is the precise opposite of the reality.

The only bit that's true is that there has indeed been a rise in the so-called 'career politician' in recent years. MPs *are* now more likely to see politics as their main profession and to come into the Commons without having done a substantial 'proper' (by which is meant non-political) job beforehand, although there are still plenty of MPs for whom this cannot be said. But the effect of the rise of the career politician has not been, as is so often claimed, to induce loyalty to the party. Rather, the reverse. The rise of the career politician has coincided with a *revival* in backbench independence, not a decline, with the result that British MPs in recent years have become *more* rebellious and independent-minded, not less.

Backbench cohesion in Britain was at its peak in the 1950s and early 1960s when the Commons was full of all those supposedly 'independent-minded' MPs. Indeed, the comparison to sheep found in the first paragraph is lifted word for word from *Can Parliament Survive?*, a book written by the Conservative MP Christopher Hollis, and published not in 2005, but in 1946. There were two sessions in the 1950s – two whole years – in which not a single Conservative MP defied their party whip even once. Every division in the House of Commons in those two years – all 407 of them – saw complete unanimity amongst the government's backbenchers. Today's whips would be green with envy at the thought of such behaviour. Similarly, in the 25 years between 1945 and 1970, there was not a single government defeat in the House of Commons caused by MPs defying their party whips. (The handful of defeats that did occur were caused by poor organisation on the part of the whips or as a result of tactical manoeuvres by the opposition.) The nineteenth-century French politician and writer Charles, Comte de Remusat once declared that unanimity was 'almost always an indication of servitude' and, by that definition, MPs in the 1950s were servile to excess. Backbench cohesion began to weaken in the late 1960s and 1970s, at exactly the same point as those much-derided career politicians began to enter Westminster in such numbers.

One group of politicians who grew particularly used to being dismissed as ineffectual were the Labour MPs elected en masse in 1997. After Labour's first landslide, they got used to being described as timid, sycophantic, acquiescent and cowardly. They acquired a reputation for excessive cohesion, mindless loyalty and a distinct lack of backbone. As well as sheep, they were regularly compared to poodles, clones, robots or – most bizarrely of all – daleks. Singled out for especially acidic criticism were the newly elected Labour women, elected in then record numbers in 1997, and who were said to be particularly loyal. They were compared to the Stepford Wives – although the Conservative MP Ann Widdecombe complained that the comparison was unfair to the Stepford Wives. The charge laid against most previous Labour leaders was that they were not in control of their party; after 1997 the complaint was that the leadership was too much in control.

But during Labour's second term in office a transformation appeared to come over the Parliamentary Labour Party (PLP). Almost overnight it appeared to develop some attitude and some backbone. In the first four years of the Blair government Labour MPs acquired an unenviable reputation for asking patsy questions to Tony Blair during Prime Minister's Questions (PMQs), in what occasionally became a cringe-making competition in sycophancy. It wasn't that Labour MPs were the first to do this – the practice had been rife under the Conservatives, many of whose MPs could toady with the best of them – yet Labour MPs certainly took the practice to new lows. But on 4 July 2001, during one of the first PMQs of the new parliament, things suddenly seemed very different. A Prime Minister who had just delivered a second consecutive landslide election result for the first time in his party's history might have expected a relatively easy ride from his MPs: a smidgen of praise perhaps, some soft-ball congratulatory questions, a few pats on the back. Instead he got a remarkably assertive series of questions – several of which appeared to leave him taken aback by their ferocity. David Winnick and Dennis Skinner both challenged the proposed changes to incapacity benefit, Skinner describing the govern-ment's previous benefit reforms as 'not the brightest thing my Right Hon. Friend did', and Chris Mullin launched a full-on assault on US foreign policy, including what he called the 'madcap' missile defence scheme. Simon Hoggart, parliamentary sketch-writer for the *Guardian*, said it was 'as if all those wretched soldiers in the trenches of the Somme had climbed out to tell General Haig that the time had come to rethink his strategy. Or just sod off.' Another journalist jokingly described it as 'Day One of the Intifada'.

The troops continued mutinying throughout the parliament. More than a hundred Labour backbenchers joined forces to block a government attempt to dump two occasionally trouble-some select committee chairmen, Gwyneth Dunwoody and Donald Anderson. May 2002 saw the government forced to back down over its plans for Lords reform in the face of backbench pressure – pressure which included a rumbustious private meeting of the PLP at which the then Lord Chancellor, Lord Irvine, was given a good going over by Labour MPs. And then there were the record-breaking rebellions over Iraq, foundation hospitals, and student top-up fees. The rebellions in 2003 over the introduction of foundation hospitals broke the record for the largest health policy rebellion ever by Labour MPs against their own government. In 2004 the 72 Labour votes against the second reading of the Higher Education Bill, the Bill that introduced top-up fees, was precisely double what had until 2001 been the largest education rebellion ever by Labour MPs. And the rebellions over Iraq – the largest of which, in March 2003, saw 139 Labour MPs vote against their whip – were larger than any previous foreign policy or defence rebellion against a Labour government. Indeed, the Iraq revolts were the largest rebellions by MPs of any governing party – Labour, Conservative or Liberal – on any type of policy for over 150 years. To find a larger backbench revolt than Iraq, you have to go back to the middle of the nineteenth century, when the franchise was enjoyed by just 5 per cent of the population, and before anything which even vaguely resembled today's political parties had been formed. In 1846, Sir Robert Peel saw two-thirds of Conservative MPs vote against their own administration's plans for repeal of the Corn Laws, with just a third backing him in the division lobbies. But since then, since the beginnings of modern British politics in other words, there had been nothing to match the Iraq revolts.

And those were just the best-known backbench revolts. In the four years after 2001 there were also rebellions over anti-terrorism legislation (repeatedly), community health councils, smacking, asylum and immigration (again, repeatedly), faith schools, living wills, trial by jury, gambling, the fire-fighters, the Housing Bill, organ donation, the Enterprise Bill, the European constitution, ID cards, and banning incitement to religious hatred. On top of those, there were a multitude of smaller, more isolated, revolts, sometimes consisting of a lone MP, sometimes seeing just a handful of rebels go through the division lobbies in defiance of their whips.

'It's now a rebellion a week,' complained a whip midway through the parliament (although it was, in fact, more like two a week). Collectively, these rebellions involved more than 200 Labour MPs, rebelling on 259 separate occasions, more than in any other postwar parliament save that between October 1974 and 1979. But the Wilson/Callaghan government of 1974–79 lasted five years, whereas the second Blair government covered just four. Measured as a percentage of the divisions (votes) to occur in the parliament, the period from 2001 to 2005 tops the postwar lists. Labour backbenchers rebelled in 20.8 per cent of votes, a higher rate of rebellion than in any other parliament since 1945.

So instead of complaining about sheep, the media's focus after 2001 shifted onto the extent to which Labour MPs were now willing to defy their leadership. These are just a handful of newspaper headlines, taken semi-randomly, from the 2001 parliament:

'Army of Labour rebels grows' (*Guardian*)
'Party in a panic over growing band of rebels' (*Daily Telegraph*)
'Blair may be held hostage by rebels who cannot lose' (*The Times*)
'What can Mr Blair do about all his revolting backbenchers?' (*Independent*)
'Will the poodles bite Blair?' (*The Times*)
'Blair battered by rising tide of rebellion from back benches' (*Independent*)
'Rebellious MPs control make-or-break moment' (*The Times*)
'Blair mauled by own MPs' (*Sun*)
'Mood of revolt spreads as Labour backbenchers cast aside slavish loyalty' (*Guardian*)

As Peter Oborne pointed out in the *Spectator* in 2004, with the government struggling to enact its proposals for the funding of higher education: 'Tony Blair has achieved the impossible. Three years after winning a landslide majority of 160, he is forced to conduct his business as if he were leader of a minority government.' It was, Oborne concluded, 'a failure of party management on a heroic scale'.[1]

One of the aims of this book is to explain this transformation. How had a group of politicians routinely dismissed as second rate and cowardly become so rebellious? It was certainly not because of any change in personnel. Only a handful of seats changed hands in the standstill election of 2001 and so 85 per cent of the Commons was the same after the 2001 election as it had been before. The people who caused so much trouble in the four years after 2001 were almost exactly the same ones who had been dismissed as sheep for the preceding four years. Why were they so acquiescent before, yet so rebellious after 2001? What had happened? How had Tony Blair managed to mislay a majority of over 160?

★ ★ ★

Another of the standard criticisms frequently made about Westminster's politicians is that they demonstrate a high level of party discipline compared to parliaments in other democracies. And so, critics argue, whilst they may well be more rebellious today than British MPs of yesteryear, they are still pretty feeble in comparison with those in other parliaments.

The evidence for this is always the US Congress, which is known for its extremely low levels of party cohesion, and where even the most rebellious of British MPs would seem like a spineless toady. But the US Congress is an atypical legislature, like almost no other parliament in the world, and it witnesses atypical behaviour (although note that cohesion is increasing even on Capitol Hill). Comparing Westminster with the US Congress is a pointless exercise. It's like comparing normal sexual activity to that seen in the movies – you are just bound to be disappointed. If, however, you compare the British House of Commons with the comparable chambers of most western European parliaments, you soon see that there is nothing exceptional about Westminster at all. In fact, compared to the parliaments in several European countries – such as Belgium, Portugal and most of Scandinavia – the Commons sees relatively low levels of cohesion. Several don't allow for any backbench dissent at all, with the party leaders casting votes on behalf of the entire party.[2] Give British whips the chance of such power and they'd grab it hungrily with both hands and heartfelt whoops of joy.

Similarly ignorant are all those claims that Parliament has become an irrelevance, a body which merely rubber-stamps decisions made by the executive. For all the talk of the decline of Parliament – which has in fact been an ever-present complaint of the last hundred or so years, not some invention of the last eight – the way MPs behave in Parliament remains important. Of course, the impact MPs have on the majority of policy decisions is usually limited. The 'first-past-the-post' electoral system used for Westminster elections usually generates exaggerated majorities for the governing party, which, when coupled with high levels (in absolute terms) of cohesion within the parliamentary parties, means that it is extremely rare for governments to see their legislative proposals defeated within Parliament; even minor amendments are very unlikely to be passed unless supported by the government.

This, though, is hardly new. Parliament has been of marginal importance in the making of policy in the UK for over a century now, and there is relatively little evidence – as distinct from assertion – that it has less impact on policy now compared with, say, 40, 50 or 60 years ago. As the academic writer Hugh Berrington has shown, even the so-called Golden Age of Parliament in the mid-nineteenth century was not quite as brilliant as traditionally thought. 'The consequences of back-bench independence', Berrington wrote, 'have been grossly exaggerated by some commentators.'[3] It was in 1882 that W. S. Gilbert wrote in *Iolanthe* perhaps the most famous dismissal of party behaviour:

When in that house MPs divide
If they've a brain and cerebellum, too
They've got to leave that brain outside
And vote just as their leaders tell 'em to.

Four years before that, in *HMS Pinafore*, Gilbert had produced the equally scathing 'I always voted at my party's call | And I never thought of thinking for myself at all'. By the end of the nineteenth century, party votes – those in which 90 per cent or more of the members of one party vote one way, facing 90 per cent or more of the members of the other principal party – were the norm in the Commons.[4] Blaming any of today's politicians for this is about as sensible as blaming them for the loss of the American colonies.

The second mistake made by those who dismiss Westminster is to assume that marginal or sporadic influence on policy is the same as no influence. MPs may not *make* policy, but they do constrain (and occasionally prod) government. All but the most technical of decisions are affected by some considerations of party management. John Major was forced to tack and trim for the entire five years from 1992 to 1997, most obviously over Europe, where his freedom of manoeuvre was limited by Conservative Eurosceptic MPs, but also in a range of other areas where the government withdrew or modified policies in the face of parliamentary opposition. The same has been true of almost all recent governments. Even Major's predecessor, despite her image as a stern and unbending premier and despite enjoying very large majorities for most of her time in No. 10, was also often willing to make concessions to her backbench MPs, in order to get her policies through. In the 1970s, Edward Heath, Harold Wilson and James Callaghan were all repeatedly forced by their own backbenchers to withdraw or amend policy. And as Ronald Butt's magisterial 1967 work *The Power of Parliament* showed, this was merely the continuation of a long tradition of backbenchers managing to influence government through overt or covert pressure.[5] Even with a majority of a hundred, for example, Harold Macmillan was continually worrying about the behaviour of his MPs.

Even if Parliament usually plays a limited role in policy-making, there are issues where its role is far more significant – so-called free votes, those on which the party managers do not provide instructions for their MPs. Since Labour was elected in

1997 there has been a regular procession of high-profile free votes coming before the Commons, covering such topics as embryo research, capital punishment, euthanasia, gun control – and, most obviously of all since 1997, the two Hs: homosexuality and hunting. Here, the executive remains (ostensibly) neutral and the issues are left to parliamentarians to decide. As a result, rather than being peripheral, the legislature, and the legislators within it, becomes central. The formulation of British public policy as a whole may be post-parliamentary but when dealing with issues of conscience it remains firmly parliamentary.

MPs also matter for symbolic reasons. Who cares if Joe Bloggs, Labour Party member, moans about the things that the government is doing (at times it appears that Labour Party members are never happier than when moaning about the things that the government are doing)? But if Joe Bloggs MP says something that deviates from the party line, then that is something else entirely. It is a 'split', in which Bloggs is inevitably presented as 'slamming' the government. Few members of the British media follow US President Herbert Hoover's injunction that 'honest differences of views and honest debate are not disunity. They are the vital process of policy-making among free men.' Deviations from the party line are instead always pounced upon as evidence of disunity. This too had been clear for much of Major's premiership: the media focused with a searing intensity on the divisions within his parliamentary party, and the term 'Conservative Party unity' became an oxymoron. The Conservatives lost their reputation for unity (a reputation they had long enjoyed), with the blame for this laid squarely at the feet of the party's MPs and their behaviour. This was a lesson many of the incoming Labour MPs took to heart; the claim made by a Labour whip in 2002 that 'other than policy failure, the most damaging thing that can happen to any British government is division and disunity' was a sentiment shared by many of his backbench colleagues. Parties that want to appear united need their MPs to appear united.

But the easiest retort to those who argue that Parliament – and especially the Commons – doesn't matter any more is to look at all the effort that goes into trying to ensure that MPs vote together and that rebellions are limited. The various activities of the Whips' Office – which are discussed at length in the following chapters – are not proof of a disregard for Parliament, but of a concern on the part of the party hierarchy about the behaviour of its MPs. Take, for example, the various procedural shenanigans that whips occasionally employ in order to avoid a vote, or when they otherwise attempt to minimise expressions of dissent by swamping the debate with pro-government speakers. Ditto for when the whips try to apply pressure to an MP, stressing the damage that a rebellious vote might do to his or her career. However unpleasant these tactics might appear to slightly naïve, namby-pamby purists, they are all evidence of a belief by the whips that they *need* to minimise the appearance of division.

Just look at the amount of effort that went in to trying to win votes in the 2001 parliament. One of the striking features of the events recounted in this book is the amount of sheer hard work that was put in – by whips and ministers, going right up to the Prime Minister – into winning key votes. For a government that is widely believed to think Parliament an irrelevance, the Blair government went (and still goes) to great lengths to prevent rebellions taking place. For a government that supposedly ignores and disdains Parliament, it expends considerable energy trying to keep the visible signs of discontent to a bare minimum. Why persuade, cajole and negotiate (and, just occasionally, trick and bully) if you do not care? Another of the aims of this book, then, is to try to counter some of these myths – and to explain a bit of the reality behind what goes on in Parliament. Those who like their politics like a Jerry Bruckheimer film – full of goodies and baddies – will probably not like this book.

As Labour is the current party of government the book largely focuses on Labour MPs, although there are appendices detailing rebellions by Conservative and Liberal Democrat MPs, and most of the book's arguments were equally true of the Conservatives when they were in power. The next chapter (Chapter 2) explains some of the motivations for rebellion and for loyalty. Just as it is simply not true that MPs today are less independent than they used to be, it is also not true that MPs only vote their party line because they are too frightened to do otherwise. Nor is there some easy distinction between loyalist MPs (scaredy-cats) and rebels (bravehearts). Furthermore, it is untrue that when the government wins votes it does so because the whips employ thumb-screws and bribery to bully MPs into voting for things that they otherwise would reject out of hand. Chapter 3 provides some of the main backbench revolts from Blair's first term between 1997 and 2001 – when Labour MPs gained their reputation for excessive loyalty. The following five chapters (Chapters 4 to 8) provide examples from the second term. The aim is not to provide details of every rebellion during the Parliament (given the frequency with which Labour MPs were defying the whip between 2001 and 2005, such a book would be at least twice the size of this one) but instead to focus on the key examples. The chapters on the 2001 Parliament are broadly chronological, beginning in Chapter 4 with the dispute over select committee nominations in 2001, and ending in Chapter 8 with the Prevention of Terrorism Bill. After each chapter there is a short free-standing section examining particular individuals or groups of rebels – such as the first ever Labour rebel, the most rebellious, the ex-ministers, the much derided women from the 1997 intake, and the 2001 intake.

This book doesn't assume too much knowledge about parliamentary procedure or practice – but it does assume that the reader knows the basic stages that a Bill goes through in the Commons before becoming law (second reading, to committee, to report stage, to third reading), and that Bills go through both the Commons and the Lords. The Lords cannot block Bills indefinitely, but – as will become clear throughout the book – it is becoming increasingly obstructive. And the tendency for controversial Bills to ping-pong between Commons and Lords provides yet more opportunities for backbenchers to stick their oar in. For those unfamiliar with parliamentary terms, a simple glossary is provided in Appendix 1.

★ ★ ★

The assumption made within the government Whips' Office shortly after the 2001 election was that the size of the government's majority meant that it should be able to make it through the four years of the Parliament without being defeated on a whipped vote. The whips anticipated difficulties with one or two proposals, but none of these problems appeared insurmountable. They knew that things were going to be tougher than they had been in the first Blair term, but they were still confident that with enough work and the right approach they would reach the end of the Parliament without suffering a defeat. They therefore attempted an ambitious longer-term strategy: to look ahead to Labour's third term. The goal of the second term should be to nurture good relationships with backbenchers and to prevent the habit of rebellion from becoming too widespread, so that if Labour managed to win a third term – with what they assumed would be a reduced majority – the whips would have credit in the bank with Labour backbenchers, which they could then use to get legislation through, even with that smaller majority.

It didn't work. Instead of constraining it, the events of the 2001 Parliament made backbench rebellion a relatively common-place activity – one engaged in by the majority of Labour MPs, and one which few backbenchers had not taken part in at some point. Unfortunately for the whips, the rebellions didn't involve the same old same old, rebelling over and over again. As the Parliament progressed, and as rebellion followed rebellion, so the rebel cause gathered new recruits. At the beginning of the 2001 Parliament, there were 111 Labour MPs sitting on the government benches who had rebelled against the Blair government during its first term. Four years later, as the Parliament came to a close, that number had more than doubled, to 229. It was not exactly what the whips had been aiming for. Asked in 2005 whether he thought their strategy had been a success, one whip replied (with a laugh), 'I'm not sure it worked,' adding that what he called 'the threshold of rebellion' had been crossed by most Labour MPs.

The bit that the Whips' Office got right, of course, was that Labour did then win a third term and with a much reduced majority. Labour lost 47 seats in the election of May 2005, and the government saw its majority fall to 66.[6] Historically, this is not a particularly small majority; of the full-length Parliaments after 1945, it is larger than the majority enjoyed by Churchill in 1951, Eden in 1955, Heath in 1970, Thatcher in 1979 or Major in 1992; those involved in the Wilson/Callaghan government of October 1974–1979, which limped on for five years either with a majority in single figures or no majority at all, would have sold their souls for a majority of 66. But for a government which has occasionally struggled to get its legislation through with a majority of over 160, 66 seems a worryingly small figure. Instead of requiring over 80 rebellious MPs to defeat the government, it now requires fewer than 40.[7] And even after the retirements and defeats of the 2005 election, there are plenty of Labour backbenchers who defied the government repeatedly until 2005, and who are odds on to do so again during Labour's third term.

The government therefore began the 2005 Parliament knowing that it was in for a much tougher time in the Commons – exactly what the whips had been aiming to avoid when the 2001 Parliament had started, and what most observers in the 1997 Parliament, when all the sheep and clone references were so common, would have thought impossible. The final aim of this book, therefore, is to look ahead (in Chapter 9) to Labour's third, and most difficult, term. Can Tony Blair govern with a majority this small? And can Gordon Brown – Blair's most likely successor as Prime Minister – manage any better?

This, then, is the story of how a parliamentary party routinely dismissed as feeble and hopeless has now become one of the government's biggest headaches. It is the story of how Blair mislaid his majority.

# Herbert Dunnico and Dennis Skinner

No previous Labour Prime Minister would have been particularly surprised to discover a Labour government facing difficulties with its backbenchers. They would have thought it all pretty much par for the course. From Ramsay MacDonald onwards, the PLP has not been a tightly disciplined organisation but rather a fractious and troublesome bunch, which soon acquired what police officers call 'form'.

Indeed, it took just nine days from the formation of the first Labour government in 1924 to the point when one of its own MPs voted against it. The first Labour rebel was the Rev. Herbert Dunnico, the MP for Consett, County Durham. It is one of history's little ironies that Dunnico's constituency is largely (though not entirely) the same as the Durham North West constituency of the current Labour Chief Whip, Hilary Armstrong. There are few MPs with Dunnico's background now left in the Commons – not least because we no longer send children down the mines at twelve. Dunnico started work in a factory aged ten, and then went down the pit two years later. Following adult education study at University College Nottingham, he helped found the Free Church Socialist League in 1909 and became secretary of the Peace Society in 1915. He was a Baptist minister, a town and county councillor, and then entered the Commons in November 1922. And on 21 February 1924 – nine days after Parliament resumed – he became the first Labour MP ever to vote against a Labour government. The subject? The MacDonald government's programme of light cruiser construction.

Dunnico's rebellion was merely the first of several revolts that the Labour government of 1924 suffered over defence and foreign affairs (a subject that has caused problems for almost every Labour government since MacDonald's time); there were repeated revolts during the passage of the Army and Air Force (Annual) Bill of 1924, the biggest seeing 68 Labour MPs vote to abolish the death penalty for military offences. The largest rebellion of the 1924 Parliament, though, came over the right of strikers to claim unemployment benefit (benefits, as all Labour's Chief Whips will testify, being another perpetual source of discontent amongst Labour backbenchers); it involved 73 Labour MPs – almost 40 per cent of the PLP.[8]

MacDonald's second government of 1929–1931 similarly struggled against the backdrop of ever-rising levels of unemployment, from 1.5 million at the beginning of 1930 to nearly 2.75 million by the middle of 1931, and the issue that caused most dissent was once again that of unemployment benefit.[9] A string of 39 rebellions took place on one Bill, the Unemployment Insurance (No. 3) Bill, which imposed restrictions on the entitlement to benefit; the legislation became known as the Anomalies Bill, and it was opposed by a determined group of Labour MPs. On 15 July 1931 Labour backbenchers opposed the Bill in more than 30 straight divisions, one after the other, with the first vote held on the Wednesday afternoon at 3.48 p.m., the last the following morning at 9.27 a.m. The debate then adjourned one minute before ten o'clock, with rebel Labour backbenchers having spoken in relays throughout the night.[10]

Up until 1997, each postwar period of Labour government saw more backbench rebellions than its predecessor: 84 between 1945 and 1951, 110 between 1964 and 1970, while the Wilson/Callaghan government of 1974–79 witnessed an astonishing 317 revolts, almost a threefold increase on the preceding period, and almost as many as had occurred in every single previous Labour government combined.

## The 30 most rebellious Labour MPs of all time

| Name | Number of votes against Labour whip in government |
|---|---|
| **Dennis Skinner*** | **273** |
| **Jeremy Corbyn*** | **212** |
| **John McDonnell*** | **194** |
| Ian Mikardo | 163 |
| **Audrey Wise** | **161** |
| **Brian Sedgemore** | **157** |
| **Andrew Bennett** | **151** |
| Russell Kerr | 144 |
| **Lynne Jones*** | **140** |
| **Tam Dalyell** | **135** |
| **Bob Marshall-Andrews*** | **134** |
| **Alan Simpson*** | **134** |
| Jo Richardson | 132 |
| John Lee | 126 |
| Eric Heffer | 125 |
| Sydney Bidwell | 123 |
| Stan Newens | 123 |
| **Dennis Canavan** | **120** |
| Martin Flannery | 120 |
| **Kelvin Hopkins*** | **119** |
| **Robert Wareing*** | **119** |
| **Kevin McNamara** | **117** |
| Max Madden | 112 |
| **Harry Barnes** | **108** |
| Joan Maynard | 105 |
| Frank Allaun | 104 |
| George Rodgers | 104 |
| Stan Thorne | 103 |
| Eddie Loyden | 101 |
| James Lamond | 100 |

Note: bold type indicates an MP between 1997–2005; an asterisk indicates an MP who is still in the Commons. Figures correct as at the end of the 2005 Parliament and record votes cast against the whip while Labour was in government.

At the same time as the rebellions increased in frequency and size, so did their effect. Although previously a government might amend or withdraw its policy as a result of backbench opinion and pressure – as Harold Wilson was forced to with both *In Place of Strife* and the Parliament (No. 2) Bill in the 1960s – until 1974 no Labour government was ever defeated by its own MPs voting with the opposition. Indeed, although Labour MPs often proved willing to vote against their own government, they had rebelled in large numbers mostly on occasions when the Conservatives were either abstaining from voting or else voting with the Labour government. Before 1974 Labour MPs might have been prepared to bark – sometimes quite loudly – but they never bit. Between 1974 and 1979, however, Labour MPs began to bite – and frequently. There was a much greater willingness on the part of Labour rebels to vote in a whipped Conservative lobby. The size of the government's majority during this period – a minority in February 1974, a majority of just three after October 1974, slipping back to a minority in April 1976 – meant that one or more Labour MPs voting with the opposition could risk Labour's majority. As a result, the government went down to 59 separate defeats. Of these, 36 could be attributed to the government's minority status, but 23 were caused by its own backbenchers voting with the opposition. To put this figure into its proper context, note that during the 67 years between July 1905 and March 1972 there had been just 34 defeats. In a mere five years, therefore, the Labour government of 1974–79 suffered nearly double the number of defeats seen in almost 70 years.[11] It was evidence of a quite remarkable change in behaviour. Writing in 1970, Ergun Ozbudun had noted 'occasional deviations' from the norm of party cohesion in Britain. Such deviations were always more common under Labour than under the Conservatives; and by the 1970s they had long since ceased to be merely occasional.[12]

## The Rebels

Dunnico may have been the first Labour rebel, but he wasn't the most rebellious. That honour – if it is an honour – goes to Dennis Skinner, the MP for Bolsover since 1970. Like Dunnico, Skinner is an ex-miner – although unlike the Rev. Dunnico, Skinner also had a brief career as a club singer, imitating Al Jolson, Johnny Ray and Frankie Laine. As an MP, he became known as the 'Beast of Bolsover' – a nickname given him by a fellow Labour MP, Andrew Faulds – although it was a curious label, since Skinner's strength as a parliamentarian comes from a combination of industry and wit rather than mere aggressiveness. Skinner went through the lobbies against the Wilson and Callaghan government on a whopping 156 occasions, more than any other Labour MP in the 1970s; combined with more than 100 votes cast against the Blair government since 1997, Skinner's total comes to 273 votes cast against Labour governments by the time of the 2005 election. This is even more remarkable given that he was seriously ill for much of the second Blair term, with both cancer and heart difficulties. 'I go and make speeches about the wonderful health service,' he jokes. 'All those thousands of new nurses – I've met a lot of them myself!'

There are only 30 Labour MPs who have voted against a Labour government on a hundred or more occasions, listed in the table above. Skinner tops the table by a long way, followed by Jeremy Corbyn (the only other Labour MP to have broken the 200 barrier by the time of the 2005 election). For those who cling to the myth of the independence of the past and the spinelessness of the present, it might be a surprise to see that exactly half the most rebellious Labour MPs of all time have been in the Commons since 1997; they include eight of the ten most rebellious Labour MPs of all time. And the three most rebellious – Skinner, Corbyn, and John McDonnell – are still in the Commons, and around to cause Blair difficulties in the future.

# 2

# It's a bit more complicated than that

*Reasons for cohesion – The truth about whipping – The desire to negotiate*

> We expect our whips to deal with the colleagues in an adult and amiable fashion. Where there are differences on the issues, we expect our whips to confront these concerns at the intellectual and policy level. Conversation, not coercion, is the keynote. – Keith Hill, Deputy Chief Whip, 2001–03

> Keith did all this stuff about how we had to be nice to people, and enjoy intellectual arguments. I said, 'Does that mean that we can't beat people up any more?' – Labour whip, 2003

Nothing obscures the sensible discussion of MPs' behaviour more than the idea that there are two simple and clear-cut categories: there are loyalists, and there are rebels. Rebels are inevitably brave and independent-minded political Valiant-for-Truths, the sort of people who stick to their principles, the sort you'd want next to you in the trench. Loyalists, on the other hand, are spineless, gutless, cowardly swine, who believe in nothing but toadying to the powers that be for their own advancement.

The truth is a teeny-weeny bit more complicated than that. For sure, some of the rebels are just like the stereotype: thoughtful, brave and honest; some of them *have* sacrificed their personal advancement for their beliefs. But others are self-obsessed and egotistical, the sort of people who read press cuttings about themselves out to other people. When they rebel it's not from deep conviction but from a corrosive bitterness at their failure to progress beyond the back benches. Ironically, in the case of some Labour rebels, given how easily they will condemn the Blair government for not being sufficiently left wing, their rebellion is frequently motivated by a failure to believe in the value of cooperation and the need to put the common good above their own selfish interests. Whisper it: some are simply too dim to understand the impact of government policy.

The same applies for 'loyalists'. Sure, some are cringing lick-spittles, interested only in their own advancement and willing to say or do anything to achieve it. But others have principles that are just as deep as those held by the rebels. They vote the party line not because someone forces them to or because they are too scared or ambitious to do otherwise, but because they happen to agree with what the government is doing. On those occasions when they don't agree, they believe in subjugating their own views and interests for the good of the party.

In short, rebels are not better than loyalists or vice versa. Voting against the party line is neither a Good Thing nor a Bad Thing. Voting against the party is not necessarily brave (although at times it can be); toeing the party line is not necessarily a sign of subservience (although again, at times it can be). As will become clear throughout this book, MPs can vote with, or against, the party line for the best and the worst of reasons.

★ ★ ★

The propensity of MPs, of whatever party, to vote the party line should not be surprising. There are considerably more factors contributing to unity amongst British parliamentarians than there are to disunity.

Let's start with two statements of the blindingly obvious – but which far too many critics of the whipping system overlook.

First, Labour MPs are in the same party as other Labour MPs. And second, this is because they share roughly the same views on issues, the same beliefs, the same values. This isn't to pretend that British political parties are chock full of people in wholesale agreement with one another; there are plenty of differences, disagreements and disputes, as any scan of British political history would reveal. The PLP is hardly the sort of organisation to engage in group hugs. The Conservative parliamentary party, too, has known the odd ding-dong in its time. But on the whole, all things considered, taking one thing and another into account, and indulging in a bit of a sweeping generalisation, MPs of the same party tend to agree with one another. Or, more accurately, they agree with one another more than they agree with MPs from the other parties.

The best evidence for this is what happens when the whip is removed, and MPs are left to their own devices – so-called free votes. Critics of Parliament love free votes, the idea of the normally chained MP set free from the evil whip in some temporary act of liberation, like 'so many heirs of Spartacus' in Peter Jones's lovely phrase.[1] And when free votes are held on issues such as fox-hunting or abortion or capital punishment, it is common to hear the issues described as 'cross-party', 'non-party' or (even more ludicrously) 'above party'. Yet look at the voting. Look what happens when MPs are freed from the 'constraints' of the party whip. They *still* end up voting with members of the same party; Labour MPs go into one division lobby with other Labour MPs, Conservatives go into the other lobby with other Conservatives.

Take, for example, perhaps the most interesting free vote of the 2001 parliament, one of the many to happen over fox-hunting (a saga covered in more detail in Chapter 8). By November 2004 the parliamentary marathon over fox-hunting had been going on for seven years, but No. 10 still thought it was possible to engineer a compromise over the issue, this time by backing a scheme of licensed hunting for pest control where it could be shown that no other method would cause less suffering.

An amendment to the Hunting Bill was duly moved by the Welsh Labour MP Huw Irranca-Davies on 16 November 2004, and was then heavily voted down by the Commons (as everyone except those in No. 10 knew it would be), by 321 votes to 204. The Prime Minister voted in favour of Irranca-Davies's amendment – but he was one of just 25 Labour MPs to do so. In the other division lobby, opposing the compromise and insisting on a total ban, were the broad mass of the PLP, a total of 297 Labour MPs. The Prime Minister therefore voted on the side of just 8 per cent of the Labour MPs to have voted. Facing him were the remaining 92 per cent.[2] The split amongst Conservative MPs was similarly one sided: just 2 per cent opposed the compromise, 98 per cent supported it. So without being told how to vote, 92 per cent of Labour MPs went into one lobby, whilst 98 per cent of Conservative MPs went into the other lobby. Similarly stark splits can be seen on most free votes. Look at the 1990 votes which gave us the current abortion law, with its time limit of 24 weeks. Two-thirds of Labour MPs voted to keep the limit at 28 weeks – compared to just 5 per cent of Conservative MPs. The more restrictive option of 22 weeks was supported by 64 per cent of Conservatives, but just 15 per cent of Labour MPs. Or how about the votes on lowering the age of homosexual age of consent to sixteen in February 2000? Just 2 per cent of Labour MPs voted against sixteen compared to 90 per cent of Conservatives. There's precious little that's non-party about that!

There are, of course, some exceptions. Some free votes split one of the two main parties (although there are few issues that split both of them at the same time) and the Liberal Democrats are particularly prone to splitting on these sorts of issue.[3] But on the whole, even when the whip is off, no instructions have been given, and MPs can vote how they like, the single best piece of information that will help you predict how an MP is going to vote is their party label. Pretending otherwise is just part of the slightly silly but remarkably persistent aversion that exists towards political parties. Writing at the beginning of the twentieth century, Sidney Low noted that the easiest way to get a round of applause at a public meeting was to claim that something was non-partisan. 'No sentiment', he said, 'is likely to elicit more applause at a public meeting, than the sentiment that "this, Mr Chairman, is not a party question, and I do not propose to treat it from a party standpoint".'[4] Not much has changed since.

★ ★ ★

By the time someone becomes an MP they will have been a member of their party for years, usually decades. And not just a sitting–on–their–arse–in–front–of–the–telly–having–paid–their– membership–fee–by–direct–debit type of member either. Those who become MPs will have been amongst the most active members of their party. By the time they reach Westminster, they'll have put in hours, days, weeks of unpaid work on behalf of the party. They will have canvassed, donated money, delivered leaflets, and attended meeting after godforsaken meeting. Labour MPs will have held office in Young Labour or Student Labour or Trade Unionists for Labour (and sometimes all three), or they'll have been secretary or treasurer or chair of their constituency party (and sometimes all three). They'll have taken part in election campaigns that they'll have won and others that they'll have lost. In other words, by the time anyone becomes an MP, they've been with the party through thick and thin – and in the case of Labour members, more thin than thick.

This all leaves its mark. It means that for most MPs, going against their party is not an easy thing to do. It is rarely done lightly. This, for example, is one of the most rebellious Labour MPs of all time talking about the Conservatives: 'I hate the bastards. I want us to win every inch of the way. I bleed when we lose.' So does he have qualms about rebelling? 'All the time, all the time. I've never voted against the government lightly.' Another of the most rebellious MPs confessed that before rebellions she feels sick and has sleepless nights. 'I hate it,' she said. A third described it like this: 'It really upsets me. I feel awful. I always feel guilty going into the lobby with them. I think, "What the hell am I doing in here with this lot?"'

The thought that they may do something to damage their party is not a pleasant thought for most MPs. 'Have you read John O'Farrell's book [*Things Can Only Get Better*]?' asked one newly elected MP in 2001. 'That is my life. I spent the majority of my life under a Conservative government, working in the public sector, and saw the devastating effect of the Tories. Rebellion weakens your government and therefore increases the chances of bringing in another government.' Another MP, with more parliamentary experience under his belt, put it like this:

I could never vote against the government. The last time we behaved like this, we got the Tories for eighteen years. They destroyed my city, simply destroyed it, ripped the top off. We've just about repaired the economic damage, but we've not even begun to repair the social damage that they did.

As he finished speaking, furious nodding – like a sequence of minor epileptic fits – ensued in the surrounding group of Labour MPs, all of whom felt the same.

Add to this the fact that in Britain, with rare exceptions, we vote for parties, rather than individual candidates. Nearly all MPs know that they were elected because of their party label, not who they are. It wasn't their scintillating wit or intellect or oratory that got them a place at Westminster. It was the party. Party is their ticket to ride, and without it, they are nothing. And most MPs – except the most stunningly pompous – know it. 'I'm not here as an individual,' said one of the 2001 intake. 'I stood on a Labour Party ticket, warts and all. No one voted for me because they think I'm a great bloke.' 'It's a collective,' said another MP from the 2001 intake. 'People didn't vote for Bob Marshall-Andrews, they voted for the Labour Party. And so he should vote for the party line. If Alice Mahon was leader of the Labour Party,

I wouldn't rebel.' Then he paused, before adding, 'Well, I'd like to think I wouldn't.'

There are some MPs who take the party-centred realities of British politics to what they see as their logical conclusion, regarding themselves as the delegate of the party, in Parliament merely to do the party's bidding. Between 1966 and 1970, there were Labour backbenchers who, according to J. R. Piper's study, 'held a role conception that did not entail open rebellion under any circumstances'. They included some backbenchers 'who saw themselves as no more than passive instruments of the party leadership'.[5] There were some Labour backbenchers with a similar role conception between 1997 and 2001, although the numbers were tiny even then, and have diminished yet further since. Several of the MPs who declared (albeit privately) soon after 1997 that they would never vote against the party have since been found trooping through the division lobbies in defiance of their government. Those who would vote the party line come what may are almost non-existent on the Labour benches.

But for most 'The Party' still looms large. Their default setting is to vote with their party. Decisions to deviate from that are not taken lightly. As one rebel put it, 'a gut feeling that something's wrong isn't good enough.' To move beyond that gut feeling, to the point where an MP is prepared to challenge the government, usually requires an in-depth knowledge of a topic, something which MPs possess on only one or two areas of policy.

★ ★ ★

The procedure for most votes in the Commons is fairly straight-forward, if distinctly low tech.[6] The Speaker calls a voice vote: 'The question is that the amendment be made. As many as are of that opinion say aye, to the contrary no.' If the voice vote is uncontested, then no formal vote is held. But if there are shouts of both aye and no, then a formal vote takes place. This is known as a 'division', because MPs divide into one of two lobbies (aye or no), with their vote being recorded as they walk through. The voting figures are then announced in the chamber and the voting lists published in the official record, Hansard, both in print and online, the following day.

Each vote takes an average of between twelve and fifteen minutes to complete, and as a result the voting system is a regular target of parliamentary reformers, who wonder why MPs vote in such a time-consuming way, and suggest clever new-fangled replacements – such as swipe cards or push buttons – to replace the existing system. Part of the reason why the system remains unchanged is the astonishing institutional inertia that exists at Westminster, something which should never be under-estimated in any discussion of parliamentary reform. But it is not the only reason. Many MPs like the existing system; voting may take a long time, but because ministers and shadow ministers also have to vote, it forces them to spend time in close proximity to their backbenchers, and whilst there MPs can badger them and try to persuade them of their current pet cause. Many MPs fear they would lose that level of contact if the system was reformed.

The exact number of divisions per session has varied dramatically over the postwar period, but every Parliament since October 1974 has seen at least 1,200 divisions.[7] As a result, British MPs spend a lot of their time voting. An average length parliament would spend 270 hours of its business voting, and an MP who spent, say, 20 years in the Commons, and who voted in, say, 60 per cent of divisions, would, by their retirement, have spent 810 hours – just over a month of his or her life – walking through the division lobbies.

A more revealing statistic, however, would be the number of times that MPs know what they are voting on. The claim that MPs frequently vote in almost total ignorance of the subject under discussion usually produces gasps of horror from voters. But it's true. It's also perfectly reasonable. With around 300 votes per year, it is next to impossible for an MP to know much about each vote. As one MP put it, 'we're only human. It's just not humanly possible to know about everything you're voting for.

It's like Pavlov's dog. The bell goes and off we go. Sometimes you're in the lobby and you think, "I wonder what despicable piece of legislation I'm voting for tonight!"' Another MP – bright and very conscientious – estimated that he knew the subject of one vote out of the twelve that had taken place that week. Even if they take the time to find out the topic under discussion, it would be practically impossible to find out much about the issue in order to make an informed decision about how to vote. Given that, many argue that it's much more sensible to know almost nothing about the issue at all.

If you disagree, try this little test. Here's one amendment, picked completely at random, which was moved to the Finance Bill in June 2005. The proposed amendment was to insert the following clause into the Bill:

**Appeals against a notice issued by the Commissioners of Her Majesty's Customs and Revenue under section 24 or section 26.**
1. Any company to whom a notice has been given under section 24 or 26 may within 30 days by notice to the Special Commissioners appeal on the grounds that section 24 or section 26, as appropriate, does not apply to the company in respect of the transaction or transactions in question, or that the adjustments directed to be made are not appropriate adjustments.
2. If the Commissioners or the company are dissatisfied with the determination of the Special Commissioners the company or the Commissioners may, on giving notice to the clerk to the Special Commissioners within 30 days after the determination, require the appeal to be re-heard by the tribunal, and the Special Commissioners shall transmit to the tribunal any document in their possession which was delivered to them for the purposes of the appeal.
3. Where notice is given under subsection (2) above, the tribunal shall re-hear and re-determine the appeal and shall have and exercise the same powers and authorities in relation to the

appeal as the Special Commissioners might have and exercise, and the determination of the tribunal thereon shall be final and conclusive.

4. On an appeal under subsection (1) and (3) above the Special Commissioners or the tribunal shall have power to cancel or vary a notice under section 24 or section 26 of this Act, or to vary or quash an assessment made in accordance with such a notice, but the bringing of an appeal or the statement of a case shall not affect the validity of a notice given or of any other thing done in pursuance of those sections pending the determination of the proceedings.

That's one of the shorter and simpler amendments. Others go on for pages. But even if you can understand the four paragraphs above (and they're not actually that complicated if you concentrate), before you could make a decision on what you wanted to do about the issue you'd also have to understand section 24 and 26 of the Bill to which the amendment applies.

So – just to help you – here's Section 24:

**Deduction cases**

1. If the Commissioners for Her Majesty's Revenue and Customs consider, on reasonable grounds, that conditions A to D are or may be satisfied in relation to a transaction to which a company falling within subsection (2) is party, they may give the company a notice under this section.

2. A company falls within this subsection if—
   a. it is resident in the United Kingdom, or
   b. it is resident outside the United Kingdom but is within the charge to corporation tax.

3. Condition A is that the transaction to which the company is party forms part of a scheme that is a qualifying scheme.

4. Condition B is that the scheme is such that for the purposes of corporation tax the company is in a position to claim or has claimed an amount by way of deduction in respect of the trans-

action or is in a position to set off or has set off against profits in an accounting period an amount relating to the transaction.

5. Condition C is that the main purpose, or one of the main purposes, of the scheme is to achieve a UK tax advantage for the company.

6. Condition D is that the amount of the UK tax advantage in question is more than a minimal amount.

7. A notice under this section is a notice—

   a. specifying the transaction in relation to which the Commissioners consider that conditions A to D are or may be satisfied,

   b. specifying the accounting period in relation to which the Commissioners consider that condition B is or may be satisfied as regards the transaction, and

   c. informing the company that as a consequence section 25 (rules relating to deductions) has effect in relation to the transaction.

8. Nothing in this section prevents the Commissioners from giving a company falling within subsection (2) a notice under this section as regards two or more transactions.

9. Schedule 3 makes provision about what constitutes a qualifying scheme.

And here's Section 26:

### Receipts cases

1. If the Commissioners for Her Majesty's Revenue and Customs consider, on reasonable grounds, that conditions A to E are or may be satisfied in relation to a company resident in the United Kingdom, they may give the company a notice under this section.

2. Condition A is that a scheme makes or imposes provision ('the actual provision') as between the company and another person ('the paying party') by means of a transaction or series of transactions.

3. Condition B is that the actual provision includes the making by the paying party, by means of a transaction or series of transactions, of a payment that is a qualifying payment in relation to the company.

4. Condition C is that, as regards the qualifying payment made by the paying party, there is an amount that—

    a. is available as a deduction for the purposes of the Tax Acts, or

    b. may be deducted or otherwise allowed in respect of the payment under the tax law of any territory outside the United Kingdom, and does not fall to be disregarded as described in subsection (5).

5. An amount is to be disregarded if or to the extent that it is, for tax purposes, set against any income arising to the paying party from the transaction or transactions forming part of the scheme.

6. Condition C is not to be treated as satisfied if—

    a. the paying party is a dealer,

    b. in the ordinary course of his business, he incurs losses in respect of the transaction or transactions forming part of the scheme to which he is party, and

    c. the amount by reference to which condition C would, but for this subsection, be satisfied is an amount in respect of those losses.

7. In subsection (6), 'dealer' means a person who is a dealer in relation to a distribution within the meaning of section 95(2) of ICTA or who would, if he were resident in the United Kingdom, be such a dealer.

8. Condition D is that at least part of the qualifying payment is not an amount to which subsection (9) applies.

9. This subsection applies to an amount that is, for the purposes of the Corporation Tax Acts—

    a. income or gains arising to the company in the accounting period in which the qualifying payment was made in relation to the company,

    b. income arising to any other company resident in the United Kingdom in a corresponding accounting period, or brought into account by a company as a credit for the purposes of Chapter 2 of Part 2 of FA 1996 by virtue of section 91A of FA 1996 (avoidance involving shares subject to outstanding third party obligations).

10. Condition E is that the company and the paying party expected on entering into the scheme that a benefit would arise as a result of condition D being satisfied (whether by reference to all or part of the qualifying payment).

11. A notice under this section is a notice—
    a. informing the company of the Commissioners' view under subsection (1),
    b. specifying the qualifying payment by reference to which the Commissioners consider conditions B to E are or may be satisfied,
    c. specifying the accounting period of the company in which the payment is made, and
    d. informing the company that as a consequence section 27 has effect in relation to the payment.

12. For the purposes of this section a payment is a qualifying payment in relation to a company if it constitutes a contribution to the capital of the company.

13. For the purposes of this section the accounting period of a company ('company A') corresponds to the accounting period of another company ('company B') if at least one day of company A's accounting period falls within company B's accounting period.

If you were being honest, in order to understand these two sections properly, you would also need to have understood the other pieces of law referred to in them. But you can be spared those – the point's clear enough. Even if you managed to get your head around that particular issue, next week it would be sheep-farming or fluoridation of water or immigration legislation or social security and so on, through roughly 300 votes each year. Given the complexity of much legislation, and given the party-centred realities of British politics, it's therefore perfectly rational for MPs to defer to their party managers and vote in total ignorance of the subject much of the time.

It's not that they do so all the time. All MPs have opinions on matters of high-profile policy – they all know what they are doing and why on the controversial issues – but they are much less likely to have nuanced positions on the more detailed aspects of legislation, and, as Hugh Berrington once noted, it is 'the steady conformity which Members display on obscure clauses and complex amendments which is the more important for the day-to-day working of government'.[8] Or, as one MP bluntly admitted, 'I go through the lobby a great number of times not knowing a fuck about what I'm voting for.'

As Paul Flynn, the Labour MP and sometime rebel, puts it in his entertaining book, *Commons Knowledge*, MPs are therefore 'grateful for the sheepdog herding of the Whips who direct them safely into the lobby of righteousness and truth'.[9] But this herding is not the conventional view of the whip: bullying poor MPs into voting for things they would rather reject. It's not creating cohesion through discipline. Rather, it is ensuring cohesion amongst those who are quite happy to be cohesive. 'We are just here to help,' the whips sometimes say.

\* \* \*

Sometimes the herding breaks down and the MP is directed into the wrong lobby (see Appendix 2); several cases of what look like dissenting votes are, in fact, just MPs ending up in the wrong division lobby by mistake. However embarrassing they are for the MPs concerned, such mishaps usually have no substantive impact. With a majority such as the one enjoyed by Labour between 1997 and 2005, one vote here or there rarely made much difference. But they could – and occasionally did. In 2003 the Commons held a series of votes on Lords reform. The

Commons rejected every option put before it – ranging from abolition of the upper chamber, to a Lords that was 100 per cent elected, to a Lords that was 100 per cent appointed. Every option was voted down, leaving the Commons without an opinion on the issue. When the voting had finished, a frustrated Leader of the House, Robin Cook, said that it might be a good time to 'go home and sleep' on the events of the day.

Few people came out of the episode in a good light. The Commons did not appear to be able to make what to most outsiders seemed like a simple decision. The Prime Minister had had his position – for a fully appointed House – rejected by the majority of his own MPs (including four of his Cabinet ministers and 21 other ministers). The Leader of the House had seen his own position (for a wholly or largely elected Lords) rejected, and – less noticed but still significant – the Conservative leader, Iain Duncan Smith, had seen the majority of Conservative MPs who voted oppose his party's position for an 80 per cent elected Senate. The only winners – albeit largely by default – were those who wanted an all-appointed House. They had lost the vote in the Commons by a substantial margin but the outcome was effectively exactly what they wanted.

With all that embarrassment floating around, one small group of MPs escaped, largely unnoticed. The option that came closest to succeeding was that for a House of Lords that was 80 per cent elected, 20 per cent appointed. It failed by just three votes. But at least four MPs voted against it by mistake, despite supporting it.[10] The votes had been supposed to take place in a particular sequence: with the 80 per cent appointed option being followed by the 80 per cent elected option. But 80 per cent appointed – which had originally been the position of the government – was negated on a voice vote, with not a single MP voting for it, and so there was no division. As a result, when the division bells next went, these four MPs thought they were voting on the 80 per cent appointed option, and walked through the no lobby by mistake. Those four mistaken votes were the difference between that option winning and losing, between the Commons plumping for a largely elected upper chamber or for nothing at all. Had those four MPs paid slightly more attention to what was going on, the day would not be remembered as quite the farce that it currently is.

* * *

But even when they do know what they're voting on, and even when they know that they don't like it, MPs still might not defy the whip. Why?

The first explanation is the conventional one: the whips. The frighteners go on, and MPs buckle under the pressure. Whips have long been the pantomime villains of Westminster politics – a combination of arm-twister, bully, and Machiavelli, whose sole role is to intimidate poor unsuspecting MPs into carrying out evil deeds on behalf of the government. The sort of people who tie damsels to train tracks whilst twiddling their moustache, whips stamp on any signs of independence, and demand sheep-like obedience from our MPs. Tales of the tricks used by the whips to 'persuade' MPs are legion. They include the infamous 'Black Book', in which Conservative whips used to keep details of the financial and sexual peccadilloes of their MPs. Jeremy Paxman's otherwise dreadful book on British politicians, *The Political Animal*, includes this example of how such information could be used:

> Somewhere in central London is a safe containing a brown envelope. Inside the envelope is a photograph. It shows a well-known politician, a tireless campaigner for 'family values', in what used to be called a 'compromising position'. He is naked. There are a number of women – also naked – in the photograph. It also includes a dog . . . The photograph has been taken out of the safe only once, when the MP at the centre of the picture had threatened to rebel over a piece of legislation. He was invited to the whips' office and offered a drink. Then he was tossed the

envelope. He opened it, blanched, and spent the rest of his political career doing what he was told.[11]

The reality, though, is usually much less salacious or exciting, and most academic accounts of Parliament have therefore tried to stress the more prosaic functions of the whips as party managers, organising those who want to be organised, providing a channel of communication from leaders to led and vice versa, and who – when push comes to shove – are not half as powerful as the mythology makes out. But none of this can complete with the intrigue, the downright sexiness, of the myth. It is just much more exciting to believe that the whips are all like the fictitious Francis Urquhart – omnipresent, omniscient, omnipotent – than to face the more mundane reality.

When the Prime Minister appointed Hilary Armstrong as Chief Whip shortly after the 2001 election, he told her that he wanted her to do the job 'politically'. He meant that the whips were to go out and argue the case for policies with backbenchers, not just attempt to bully them into submission. Keith Hill, the Deputy Chief Whip from 2001 to 2003, explained this succinctly: 'We expect our whips to deal with the colleagues in an adult and amiable fashion. Where there are differences on the issues, we expect our whips to confront these concerns at the intellectual and policy level. Conversation, not coercion, is the keynote.'

The aim was to 'love them to death'. 'We take on the issues at an intellectual level. We brief as thoroughly as we can. We encourage the whips to talk at length.' This eschewing of what one whip labelled the 'culture of brutalism' that used to pervade the Labour Whips' Office – fists rather than photos being the currency of persuasion – wasn't a particularly moral one; it wasn't that either Armstrong or Hill were especially cuddly or limp wristed; it wasn't that they especially objected to trying to bully people into submission. It was that they just didn't think it worked any longer. As the Chief Whip put it: 'You just cannot use the old methods. Intimidation will not work.'[12]

The rise of the career politician, often blamed for the creation of subservience, has in fact had the opposite effect. Today's politicians are more demanding; they are more likely to want to influence policy, less willing simply to support policy thought up elsewhere. As the number of Labour MPs from industry declines, so the value of industrial language as a motivator has diminished, a trend that Donald Searing noticed over 30 years ago in the 1970s when he was interviewing MPs for his book *Westminster's World*.[13] The rise of 24-hour media (and a more aggressive and less deferential media at that) has given disgruntled MPs outlets for their disquiet that would have horrified most former Chief Whips. In 2003 the BBC broadcast a much-hyped drama documentary entitled *The Project*, one of whose characters was a bright young newly elected woman MP. She is both physically bullied by a hefty bruiser of a whip and then blackmailed by the Chief Whip into voting for a policy that she didn't support and which was not in the party's manifesto. As Lord Renton, a former Conservative Chief Whip, points out in his book, *Chief Whip*, 'life is not like that any longer and the BBC drama documentary was out of date before it was shown.' 'If threatened by the whips in the manner of *The Project*, the first thing most MPs would do would be to run to the media, and the media would be wholly on their side.'[14]

Today's whips are pussycats compared to, say, David Margesson, Tory Chief Whip between 1931 and 1940. Renton describes Margesson as the 'total whip'. Even on holiday, the first question to his daughter in the morning would be 'What is the programme for today?' His style of whipping could be physically brutal, treating dissenters as if they were 'defaulters on parade'.[15] Renton also describes an encounter between a young Jack Straw and the then Labour Chief Whip, Michael Cocks. As Renton indicates, the story is apocryphal, but it is still indicative of a style of whipping that simply would not work today. Straw was said to be thinking of rebelling, and so Cocks explained the party's position to him. Straw replied that he didn't find it a particularly convincing argument. At this point, Cocks seized Straw by the genitals, held onto them tight while Straw turned white in the face, and finally released him with the comment, 'Are you convinced now?'[16] They don't make them like that anymore.

It is best not to be too prissy or naïve about this. The whips do have more at their disposal than merely the power to persuade. With young and newly elected MPs they can point out what will happen to them should they insist on voting against the party, that it would be shame to jeopardise a promising career, to fail to achieve the advancement that was deserved. As one Labour MP, elected in 2001, put it, such conversations are 'not what you might call a rigorous dismissal of the empirical evidence. It's "Why are you doing this? You're throwing your whole fucking career away." That's the currency they deal in.' For those not interested in future ministerial office there is always the lure of better office space, time to go on overseas trips or be otherwise absent from the House, or positions on the more prestigious select committees (or, for those who sin, the purgatory of the delegated legislation committee or some similar monstrosity). These are all things that the whips either control or (at least) heavily influence and troublesome MPs will find them less accommodating. These trade-offs go on all the time; as one long-serving whip said, 'if you get into the business of asking the whips for things, then you've got to give something back. And you've only one thing to give: your vote.' The MP who swapped his vote on one of key issues during the 2001 Parliament for two weeks' holiday is an example of this trading at its most bare faced – and its least edifying.[17] But blatant cases like this are rare. Most of the relationships between whips and backbenchers are more subtle than this, more nuanced, based on the building up of reciprocal relationships (what Searing described as 'the norm of reciprocity').[18] In the same way that most confessions to the Spanish Inquisition came when the torture implements were shown to victims, most MPs are well aware of the realities of political life; they don't need them spelling out.

Not that heavy-handed methods have vanished entirely. Not all the whips favoured the new approach. 'Keith did all this stuff about how we had to be nice to people, and enjoy intellectual arguments,' said one junior whip. 'I said, "Does that mean that we can't beat people up anymore?"' And at various points throughout the Parliament there were complaints that whips were pushing the limits of what was acceptable. Much depended on the individual whip. Some were natural good cops, favouring tea and sympathy. Others were born to play hard, and were not averse to dishing out abuse. 'They shout at you, they scream at you, say, "You tosser,"' complained one MP. One whip dismissed claims that this was bullying – 'That's panic, not bullying' – and it was all a long way from what would have been considered perfectly acceptable even just 20 years before.

\* \* \*

Just after the 1966 election, at which Labour leapt from a single-figure majority to one just three seats shy of a hundred, Harold Wilson was interrupted by a visitor while practising his putting at Chequers. 'How's your handicap?' the visitor asked. 'Gone up from three to 97,' replied the typically astute Wilson.[19] Large majorities such as those 'enjoyed' by Labour since 1997 may make defeat less likely, but they bring problems of their own – and have the potential to be a huge headache for the whips.

A large majority means that MPs can break ranks in numbers, safe in the knowledge that they will not defeat the government. Small majorities, by contrast, require self-discipline from MPs. And, because MPs in large majorities know they can rebel in numbers, it becomes harder to discipline them. Small rebellions invite isolation and punishment. But, as became very clear early on in the 1997 Parliament, party managers are virtually powerless to take action after the fact against a significantly large group of dissidents. Once a potential rebellion attracts a critical mass of MPs, it becomes much more difficult to stop other sympathisers joining the fray.

A large majority also reduces the whips' power of patronage yet further. At the most basic level, the larger the parliamentary party, the smaller the proportion of the 'payroll vote', those hundred or so ministers and parliamentary private secretaries (PPSs) whose votes can be taken for granted. Governments of all shades have, in recent years, tried to push the extent of their patronage as far as it can go – by having unpaid ministers, for example, or by expanding the number of PPSs. A PPS is the lowest level in the governmental food chain, a sort of aide-cum-gofer, whose job is to help their minister, especially by liaising with backbench MPs. PPSs are neither paid nor officially ministers yet they are still bound by collective responsibility and expected to vote with the government – and to resign if they do not. Their numbers have been steadily expanding over recent years, and even when we'd reached what most people thought was saturation point – when almost every member of the government at minister of state level or higher had at least one PPS – the Blair government stumbled onto a clever wheeze: to appoint 'team' PPSs, to cover departments and to report to ministers collectively, rather than being linked to individual ministers. The DTI even decided that it needed two team PPSs in addition to the four that it already had for its three ministers of state and the Secretary of State. Depending on who you talk to, team PPSs were either a valuable attempt at improving the liaison between front- and backbenchers – or an embarrassing set of vacuous sinecures to placate the otherwise passed over.

Still, there are limits to how far such creative constitutional tinkering can go – and the more MPs a party has inevitably means more disappointed and disgruntled MPs. As one party insider said despairingly, shrugging his shoulders, with so many MPs 'what the fuck do you do?' To begin with, a new MP might be kept in line with the promise of office in the future, but once enough of their colleagues begin the climb up the ministerial ladder, even the most thick skinned will realise that there is unlikely to be jam tomorrow. By 2001 quite a few of Labour's *mass de manoeuvre* from 1997 had come to precisely that conclusion – with damaging consequences for the government.

★ ★ ★

Even when they know what they're voting on, even when they know that they don't like it, even if they are not worried about the cost to themselves, well, then still to come are the multitude of meetings with ministers to explain the policy and to discuss possible solutions.

The former Conservative Eurosceptic MP Teresa Gorman provides a good example of this. When an MP, she had been invited to No. 10 for a discussion with the then Prime Minister, John Major:

> Suddenly John leant across, took hold of my left hand, and placed it between his two hands. He looked me straight in the eye and said, 'There's something which I want you to do which means a very great deal to me.' He began very gently stroking the side of my hand with his thumb. My mind began to race. I didn't know what to think. 'I'm going to ask you something and I want you to think very carefully before you answer me.' I nodded. I could feel my heart beating a little faster . . . Was he coming on to me? Suddenly I was excited and apprehensive. I knew the civil servant would not come in, but what about Norma? She might be in the flat upstairs, and then what? . . . Surely, he wasn't going to proposition me?

Thankfully for all concerned, he wasn't:

> 'In the next session of Parliament, we are going to debate an increase in the European budget and it's very important not to have another showdown over the amount. It's only £75 million.' Now it was his turn to take a deep breath. 'So, Teresa, I want your assurance that you will vote with the government this time.'

Her answer: 'No, Prime Minister.'[20] It is difficult (impossible, even) to imagine Tony Blair trying to sweet-talk Gwyneth Dunwoody in quite the same way.

It's when the conversations move away from hand-stroking and onto potential changes to the legislation that the tactic is more likely to succeed. If the minister is prepared to negotiate, then many would-be rebels feel the need to do the same. 'If the government gives way, and yet we still rebel, then what is the incentive for the government to give way in the future?' Or, as another MP put it, 'if you go saying [that] you are definitely going to vote against the government, then what's the point of them talking to you?' And the fact that ministers might be willing to negotiate on one issue helps dampen the extent to which MPs are willing to rebel on others. Most backbenchers choose their rebellions carefully, in order to avoid being seen as too troublesome. As one occasional rebel put it, 'I set myself a rule . . . If I am to be regarded as normally loyal, it would take quite exceptional circumstances for me to vote against . . . I try to keep the currency of dissent at its full value.'

An MP who led one of the larger rebellions during the 1997 Parliament confessed that he had remained loyal on a particular issue so that he would have more kudos with the whips ('I don't want to get a name as a serial campaigner'), a point he made explicitly to the whips in order to increase his bargaining power with them. Other MPs argue in terms of credit chips, bullets or Brownie points. You use them wisely, rebelling only when it matters, so as to have maximum ammunition for those occasions when you really want to pressurise a minister into doing something. This view is common, right across the parliamentary party, regardless of the MPs' background. Here are verbatim quotes, from five Labour MPs, who differ hugely in their background, their position within the party, and the type of seats for which they sit. But notice the similarity in the way they view their relationship with the government:

If you dig a trench and oppose from the start, (1) you weaken the government, and (2) you throw away your bargaining chips . . . It's bad politics.

Not devaluing the currency of opposing the government by doing it too often. If you rebel when you feel really strongly, that's one thing. But if you do it when you're less adamant . . . You need to pick your time, if you want to have an impact. It's important to pick your target carefully.

You must demonstrate that you will rebel, but that you'd prefer not to. There is no point in being Jeremy Corbyn. The whips just say, 'It's him again.' You have to be something in between – retaining your credibility so that they try to make you happy is the optimal position.

Everyone has their own personal style and tone. You won't influence the government by being seen as the usual suspects. The tone must not be damaging to the party. But unless the government believed you would vote against, you wouldn't have the leverage.

Most politics is about negotiation, discussion and debate. If you run out of credit, you are discounted. It's a waste of time. If you rebel too often, you lose your bargaining power.

There are a handful of MPs who don't view things like this – 'You can't afford to compromise. It'd destroy my reputation if it ever got out that I'd compromised' – but most, even many of the most rebellious MPs, believe that rebellions have to be rationed to have their full impact. They see their vote as something to negotiate over with the whips. Most MPs are able to quote example after example where they have made a difference through arguing with ministers behind the scenes, but without rebelling. Or, as one long-serving MP put it, there's no point grandstanding. I mean, anyone can go in, shoot their mouth off, vote against the government. And that feels really good. You're a hero to people outside, because you voted against the government. But it lasts about 24 hours. And then you start to think, 'What did I achieve?' I'd rather achieve something. I came into politics to achieve things, not to make gestures. I'm not into gestures.

★ ★ ★

What about the constituency? At what point do the concerns of the voters come into all of this? The short answer is that most of the time they don't come into it very much at all.

This does not mean that MPs are not responsive to their constituents. In fact, all the evidence is that MPs today are much more responsive to constituents' queries than they ever used to be – spending an ever-increasing amount of time, effort and money keeping in touch with their constituents and dealing with their concerns.[21] In fact, it is getting to the point where many observers have started to question whether MPs are not spending far too much time dealing with their constituents' problems and concerns at the expense of their work at Westminster.[22] This responsiveness takes the form of surgeries held, letters answered, casework dealt with – dealing with social security issues, or planning disputes or housing cases or any number of esoteric concerns (most of which, ironically, the MP usually has absolutely no control over). What is much less common is to see an MP vote one way or the other because an issue is of particular concern to his or her constituents. It occasionally happens; debates on asylum and immigration, for example, often see MPs with large immigration caseloads taking a particular interest – and sometimes being more likely to defy their whips as a result. Every now and again, there is an issue with a particularly sharp constituency focus (in July 2004, for example, there was a rebellion when the government fined Nottingham City Council for overspending – two of the city's three MPs voted against the government).[23] But most issues don't have a particular 'constituency' dimension, and so cases like this are pretty rare.

More generally, there is often an assumption that MPs in marginal seats will be more responsive to the concerns of the voters, more likely to rebel when the government is trying to push through a controversial piece of legislation. In fact, there is almost no difference between the behaviour of MPs in marginal seats and those in safe seats. MPs in all seats will be worried about the costs of an unpopular policy – because they will prefer to see their party in power rather than in opposition – and whilst MPs in the most marginal seats might be more concerned about the government's unpopularity, they might also be especially concerned that their party should not appear divided. Voters frequently say that they want more independent MPs – but they also say that they do not like divided parties. MPs in marginal seats are well aware of the tension between the two. One Labour MP, sitting for one of the most marginal seats in the country, argued that the biggest threat to his seat was 'posed by disunity'; he said he felt 'wholly let down' by the behaviour of those who were voting against the government.[24]

OK, say the critics, but shouldn't MPs do what voters want, regardless of the type of seat they sit for? It is one of the fundamental issues in political representation – whether an MP should be a delegate (doing what the voters want, regardless of their own preferences) or whether they should be a representative in the Burkean tradition, doing what they think is best for the voters, even if it is not what the voters themselves want. Edmund Burke (1729–97) was MP for Bristol, and in his famous speech to his electors he argued: 'Your representative owes you, not his industry only, but his judgment; and he betrays instead of serving you if he sacrifices it to your opinion.'

On most issues, of course, the question is redundant. On most issues the public don't have a view for MPs to listen to. What, for example, do you think the public view was on the proposed amendment to the Finance Bill discussed above (pp. 29–30)?

Even on those issues where there might be a public view, how is the MP supposed to know what it is? For sure, they could take heed of the letters, emails and phone calls they get – but if they did that, then the Catholic Church and the League Against Cruel Sports would be the two most powerful organisations in the country. Ditto for marches, petitions, and other protests. If demonstrations were representative of the population, the Socialist Workers' Party would permanently be in government. MPs are well aware that these are not representative of the wider views of the public, and they (rightly) act accordingly.

Of course, there are some issues (albeit a very small number) where thanks to opinion polls we know what the views of the public are (although polls, of course, can provide different answers depending on how and when the questions are posed). Yet Burke's legacy is strong. Most MPs would still say that they should do what they think is right, even if they know they are going against the wishes of the voters. They'll argue that the voters will get their chance to pass judgement at the next election. And if they don't like what the MP has done, they can turf them out. For his part, Burke only lasted one term as MP for Bristol – before the voters decided that they'd manage without his industry or his judgement.

And across all of this, once again, is The Party. It's a fairly simple calculation. If you are a Labour MP, then you believe that it is better for the country to have a Labour government than a Conservative government – because (as you see it) a Labour government brings sunshine and happiness to all whereas a Conservative government grinds down the poor and spreads misery across the land. So, if your party decides to do something stupid you will try to dissuade it. You might even be prepared to vote against it. But you'll be unwilling to do anything that might damage it – and thus make it more likely that the other party will get into power – because that would not be beneficial for the country. In such cases, the interests of party neatly coincide with those of constituency and country.

\* \* \*

At the beginning of *Slaughterhouse-Five*, Kurt Vonnegut records the reaction of a colleague when told that he intended to write an anti-war book: 'Why not write an anti-glacier book?' His argument was that wars, like glaciers, cannot be stopped. At a somewhat less dramatic level, the same can be said of backbench cohesion. Party discipline within Parliament developed in tandem with the growth of extra-parliamentary political parties; and extra-parliamentary political parties developed because of the growth of the franchise. One led inexorably to the other. Legislative cohesion – the tendency of MPs of one party to vote with one another – is therefore a consequence of the growth of the franchise and the extension of democracy. The precise level of cohesion will wax and wane, according to circumstances (and at the moment, it is on the wane), but cohesion is a fundamental of parliamentary life. It is, and should be, an MP's default setting, and it is not going to go away. So stop moaning about it.

Rather than self-flagellating about the supposed lack of independence on the back benches we should perhaps all grow up a bit and cease to be amazed that most of the time MPs of the same party prefer to vote together and for the party under whose colours they won their seats. On those occasions when they have disagreements with the party, there are many different reasons why an MP might not rebel. For sure, some of these are about ambition, venality and feebleness. But the others are more complicated, and more positive than this. To focus on the weakness of MPs and the disciplinary power of the whips – to see them as Westminster's answer to the Krays, ruling their manor through intimidation and bribery – is a quite monumental failure to understand the realities of parliamentary life.

# Jeremy Corbyn and Siôn Simon

The most rebellious Labour MP between 2001 and 2005 was Jeremy Corbyn, the MP for Islington North, who voted against the party whip on 148 occasions. This will be little surprise to Westminster-watchers: he was also the most rebellious Labour MP between 1997 and 2001. Once described as 'the nearest thing Parliament has to 'Greenham Common Man', Corbyn looks a bit like a 1970s Open University lecturer who's wandered into the Commons by mistake. He is Old Labour, and proud of it. He once claimed that he did not vote against the party willy-nilly, only being willing to defy the whip over three types of issues: war and peace, issues of liberty and social-economic policy. Point out to him that this covers almost everything that the government could possibly do, and he laughs, 'I suppose it does.'

Corbyn rebelled when the government tried to restrict debate over the nomination of select committees; he rebelled over the Anti-Terrorism, Crime and Security Bill, over the Education Bill, over the Nationality, Immigration and Asylum Bill and over the NHS Reform and Health Care Professions Bill; he rebelled over Iraq and over the fire-fighters and over the railways; he rebelled over the Criminal Justice Bill, the Health and Social Care (Community Health and Standards) Bill, over the Asylum and Immigration (Treatment of Claimants) Bill and over the Higher Education Bill; he rebelled over the Gambling Bill, the Children Bill, the Housing Bill and the Serious Organised Crime and Police Bill; he rebelled over the Identity Cards Bill and – last but certainly not least – he rebelled over the Prevention of Terrorism Bill. In short, Corbyn took part in almost all of the major rebellions involving Labour

MPs in the four years between 2001 and 2005.

At the other end of the spectrum is Siôn Simon, the Labour MP for Birmingham, Erdington, and previously a columnist for the *Spectator* and the *Daily Telegraph*. Simon is both sartorially and ideologically far removed from Corbyn. He eschews facial hair and would doubtless view a brown corduroy jacket as the work of the Devil. Simon is as much New Labour and proud of it as Corbyn is Old. Since becoming an MP in 2001, he has never voted against his party whip. Even on the key occasions where MPs were allowed free votes but where the preferences of the leadership were known – such as votes on House of Lords reform in 2003 – Simon was to be found voting with the leadership. Halfway through the 2001 Parliament, he was identified as one of the five most loyal members of the new intake, something he was not at all apologetic about. 'I haven't wanted to vote against the government,' he said. 'I agree with them, even to the extent that on the Lords votes I voted as I saw it, which turned out to be the same as Blair. I have been voting the government line; I've also been voting my conscience.'

But his apparent loyalty to the party line does not simply result from a happy coincidence of his views and those of the leadership; it is also because he doesn't think the job of a Labour MP is to rebel against the party. 'It's the job of a Labour MP to support the government. People didn't vote for me, they voted for Labour and a particular type of Labour. They're voting for Tony Blair more than Siôn Simon.' Not for him stand-offs with ministers over legislation. 'It would go against the grain to start going up to ministers and insisting on rewriting policy. It's not the role of the backbench MP to decide policy. That's what we have ministers for.' He doesn't describe those who vote against the party whip as 'rebels' because it is too romantic a phrase, which conjures up images of brave fights against evil aggressors. He prefers 'deserters'.

Yet the reality is that Corbyn and Simon are not all that different. Whether they like it or not (almost certainly not), much more unites them than divides them. Corbyn's 148 votes against the government constitute just 12 per cent of the 1,246 votes to have taken place during the Parliament. Even allowing for those votes from which he was absent, and the various free votes given by the whips, Corbyn was still much more likely to vote with the government than against it. He once made this point to his whip, arguing, 'I'm with you in 99 per cent of cases.'[25] To which the whip's response was: 'Yes, Jerry, but not in the 1 per cent that matter.' Similarly, Simon may eschew stand-offs with ministers, but he does still seek to influence them. 'It's quite easy to be independent – to speak, think independently, against the government – without *voting* against.' And he still reserves the right to vote against the government, especially if the matter affects his constituency – something which, he says, 'overrides everything'.

Even the most 'loyal' MPs, therefore, reserve the right to rebel. And even the most rebellious MPs are overwhelmingly 'loyal' – which is one of the reasons why so many of them dislike being described as 'disloyal'. And Corbyn and Simon are at the extremes – and they know it. By the end of the 2001 parliament, 218 Labour MPs had voted against their whips at least once. Totally loyal backbenchers such as Simon were relatively rare. There were just 36 Labour MPs who sat on the backbenches for the entire 2001 Parliament and who hadn't rebelled by the time of the 2005 election.

Similarly, few of the 218 Labour rebels had voting patterns that resembled those of Corbyn. The table below lists the 30 most rebellious Labour MPs during the 2001 Parliament. The only MP to have a voting record similar to Corbyn's was John McDonnell, the MP for Hayes and Harlington (135 dissenting votes). But McDonnell and Corbyn stand out as atypical even when compared with most other rebels. After the two of them, there's a fairly sharp fall away to the only other two MPs to have voted against the whip on more than a hundred occasions during the 2001 parliament – Lynne Jones (103) and Bob Marshall-Andrews (102). Below them, there were three MPs who cast over 90 dissenting votes (Brian Sedgemore, Robert Wareing and Alan Simpson) and two in the 80s (Kelvin Hopkins and Harry Barnes). By the time you've reached the 20th most rebellious Labour MP – the then Father of the House, Tam Dalyell – you are down to 53 dissenting votes, less than half the number cast by Corbyn. By the time we reach the 30th most rebellious MP – the less well-known Jim Cousins – we have dropped to 33 rebellions.

It is worth bearing in mind what some of these figures mean in percentage terms. Take someone like Alan Simpson, one of the ten most rebellious Labour MPs and the former secretary of the Socialist Campaign Group. About as anti-Blairite as it is possible to be, in the four years from 2001 to 2005 he voted against his whip on 96 occasions – or in 8 per cent of votes. The figure for Dalyell – an MP who described Tony Blair as the worst prime minister he'd seen in his 33 years in Parliament, and whom he came close to describing as a war criminal – was 4 per cent. The figure for Cousins was just 3 per cent. And these are the *most* rebellious Labour MPs.

Below them, the number of rebellions cast by Labour MPs drops yet further. Some 60 per cent of the 218 Labour MPs to vote against the whip between 2001 and 2005 did so on fewer than ten occasions; over a third did so on fewer than five occasions. Just one in five of the rebels rebelled on 20 or more occasions, and the median number of votes cast against the whip by a Labour rebel MP was seven. As a percentage of the 1,246 votes held, seven dissenting votes constitutes a vanishingly slight 0.56 per cent. In other words, the average rebel rebels once every 200 parliamentary votes.

## The 30 most rebellious Labour MPs, 2001–2005

| Rebel ranking | Name | Constituency | Votes against the whip, 2001–05 |
|---|---|---|---|
| 1 | Jeremy Corbyn | Islington North | 148 |
| 2 | John McDonnell | Hayes & Harlington | 135 |
| 3 | Dr Lynne Jones | Birmingham, Selly Oak | 103 |
| 4 | Bob Marshall-Andrews | Medway | 102 |
| 5 | Brian Sedgemore | Hackney South & Shoreditch | 98 |
| 6 | Robert Wareing | Liverpool, West Derby | 97 |
| 7 | Alan Simpson | Nottingham South | 96 |
| 8 | Kelvin Hopkins | Luton North | 87 |
| 9 | Harry Barnes | North East Derbyshire | 81 |
| 10 | Dennis Skinner | Bolsover | 76 |
| 11 | Mark Fisher | Stoke-on-Trent Central | 74 |
| 12 | Kate Hoey | Vauxhall | 73 |
| 13 | Diane Abbott | Hackney North & Stoke Newington | 68 |
| 14 | Denzil Davies | Llanelli | 67 |
| 15 | Glenda Jackson | Hampstead & Highgate | 64 |
| 16 | Neil Gerrard | Walthamstow | 61 |
| 17 | Alice Mahon | Halifax | 58 |
| 18 | Llew Smith | Blaenau Gwent | 56 |
| 19= | Andrew Bennett | Denton & Reddish | 53 |
| 19= | Tam Dalyell | Linlithgow | 53 |
| 21 | Kevin McNamara | Kingston upon Hull North | 48 |
| 22= | Terry Lewis | Worsley | 43 |
| 22= | Mike Wood | Batley & Spen | 43 |
| 24 | Jim Marshall | Leicester South | 42 |
| 25 | Gwyneth Dunwoody | Crewe & Nantwich | 40 |
| 26 | David Taylor | North West Leicestershire | 39 |
| 27= | Peter Kilfoyle | Liverpool, Walton | 38 |
| 27= | Clare Short | Birmingham, Ladywood | 38 |
| 29 | Dr Ian Gibson | Norwich North | 37 |
| 30 | Jim Cousins | Newcastle upon Tyne Central | 33 |

# The Rebels

*Note*: Jim Marshall died in May 2004; he rebelled in 4.5 per cent of the divisions to occur until his death, which would place him on a par with Llew Smith in percentage terms. Also in any table measuring rebellion as a percentage of votes whilst in receipt of the whip would be George Galloway (who rebelled in 5 per cent of votes until his suspension from the Labour Party, on 6 May 2003, and subsequent expulsion, on 23 October 2003), and Paul Marsden, who rebelled in 10.7 per cent of divisions before resigning the whip in December 2001 (see below, pp. 101–105).

As a result, many of the 218 MPs who voted against the whip do not see themselves as 'rebels' – and plenty of them dislike the phrase. As Julia Drown, who retired at the 2005 election put it,

> the labels 'loyal' and 'rebel' – and I get called both – can be given with a critical edge (or if anything 'rebel' is seen as the good one, which seems counter-intuitive) and they are unhelpful to democracy. Being put in these boxes is extremely irritating. I don't feel any less loyal to the party or government, nor any more rebellious – I just feel rebellious to the way the terms are often used.

Similarly, anyone who told Tam Dalyell that he was a 'rebel' used to get short shrift. 'It's dissenting,' he used to bellow, 'not rebelling.' Tony Benn had similar views. He outlined his objections in a debate in November 1999, and his views are worth quoting at length:

> On welfare reform, I did not vote against the government; I voted for disabled people. I very much resent the press talking about a rebellion. There was no rebellion. There were Members of Parliament voting according to their convictions, in the interests of their constituents. Some may disagree, as people did, but those who voted for the

government were not actually voting for the government; they were voting for the changes in the Welfare Reform and Pensions Bill. I greatly resent the current personification of media coverage – the references to the 'awkward squad', the 'mavericks', the 'rebels'.

He was later to describe the use of the word 'rebels' as 'the language of Millbank Tower' (then the location of Labour Party HQ). All of this frustration is perfectly understandable. Woodrow Wyatt, the ex-Labour MP and later right-wing commentator, once described as a 'typically hypocritical British afterthought' the fact that the public liked MPs who defy their whips when the MP's deviations are appealing to them but thought that the MP should knuckle down and vote the party line when they don't agree with them.[26]

There are, of course, more neutral phrases, of which 'intra-party voting dissent' is the most accurate (and least offensive), but its drawback is pretty obvious: it's clumsy and unintelligible to most people. And so with apologies to Benn, Drown, Dalyell and others, the phrase 'rebel' (and its derivatives) will sometimes be used in this book to describe those who vote against their party whip. And, at times (and despite appreciating the connotations), 'loyal' (and its various derivations) will be used to describe those who vote with the government. But no value judgement is intended. And whichever phrase is used, the important point is to realise that there is no simple dichotomy between 'rebels' and 'loyalists'. The most rebellious of rebels are overwhelmingly loyal; even the most loyal of loyalists reserves the right to rebel; and you'll find the bulk of the PLP somewhere in between.

# 3
# Of sheep and men

*The 1997 Parliament – Self-discipline –
Benefit reform – Immigration reform*

> If it's a choice between being seen as clones or being seen as
> disunited . . . then I'd choose the clones any day. – Labour
> backbencher, 1997

Previous Labour leaders used to play down their party's rebellious streak, arguing either that things were not as bad as people
thought (probably true), or that some division was a sign of
healthy discussion (probably wishful thinking). On becoming
Labour leader in 1994, however, Tony Blair's strategy was
different: he talked up how bad things used to be, in order to talk
about how good things had become. As with the creation of
much of New Labour, this involved distorting and exaggerating
the historical record. It established a caricature of the past compared with which the present was noticeably more attractive.
And it allowed the party's supposed cohesion to be presented as
an important part of what made it new, and (just as importantly)
what made Labour different from the Conservatives, then in the
death throes of the Major government and widely seen by the
public as split.

Yet even in opposition there was plenty of evidence of
division within Labour's ranks.[1] The difference between Labour

and Conservative MPs – and it was a crucial one – was that whereas Conservative MPs appeared almost suicidally willing to broadcast their differences, even those Labour MPs known to have doubts about the Blairite project had for the most part taken what the *New Statesman* described as 'trappist-like vows', in order not to do anything to damage the party's chances of getting into government.[2] But once elected, what then? Blair might well have wanted a disciplined parliamentary party (what Prime Minister would want anything else?) but as every child soon learns, wanting is not the same as getting.

And so, when the parliamentary party first gathered together on 7 May 1997, six days after Labour's landslide election victory, the Prime Minister made it clear what role he envisaged for Labour's MPs. They had been elected to support the Labour government. There should be no lack of discipline:

Look at the Tory Party. Pause. Reflect. Then vow never to emulate. Day after day, when in government, they had MPs out there behaving with the indiscipline and thoughtlessness that was reminiscent of us in the early '80s. Where are they now, those great rebels?

The answer: not in Parliament.

When the walls came crashing down beneath the tidal wave of change, there was no discrimination between those Tory MPs. They were all swept away, rebels and loyalists alike. Of course, speak your minds. But realise why you are here: you are here because of the Labour Party under which you fought.[3]

It was to be a message the party hierarchy continually hammered home. In an article in the *Independent* in November 1998, Blair (or Blair's ghost writer, anyway) similarly argued that 'ill discipline allowed us to be painted as extremist, out of touch and divided.' Labour, he said, 'won't return to the factionalism, navel-gazing or feuding of the Seventies and Eighties, no matter how much a few people long for those heady days of electoral disaster'.[4]

But many Labour MPs were already placing a premium on the appearance of unity long before the Prime Minister lectured them. Being out of power for so long had increased the desire for discipline in Labour's ranks: it 'concentrates the mind wonderfully', as one MP put it. Or, as one Cabinet minister said, '1992 was a watershed. We'd blown it. It got to the soul of the party. If you're in politics, you're in politics to get power. They'd got the message that a divided party is a losing party.' Labour MPs had watched the Conservatives tear themselves apart between 1992 and 1997, and were determined not to do the same. As Ivan Lewis, the newly elected MP for Bury South, put it, 'disunity made a massive contribution to the eighteen years that we spent in opposition and ultimately rendered the Conservative Party unfit to govern. Disunited parties not only do themselves a disservice, but become paralysed and unable to pursue the public interest.' It is difficult to overstate just how widespread this belief was. After eighteen years in opposition, Labour MPs began the 1997 Parliament desperate not to do anything that might help send the party back to the wilderness; there was a desire amongst some of Labour's new MPs to avoid the appearance of disunity at almost any cost. As one of the newly elected MPs said in 1997, 'if it's a choice between being seen as clones or being seen as disunited ... then I'd choose the clones any day.'

So, clones it was. It was at this time that the sheep references became common currency. The reality, though, was more complicated than either Blair desired – or most of the MPs' many critics realised.

★ ★ ★

On one level, the Prime Minister's wish came true. Blair's first government managed something achieved by no other government since that of Harold Wilson's elected in 1966: it lasted the entire Parliament without being defeated on a whipped vote in the Commons. Since Edward Heath's government in 1970, every government, even the Thatcher governments elected with such large majorities in the 1980s, had gone down to a least one defeat. The scariest moment for Blair's whips had come when the government's majority fell to 25 at one point in 1999 – and that had been not as a result of a backbench revolt on a life and death issue, but as a result of a well-organised ambush by the Conservative whips on the Rating (Valuation) Bill.

There were also relatively few rebellions. Between 1997 and 2001 there were just 96 backbench revolts by Labour MPs. Since party cohesion in Britain began to weaken in the 1960s and 1970s every full-length Parliament – bar none – had seen considerably more rebellions. John Major, for example, had watched his Tory MPs rebel on 174 occasions in the preceding Parliament. Indeed, when the Maastricht Bill was undergoing its painful passage through the Commons at the beginning of the 1992 Parliament, Major suffered 93 rebellions in that session alone – almost as many in one parliamentary year as Blair suffered in the whole of his first term. The contrast of the first session of the 1992 Parliament (93 revolts) with the first session of the 1997 Parliament (just sixteen revolts) was particularly stark. From his new position on the opposition benches, Major must have looked on wistfully, imagining what his premiership could have been like had his MPs behaved like that. Nor was it just the Major government against which such a level of rebellion looked infrequent. Leaving aside the very short Parliaments of 1964–66 and February–October 1974, you have to go back to 1955 to find a full-length Parliament in which there were fewer backbench revolts by government MPs than the one elected in 1997. You are then back in the era of which a US observer, Sam Beer, wrote that British MPs behaved with a 'Prussian discipline'.[5]

Even this, though, allows us to dismiss some of the wilder claims made about the PLP's behaviour between 1997 and 2001. Compared with Conservative MPs in the 1950s, for example, the

PLP elected in 1997 was almost feral in its behaviour. Labour MPs between 1997 and 2001 rebelled roughly nine times more often than did all those 'independent-minded' Tory MPs in the 1950s. There were also, just for the record, more rebellions by Labour MPs between 1997 and 2001 than there were against the Attlee government. Moreover, as the Parliament progressed so the number of backbench rebellions began to increase, as the industrial-strength self-discipline that was so strong at the beginning of the Parliament began to wear off. The third session of the Parliament, during 1999 and 2000, saw more rebellions than the Parliament's first two put together. In part, this was because it was asking a lot for MPs to remain that self-disciplined for that long. But it was also because the imperatives for cohesion appeared to have become less important. As the Parliament progressed, it became increasingly clear that the Conservatives were not recovering in the polls, and so rebellion became less risky and far easier.

Just because, in historical terms, Labour MPs rebelled infrequently, it didn't mean they were uniformly loyal. The 1997 period still witnessed plenty of rebellions, of which three were particularly revealing: the revolts over lone parent benefit in 1997 and incapacity benefit and immigration and asylum, both in 1999.[6]

★ ★ ★

One of the early acts of the newly elected government was to announce that it was going to proceed with reforms to lone parent benefit inherited from the Conservatives. Despite widespread evidence of backbench concern about the policy, the government did not take any putative rebellion particularly seriously, with the degree of concern on the back benches not fully appreciated. Even when it became clear that there was deep unhappiness over the issue, political machismo intervened. Gordon Brown was unwilling to give way on the issue. He was said by one PLP insider to be 'up for a fight', believing that any potential rebels 'needed to learn a lesson sharp and hard'. Blair was similarly obdurate, believing that to give way would be to appear weak. As Andrew Rawnsley put it, 'if the choice was between being seen as weak and dithering or harsh and unbending, then he would choose to be seen as Margaret Thatcher rather than John Major. The cut was going to proceed.'[7]

Things were then made worse by the debate. The minister responsible, Harriet Harman, was left to defend the cuts alone. No Cabinet minister joined her on the government front bench during the debate, and she was practically friendless amongst her backbenchers too, continually being interrupted by hostile interventions. Hers was not a confident performance. One Labour MP went into the debate, not knowing how to vote, but thought that Harman's performance was so poor that she had to oppose. As well as concerns about the policy itself – one Labour MP describing it as the 'the Peter Lilley Memorial Bill', after the Conservative secretary of state who had initiated the policy – several Labour MPs stressed the government's lack of consultation over the policy. 'If the leadership are not prepared to honour their side of the deal about honest and open consultation before decisions are made,' said Ken Livingstone then a Labour MP, 'I do not have the slightest intention of honouring their rules that I should not vote against them.'

When the vote came, 47 Labour MPs voted for the rebel amendment, along with at least 20 abstentions. The rebels included four members of the payroll, all of whom had to resign their positions.[8] The rebellion was much larger than anyone had expected, and it shocked plenty of those in government. Officially, the leadership tried to shrug off the rebellion as being little more than the 'usual suspects'. A fortnight before the vote Blair had been shown a list of those threatening to rebel. 'This is the same bunch who opposed everything I've done to reform the party,' he said.[9] But the Prime Minister failed to appreciate the extent to which the policy was deeply unpopular, even with those who voted with the government. All that talk about the importance of being unified – and within months of being elected almost 50 Labour MPs were walking through the division lobbies against their own government. For those who had read their Labour Party history, this was not a good omen.

The chair of the PLP, Clive Soley, argued that lessons needed to be learned from the way the issue had been handled:

> We should all learn the importance in government . . . of identifying difficult policy decisions well in advance and alerting the parliamentary party and ministers to those difficulties. That is not an easy lesson, because there are bound to be areas of difficulty when we have been in government for only a short time.

And to some extent lessons were indeed learned from the lone parent rebellion. Government ministers began to make themselves more available for consultation with concerned MPs. Even if they varied in their willingness to make concessions, almost all ministers were more ready to listen and discuss than they had been previously. Just as importantly, the government faced a significant group of loyal MPs who had very reluctantly voted for the measure (some famously doing so in tears), and felt that the leadership owed them a favour. One MP, who had voted with the government despite grave misgivings, was told by his whip, 'Trust us, it'll get sorted.' And it was. Brown responded in his Budget statement in March 1998 by increasing child benefit by £2.50 a week above the rate of inflation, the largest-ever single increase. At no point did the government concede the principle of cuts for new lone parent claimants, but the establishment of the working families' tax credit included a childcare tax credit of up to £100 a week for the first child and £150 for two or more children, far more than anyone would have lost as a result of the benefit cut.

Superficially, the lone parent revolt was a failure. The government won the vote and the cut went ahead. But it led to some medium-term changes in policy which more than compensated. Most importantly of all, however, it resulted in a subtle change in relations between the front and back benches of the PLP. The executive was forced to realise it could not rely on coercion or self-discipline alone to deliver cohesion. Labour backbenchers realised both that the sky would not fall in if they voted against the government and that they could achieve policy change if they pressed for it. As one newly elected MP said, 'it gave us a confidence that they are not infallible.'

★ ★ ★

Before the 1997 Parliament began, there had been a conscious effort on the part of the party hierarchy to stamp down on possible rebellions. The standing orders of the PLP had been tightened, with threats of the removal of the whip or expulsion from the party for MPs who regularly defied the whip. But all talk of disciplining those who voted against the lone parent cut was soon dropped once the scale of the revolt became clear. With so many rebels, such disciplinary tactics would have been counterproductive. Indeed, despite all the rebellions that have occurred since 1997, right through to 2005, no Labour MP has so far had the whip removed or been expelled from the PLP for their voting record. Those to depart the ranks of the PLP have done so for things they've done (standing against an official party candidate, in the case of Livingstone) or said (in the case of George Galloway), not because of how they have voted. When Labour MPs vote the party line they are not doing so for fear of being expelled from the party.

Equally unsuccessful was the leadership's plan to enforce discipline by circulating the voting records to MPs' local constituency parties. The aim was that local activists – horrified at the rebellious nature of their MPs – would rise up and demand they toe the party line. Did it work? Answer: absolutely not. Local parties were much more likely to urge revolt than restraint. Labour MPs would complain that their activists had what one called the 'mindset of opposition', always seeing issues in terms of betrayal by the government. 'It's like a virus,' said one senior Labour MP, who got his first letter accusing the government of 'betrayal' just two months after the 1997 election. One MP recalled a party member who came up to her after a large rebellion (in which she had not participated) to say, 'If you're not prepared to vote against the government, what good are you?' Another MP became so fed up with pressure from his constituency party that he decided to vote against the party line on an issue – student grants, in June 1998 – just to placate his local activists. In several cases, reading out the occasions when the MP had voted against the party line produced cheers of approval from party meetings. One MP was clapped into her local party meeting and given a standing ovation after she participated in the lone parent revolt. Another MP – who had previously not enjoyed entirely harmonious relations with his local party – reported that once his voting record had been revealed to his activists, he enjoyed his easiest reselection ever.

Anyone expecting anything different had a short memory. Attempts by the Major government to use party activists to pressurise Maastricht rebels into supporting the party line had almost entirely failed – Conservative activists being, on the whole, more Eurosceptic than their MPs. And Hugh Berrington's research in the 1960s had discovered that something identical had happened in the nineteenth century, when Liberal radicals who dissented were more likely to be applauded by their caucuses than disciplined.[10] Not much had changed in over a hundred years.

* * *

During the debate over lone parent benefit several Labour MPs had flagged up concerns that the next stage of reform would be changes to incapacity benefit – more widely known as disability benefit. The publication of the Welfare Reform and Pensions Bill in 1999 showed that they were right to worry. Backbench discontent became public in March 1999 with an early day motion (EDM) put down by Roger Berry, a Labour backbench

MP and secretary of the All-Party Disablement Group; 68 Labour MPs signed Berry's EDM, the majority of them from the new intake. EDMs are routinely criticised for being useless pieces of parliamentary ephemera – so-called 'parliamentary graffiti' – and, given the thousands that are tabled each year, many of them are. But they can also be a useful mechanism by which back-benchers can make the strength of their opposition clear to the leadership, and they have now become almost *de rigueur* for any backbench revolt. EDMs do, however, have a drawback: as well as signalling to the leadership the scale of discontent, they also provide the whips with a list of which MPs are unhappy. In other words, they are both a petition and a target list. On balance, 'we'd sooner they (EDMs) weren't there,' said one whip – but when they are, the whips use them to try to target the unhappy and the disgruntled.

During the Bill's report stage, Berry moved an amendment to drop from the Bill the introduction of means-testing for incapacity benefit, as well as to excise proposals to remove benefit entitlement from those who had made no national insurance contributions in the previous two years. Again, 68 Labour MPs signed his amendment. Alistair Darling, Harriet Harman's replacement as Secretary of State for Social Security, made it clear that he had no intention of reaching any com-promise with the rebels before the vote. This, though, was a carefully chosen form of words: no compromise before the vote did not necessarily rule out compromise after the vote, and although he was keen to appear stern and unbending in public, in private Darling was more consultative and was willing to meet with potential rebels. Learning the lesson from the lone parent revolt, the government was keen at least to be seen to be listening to the anxieties of backbenchers. In the run-up to the vote, MPs were seen individually by at least one minister if they requested a meeting. Even some of those who did not request a meeting found themselves having them with senior ministers – one or more of the social security secretary, the Chancellor and the

Deputy Prime Minister – in an effort to make them back the government's position. One concerned MP went to see Darling, who in effect asked him, 'What's your price?' Another organised a group of MPs (what he called 'normally loyal people, disturbed at what the government was doing, and willing to negotiate') who went to see Darling *en masse*. The negotiations were 'tough, serious, prolonged and eleventh hour', he said, 'but I got everything I wanted.'

But Darling's room for manoeuvre was limited by the government's desire to win the case for its welfare reform programme, shifting the emphasis away from universal benefits to targeted help for those in the greatest need. As the *Guardian* put it, 'ministers agreed early on it was important not to concede ground on the main principles of welfare reform. If they backed off over this, they would be signalling weakness and this would mean further problems in the future with other welfare reform.'[11] The government claimed that they were trying to change the culture of the benefits system and any adverse publicity created by the rebellions had to be set against the need to move 'forward' on welfare reform. Concessions, therefore, could only be minor.

The government's initial plan was to bulldoze the legislation through during an all-night sitting, expecting that would-be rebels would prefer to go home to bed than stay up all night debating the intricacies of benefit reform. They miscalculated – most of the rebels stayed put – and so at 4.47 a.m., after more than twelve hours of debate, the government suddenly pulled stumps, ending the debate unexpectedly early and drawing back from a confrontation on the key vote.

The government then tried to pressurise MPs into cohesion. MPs – especially those who were not regular rebels – later complained of pressure being applied by the whips over this issue, in a way that it was not on other occasions. When the debate resumed three days later, Darling attempted to win over some of the rebels. In answer to a pre-arranged intervention about the threshold at which the 50 pence in the pound reduction in incapacity benefit would start to bite, Darling agreed that it would need to be increased. He claimed this was not a concession, that he was just making his existing intentions clear, but the point of making it explicit was to try to pacify backbenchers. It wasn't enough. When the vote on Berry's amendment eventually came, 67 Labour MPs voted against the government, and there was also a significant number of abstentions.[12] As a consequence, the government's majority was reduced to just 40. There was then a string of large, though slightly smaller, rebellions when the Bill came back from the Lords, despite the government offering further (relatively small) concessions to its backbench critics. Collectively, the rebellions involved a total of 74 Labour MPs.

The importance of the incapacity benefit revolt lies in what happened when ministers did not (or felt they could not) fully take on board the views of the PLP over an issue about which many of them felt strongly. Just as with the lone parent revolt a year earlier, and contrary to the popular image, Labour MPs were willing to rebel in substantial numbers when their concerns were not taken seriously. Coercion alone was insufficient. Negotiation was required to bring them into line. The best example of this came later that year: over benefits for asylum-seekers.

★ ★ ★

The deep concerns felt by Labour backbenchers over the contents of the Immigration and Asylum Bill were clear at the Bill's second reading in February 1999, with critical speech after critical speech. The full extent of Labour backbench concerns about the Bill was revealed a month later when 61 Labour members signed an EDM focusing on the issue of the children of asylum-seekers, arguing that 'no mother can meet the needs of a young child, over and above food and accommodation on 50 pence a day' and urging 'the government to reconsider this proposal'.

Discontent crystallised around an amendment moved by Neil Gerrard, the chair of the All-Party Group on Refugees. Gerrard's amendment sought to remove families with children from the voucher system altogether. Exactly half of the 24 signatories to Gerrard's amendment were Labour MPs elected for the first time in 1997, who were described in the press as 'flexing their muscles'. The *Observer* claimed to have learned from government business managers that the Bill had 'aroused more opposition among backbenchers than any other legislation before parliament, including welfare state reforms'.[13] Gerrard's own estimate of support for his amendment was slightly less dramatic, but he still thought it numbered 50 or so backbenchers.

Enter Jack Straw, described by one MP as 'the senior minister most often in the tea room'. Almost every section of the PLP acknowledges that Straw is good at meeting with, and negotiating with, MPs. He is, said one member of the party hierarchy, 'very adept at sounding hard line and consulting like mad with anyone who'll talk, making it difficult for anyone to rebel'. Straw seemed to attend almost any meeting at which his proposals were to be discussed, in order to present his point of view and debate with MPs. 'Jack's very approachable,' said one woman MP. 'You think it's a complete waste of time afterwards, but it never seems like it at the time.' He was a regular visitor to meetings of the left-wing Socialist Campaign Group, sometimes at his own invitation (one Campaign Group member said that they were thinking of offering him membership: 'He'd been more than some of our members.'). During one week in early June 1999, Straw appeared to be at almost every meeting being held in the Palace of Westminster. Other ministers may consult and negotiate, said one MP, 'but no one else is in Jack's league'.

As a result of these discussions, by the time the Bill returned from committee to the floor of the House, Straw had given ground. In a carefully staged series of concessions – some trailed in committee, some just before the report stage debate, some during the debate itself – the Home Secretary dealt with the concerns of his backbenchers; with an increase in payments here, a change to the immigration procedures there, he steadily chipped away at the would-be rebels until Gerrard, seeing how little support he now had as a result of Straw's concessions, decided not to press his amendment to a vote.

Straw had conceded enough to placate the rebels – but without fundamentally altering the Bill. The central part of the Bill – the voucher system – remained (only then to be scrapped shortly after the 2001 election, by which time Straw had left the Home Office). Financial support for asylum-seekers remained at 70 per cent of income support levels (although Straw sought to make it appear 90 per cent by including the provision of utensils, utility bills and bed linen in his calculations). His other concessions amounted to fairly minor changes. The only substantive change was to place on the Home Secretary a duty of care for the children of asylum-seekers, while his promises on larger families and targets were just that: promises. One Labour critic of the proposals said despairingly, 'I think that we have reached a pretty pass when, after one minister had consulted and produced some relatively minor concessions, there is dancing within the Parliamentary Labour Party.' Another critic viewed such concessions on Bills as amounting to little in reality and saw Straw as the 'arch-exemplar' of giving 'the minimum they can get away with'.

Yet the concessions had been enough. *The Times* had earlier claimed that the government was on course for its first Commons defeat over the issue. In the event, the Bill saw just four rebellions, all of them small, and only seventeen Labour back-benchers voted against any part of the Bill. Of these, just three were new MPs, those previously said to have been flexing their muscles. If the revolt over lone parent benefit was How Not to Do It, this was a textbook example of How to Do It, a classic example of how a government can negotiate itself out of trouble.

* * *

Despite its 'control freak' reputation, as a government that ignored MPs and disdained Parliament, the first Blair government was in fact rather conventional in its dealings with backbenchers, especially after the scale of the lone parent benefit rebellion in December 1997 made them realise that they could not rely solely on coercion to retain cohesion. Ministers were willing to meet with, and negotiate with, backbench critics; they didn't give concessions easily – backbenchers had to wring them out of ministers – but they did give them. As well as over asylum and immigration, the government also gave considerable ground during the passages of the Criminal Justice (Terrorism and Conspiracy) Bill, the Prevention of Terrorism Bill, and – most obviously of all – the Freedom of Information Bill. The last saw the Secretary of State – again, Jack Straw – engaging in what was effectively a seminar with his own backbenchers on the floor of the House and being prepared to rewrite bits of the Bill whilst at the despatch box.

When, however, the government did not sugar the legislative pill sufficiently, Labour MPs were prepared to revolt, and over a range of issues. Between 1997 and 2001, Labour's party managers faced discontent on a number of different fronts, often at the same time. There were twelve issues which saw rebellions of at least 20 Labour MPs. They ranged over almost all the areas of government policy; as well as welfare reform and immigration, revolts covered legal affairs, pensions, competition policy, air traffic control, civil liberties, foreign affairs, terrorism, freedom of information, and education. The rebellions seen between 1997 and 2001 were on average larger than in any Parliament between 1945 and 1966; they were larger than those seen under Edward Heath between 1970 and 1974; and larger than those seen during the four consecutive Conservative governments between 1979 and 1997.[14] For poodles, Labour MPs could bark loudly when provoked – and a great deal louder than Conservative MPs ever did.

Nor were opponents of government policy always the same people. The number of MPs prepared to vote against the government at some point in the parliament totalled 133, around half Labour's backbenchers, and far more than the easily dismissed group of the 'usual suspects'.

It was not therefore an acquiescent or timid PLP. It was not the PLP portrayed in the media, stuffed full of clones, daleks or sheep, all bereft of spine or independent thought, loyally trooping through the division lobbies. Nor, of course, was it a parliamentary party that was rebelling both frequently and in quantity – as the PLP did between 1974 and 1979 (and, to a lesser extent, between 1966 and 1970). Rather, Labour MPs were prepared to rebel, in sizeable numbers at times, but they did so infrequently. The first part of the explanation, therefore, as to how the PLP underwent such a transformation after the 2001 election – from sheep to Rottweilers – is that they had never been sheep in the first place.

# Helen Brinton and Helen Clark

Taking digs at the women MPs elected in such record numbers in 1997 has been a popular sport ever since they entered the Commons. Complaints began with their appearance, moved on to their devotion to the party line, and ended up with their supposed overall lack of achievements.[15] These complaints didn't just come from those (misogynists?) who always wanted the women to fail, but also from those (feminists?) who felt let down.

As Anne Perkins wrote in 1999, the women suffered 'derision as centrally-programmed automatons . . . being reviled for failing to rebel, condemned as careerists – in short, one great fuchsia-suited failure'. She continued:

> It was their failure to fight collectively, in particular to unite against the lone parent benefit cuts that caused such rumpus in late '97, that earned them the reputation of betraying women who needed them for the sake of their own political futures. Most damaging, it was a view shared by more experienced women colleagues.[16]

In a twist on the concept of 'critical mass' – the feminist concept that once the number of women in a Parliament reaches a certain point, then the institution will be feminised – a male Labour MP described the new women MPs as an 'uncritical mass'. Singled out as the exemplar was Helen Brinton, the Labour MP for Peterborough. A former school teacher, Brinton was first elected in 1997, and her name soon became synonymous with excessive demonstrations of loyalty – it was jokingly said that a Labour MP's loyalty to the government could be measured in 'Brintons'. She became the target of a running campaign by one of the *Guardian*'s diarists, Matthew Norman, after an appearance on BBC 2's *Newsnight* in which she had attempted to defend Peter Mandelson. It was all a bit unfair. By the end of Tony Blair's first term just eleven of the 65 women elected for the first time in 1997 had voted against their party whip. That's only 17 per cent. The figure for male MPs elected at the same time was exactly double, 34 per cent. Brinton wasn't one of the eleven, but then neither were Diana Organ, Julia Drown, Claire Curtis-Thomas, Sally Keeble, Jackie Lawrence or a host of others elected in 1997.

This difference in behaviour was first noticed during the rebellion over lone parent benefit in 1997. Of the 47 MPs to vote against the party line, just one (Ann Cryer) was a woman from the 1997 intake.[17] The majority trooped through the government lobby to cut benefit for lone parents. Here was an issue that disproportionately affected women – an issue that feminists would previously have seized with both hands as a clear-cut example of why we needed more women in Parliament – and yet the women MPs did not appear to be standing up for the interests of other women. One long-standing woman MP saw this as a 'betrayal' of all-women shortlists, the procedure by which Labour had managed to get so many women MPs into Parliament in 1997. Others – even more critical – saw it as confirmation of their belief that all-women shortlists would result in substandard MPs; if they'd been good enough, they'd have made it without needing special favours. Ann Widdecombe complained of the 'docility and absence of ability' displayed by many of the new women MPs, something she linked directly to the use of all-women shortlists:

Serious politicians arrive in the House already battle-hardened . . . Blair's Babes have arrived with starry eyes and a pager, shielded by positive discrimination from any real competition. They nod in unison behind the front bench. Some of the dear little souls have even whinged that Madam Speaker is too hard on them and indeed has caused more than one to break into tears. Can anyone imagine Bessie Braddock, Barbara Castle or Margaret Thatcher dissolving at a ticking off from the Speaker?[18]

Several of the 1997 women now look back on the lone parent vote with regret (just as many of them regret the famous photograph of them all clustered adoringly around Tony Blair). They point out that it was the first serious vote of the Parliament, that they were still finding their feet, and that had it come later in the Parliament, things would have been very different. The problems with this argument are that plenty of men from the new intake rebelled (despite similarly finding their feet) and that the lone parent vote wasn't a one-off and things weren't different later in the Parliament: the differences between the men and the women elected in 1997 remained throughout the next four years. In every single major rebellion that took place during the 1997 Parliament, the newly elected women were under-represented amongst the ranks of the rebels.

Identifying this difference was the easy bit. Explaining it was much harder. First, there was the critical explanation: these women MPs were too spineless to rebel, and not up to the job. If they couldn't stand the heat, they should get out of the kitchen – a jibe to which one responded: New Labour, New Kitchen. The second, more positive, explanation was to try to explain it away, to argue that the apparent differences in the women's behaviour were spurious, merely the result of other characteristics of the MPs, such as their age, the marginality of their seat and so on. Once we controlled for these, then all the differences would vanish. Trouble was, this didn't get you very far. It wasn't, for example, that the women were younger, and thus less rebellious. They didn't have particularly different backgrounds from the male MPs or sit for different types of seat. They weren't more or less right wing than their male counterparts. In other words, every attempt to explain away the difference found that you couldn't.[19] Nor, however, was it true that all-women shortlists were the problem. There was absolutely no difference between the behaviour of those women selected on all-women lists and those selected on 'open' shortlists. In fact, three of the most rebellious of the newly elected women in the 1997 Parliament – Cryer, Betty Williams and Julie Morgan – were all selected from all-women lists. Whatever their advantages or disadvantages, there was no evidence that all-women shortlists had brought less rebellious MPs into Parliament.

So a third type of argument – in some ways an even more positive argument – got wheeled out. For many of the 1997 women – and their supporters – the difference in their voting behaviour was proof of a different style of politics, more consensual, less macho, less confrontational. Thus Brinton wasn't feeble or second rate because she didn't rebel; she was, so this argument went, just 'doing her politics differently'. And not just differently. Better, too. This consensual and less macho style of politics was perceived by many of the women to be both distinct from, and more effective than, a style of politics involving overt rebellion – with the latter being perceived as reflecting a masculine mode of politics more concerned with gesture politics than effecting change. Thus Brinton was, in fact, a much *better* politician than all those dreadfully macho Labour men who'd voted against the government.

Apart from the retort made famous by Mandy Rice-Davies – well, they would say that, wouldn't they? – there were two more substantive problems with trying to argue a case like this. The first was that this wasn't an effect seen with all women; it was particular to that large cohort elected in 1997.

The more established women MPs, those elected before 1997, were just as likely – in some cases, more likely – to rebel as were the men. So how could this be about 'feminised' politics? This objection was swatted aside by arguing that because women had previously been such a small minority of the Commons, the longer-serving women MPs had been forced to out-macho the men in order to survive. With so few of them, in other words, women MPs had been forced to behave like men. And so it was only now, with such a large cohort of women, that these differences became clear.

The second problem – not so easily dodged – was that there was no evidence that the newly elected women were more likely to practise this style of politics than other MPs. Nearly all MPs – old and new, male and female – say that they work behind the scenes. They too take problems to ministers in private. They too have a calculating and tactical and instrumental approach to cohesion. The juxtaposition of oh-so-clever women MPs scheming their brilliant schemes with Neanderthal macho men so stoked up with testosterone that the best they can do is to blunder gruntingly through the division lobbies in opposition to their government was as crude and insulting and sexist a comparison as anything ever levelled against the women.

And then, during the second Blair term, a new problem emerged for proponents of the 'different' style of politics: the women started to rebel. The rebels included Helen Brinton – although following her marriage in 2001 she had metamorphosed into Helen Clark. As Helen Brinton she hadn't voted against the party line once. As Helen Clark, she rebelled on ten occasions, taking part in revolts over Iraq, the fire-fighters and higher education.

## Labour women MPs elected in 1997 who rebelled, 1997–2005

| Name | Votes against the whip, 1997–2001 | Votes against the whip, 2001–05 | Total votes against the whip, 1997–2005 |
|---|---|---|---|
| Ann Cryer | 16 | 17 | 33 |
| Betty Williams | 16 | 14 | 30 |
| Julie Morgan | 14 | 15 | 29 |
| Christine McCafferty | 4 | 16 | 20 |
| Barbara Follett | 0 | 19 | 19 |
| Geraldine Smith | 1 | 17 | 18 |
| Helen Brinton/Clark | 0 | 10 | 10 |
| Karen Buck | 0 | 10 | 10 |
| Linda Perham | 0 | 9 | 9 |
| Debra Shipley | 0 | 7 | 7 |
| Valerie Davey | 0 | 7 | 7 |
| Janet Dean | 3 | 4 | 7 |
| Louise Ellman | 0 | 6 | 6 |
| Jenny Jones | 6 | – | 6 |
| Diana Organ | 0 | 5 | 5 |
| Helen Jones | 0 | 5 | 5 |
| Eileen Gordon | 5 | – | 5 |
| Julia Drown | 0 | 4 | 4 |
| Claire Curtis-Thomas | 0 | 3 | 3 |
| Jane Griffiths | 0 | 3 | 3 |
| Joan Humble | 0 | 3 | 3 |
| Anne Begg | 0 | 2 | 2 |
| Sandra Osborne | 0 | 2 | 2 |
| Christine Butler | 2 | – | 2 |
| Tess Kingham | 2 | – | 2 |
| Jackie Lawrence | 0 | 1 | 1 |
| Judy Mallaber | 0 | 1 | 1 |
| Sally Keeble | 0 | 1 | 1 |
| Oona King | 1 | 0 | 1 |

*Note:* Jones and Kingham retired at the 2001 election; Gordon and Butler lost their seats.

## The Rebels

She wasn't the only one. The table above lists all the women from the 1997 intake who voted against the government between 1997 and 2005. The list is headed by Cryer, the MP for Keighley, and the widow of Bob Cryer, himself a frequent rebel whilst an MP. Of the seven women rebels left after the 2001 election, all but one (Oona King) continued to vote against the government in the 2001 parliament. They were joined by eighteen new rebels. Especially rebellious – having been entirely loyal before – was Barbara Follett, the MP for Stevenage. Another MP, like Brinton, who was once seen as the epitome of New Labour, she rebelled not once during the 1997 Parliament, but on nineteen occasions after 2001.[20] Indeed, Follett rebelled more often in the 2001 parliament than any other woman from the 1997 intake. Anyone offering odds in June 2001 that Follett would rebel more often than Cryer or Williams would not have had many takers.

Since many of the women have made it into government at various levels,[21] the rise in the rebelliousness of the women meant that by the time of the 2005 election there were just three women MPs from the 1997 intake who had neither made it onto the payroll at some level nor rebelled: Candy Atherton, Siobhain McDonagh and Christine Russell. Atherton lost her seat in the 2005 election. McDonagh and Russell then both became PPSs when Parliament resumed after the election. That leaves not a single woman from the 1997 intake stuck on the backbenches without a sniff of office and solidly loyal to boot.

# 4

# Saint Gwyneth and the Grand Old Duke of York

*Select committees – Anti-terrorism – Lords reform*

> Does my Right Hon. Friend find it bizarre – as I do – that the yoghurt- and muesli-eating, *Guardian*-reading fraternity are only too happy to protect the human rights of people engaged in terrorist acts, but never once do they talk about the human rights of those who are affected by them? – Kevin Hughes MP to the Home Secretary, November 2001

An early sign that things in Parliament were going to be different during Tony Blair's second term came in July 2001, when viewers of BBC 1's *Frost on Sunday* were treated to the sight of Donald Anderson MP and Gwyneth Dunwoody MP holding hands on live television. The cause of this early-morning tryst – one of the more disturbing sights of the Parliament's four years – was the decision taken by the government to remove Anderson from the Foreign Affairs Select Committee, which he had chaired since 1997, and to do likewise to Dunwoody from the Transport Select Committee. The government claimed that both had had a fair crack of the whip, and that the committees needed some fresh blood. Critics saw it as an attempt by the government to nobble two independent-minded select committee chairs, thus weakening Parliament's ability to scrutinise the executive. Their early-morning appearance on Frost's sofa was a sign of mutual defiance; and it was enough to put any watching whip right off their cornflakes.

Dunwoody had received a phone call from Labour's newly installed Chief Whip, Hilary Armstrong, at 11.20 a.m. on Wednesday, 11 July 2001. She had been informed that an announcement would be made about the membership of select committees in about ten minutes' time, and that she would no longer be on the Transport Committee. At the same time, the government also announced that it intended to appoint the former culture secretary, Chris Smith, to replace Anderson as chairman of the Foreign Affairs Committee. Dunwoody reacted by saying that she was 'not especially proud, but being sacked with 10 minutes' notice did not seem to me to be a very good way of conducting the government's business.'[1] These decisions did not go down well at the meeting of the PLP later that day.[2] Some of those who objected to the government's proposals did so on the personal grounds that they liked or admired either Dunwoody or Anderson. But there were also plenty of MPs who did not have much time for either Anderson or Dunwoody – considering the former to be a bit dull, the latter to be a bit of a show-off – but who objected to the government's plans on principle. The issue was not the merits of either individual, but the struggle between backbenchers and the whips over the use of patronage.

Left to its own devices, the Whips' Office would have whipped the votes – and the whips believed that had they done so they could have won.[3] But their hands were tied by comments made by the new Leader of the House, Robin Cook. Having been moved from the Foreign and Commonwealth Office after the election, Cook had declared privately that he was determined to 'leave footprints in the sand'. Almost his first public act in his new role was to intervene in the Anderson and Dunwoody affair, promising Labour MPs that they would be given a free vote on the issue, and making it clear that the Commons had the potential to reverse the decision should it so wish. He also hinted, not terribly subtly, at Cabinet-level disagreements over the decision. 'The people who took that decision', he said, 'made it on competing advice . . . If the House feels this was a wrong decision, they can put it right. This will be a free vote. We will not put any whips on, and we will not send in the payroll vote.'[4]

In private, Cook told Armstrong that he was 'hacked off' over the issue, partly because he thought it inherently wrong, but also because he had been determined to push ahead with a programme of parliamentary reform, and instead found himself defending decisions which appeared to weaken Parliament's ability to scrutinise the government. Exasperated, he noted in his diary on 12 July 2001 that:

> Gwyneth Dunwoody has been transformed by the press into a paradigm of parliamentary virtue shamelessly silenced by a ruth-less government machine embarrassed by her fearless scrutiny . . . I was already booked to appear on the *Today* programme to discuss my speech on modernisation but instead spend much of my time discussing the martyrdom of Saint Gwyneth.[5]

This was the first public indication of how Cook would fulfil his role; and until he resigned in 2003 over the Iraq war, he was to prove an activist Leader of the House, intervening in the process of Lords reform as well as attempting to give some drive and direction to the 'modernisation' of the House of Commons that had begun, somewhat hesitantly and sporadically, in the first Blair term. As a result, relations between the Whips' Office and that of the Leader of the House were never particularly good. Some of the former used to sneer whenever they used the word 'moderniser'; some of the latter used to complain that the Whips' Office was 'where they put the thickies'. 'Robin thought Hilary Armstrong was thick. And she thought he patronised her,' observed one of those close to Cook, before adding, 'They were both right.'

Those opposed to the government's plans were given further encouragement by Baroness (Betty) Boothroyd, the former Commons Speaker, who called on backbenchers to rise up: 'Here is a chance for the House to act. It can use its authority, take power away from the whips and reinstate those two excellent chairmen.' Lord St John of Fawsley, who oversaw the birth of the select committee system as Conservative Leader of the House of Commons in the early 1980s, also attacked the government's actions, describing them as 'sinister and dangerous', and saying that select committee chairmanships were 'never intended as a consolation prize for failed former ministers'.

The day after their joint appearance on Frost's sofa, the House of Commons sided with the hand-holding rebels. The government's proposed alternative membership for the Foreign Affairs Select Committee (which included dropping Anderson as chair) was rejected by 301 votes to 232. Some 234 Labour MPs voted for the motion, but 118 Labour backbenchers voted against. Twenty minutes later, MPs also rejected the proposed membership of the new Transport Select Committee (including dropping Dunwoody) by an even bigger majority of 308 to 221. This time, 221 Labour MPs supported the motion, but 125 Labour backbenchers opposed.[6] Anderson and Dunwoody were promptly reinstated onto their committees, which they went on to chair for the rest of the Parliament. The attempt to oust them had backfired. The amount of damage which either of them could have done over four years as chair of their committees was as nothing compared to the amount caused by trying to depose them. A member of the Whips' Office admitted, 'We got it wrong . . . We thought they [Labour MPs] were biddable and they weren't.' Anderson greeted the results with the claim that it was 'a peasants' revolt and a great day for Parliament'.

Some media reaction bordered on the hysterical, giving the impression, as Peter Riddell noted in *The Times*, that 'we were back in the 1640s and Speaker Lenthall was defying Charles I over the arrest of the five members'. The reality wasn't half as dramatic. For one thing, the revolt wasn't really that much of a peasants' revolt. To be sure, the 'rebels' included some previously loyal MPs, including the much-maligned Helen Brinton (now Clark) and there were some newly elected MPs amongst those voting in favour of the two committee chairs. But the vast majority of those who voted against the government – 70 per cent in each vote – had already defied the government on whipped votes during the previous parliament. Whatever else it was, this wasn't a slaughter of the innocents. The scale of the government's rebuff was made all the more impressive by the involvement of those who had been loyal previously, but the rebels alone would have been sufficient to have brought about defeat. In themselves, the votes were of only moderate importance. It is hardly as if the Foreign Affairs Select Committee has much power (or even much influence); ditto for the Transport Committee.[7] But the dispute was emblematic of the increasing willingness of Labour backbenchers to defy their front bench – and to make life harder for the government. One whip recognised the vote as 'a collective putting down of a marker'.

★ ★ ★

The Affair of Saint Gwyneth strengthened the view within the Whips' Office that the second Blair term was going to be tougher than the first – but it did not create that view. Labour MPs were, one whip recalled, 'in the most foul mood' when they returned after the 2001 election, something which became clear when the PLP gathered for its first post-election meeting. Whereas the Prime Minister had used the first meeting of the PLP after the 1997 election to lecture MPs on the need for unity, backbenchers used the first meeting after the 2001 election to lecture the Prime Minister, making it clear – in fairly robust terms – exactly what they expected from Labour's second term. 'They were', said a whip, 'very assertive'.[8]

Some of the reasons for this increased restlessness were obvious. For one thing, many of the MPs, especially those with marginal seats, were physically exhausted after months of electioneering. The idea that election campaigns are merely the four or so weeks of the formal campaign is a pretty poor fiction. Many MPs are now engaged in an almost permanent campaign, one that steps up noticeably a year or so before the election is expected. As the 2001 election approached, the Labour whips were allowing MPs with marginal seats extended time away from Westminster to press the flesh in their constituencies, with Labour's majority in the Commons being delivered by MPs with safer seats and/or those representing constituencies in London and the south-east. Those who have never done it frequently criticise the work-rate of candidates ('we've not had a single candidate knock on our door') but those with experience of elections will testify to how exhausting they are. In 1997, the sheer euphoria of Labour's first election victory for eighteen years and, for the masses of new MPs, the excitement of arriving at the Commons for the first time were more than enough to compensate. Four years later, those same knackered MPs were simply returning to a place of work.

And whereas in 1997 many of them were surprised to be at Westminster, and felt indebted to the efforts of the Prime Minister, by 2001 many of them felt that they, rather than Tony Blair, had been more important. As one member of the Whips' Office put it, 'some of them thought *they'd* done it because of things that *they'd* done in their constituency, because of how hard *they'd* worked and campaigned.' Some of the whips felt that the stress placed on localism by Labour's campaigning tactics – working the constituency permanently, including allowing MPs to be absent from Westminster for extended periods – had led to a dangerous mindset amongst some MPs, in which the national picture became secondary to the goings on in Proletown North. 'The constituency's important,' said one. 'But you're not just a super councillor. We allowed people to get into feeling that the constituency was the only thing that mattered.' Moreover, having achieved the second term – and with an almost certain guarantee that for the first time in its history Labour would be able to govern for an entire second term – one of the earlier imperatives for the praetorian self-discipline of the first four years had gone. The returning MPs were also more confident and experienced. As one MP said, talking about the 1997 intake of which she was a member,

a lot of them never expected to win. And some of them had hardly spoken to a Labour MP before. And, as far as ministers were concerned, they were overwhelmed by them, these important people, especially Secretaries of State. And as for the Prime Minister! But after a while, they got to know that these were ordinary people. They learnt that you wouldn't be burnt to death if you voted against the government. And that Secretaries of State were ordinary, fallible, people, who can make mistakes. They stopped being over-awed by office.

Alongside this, the structure of the party on the back benches had been changing. Four years of government had taken their toll. The whips had identified three groups of MPs – the so-called three 'dises' – that they expected to cause trouble. First, there were what they called the perennial *dis*senters (largely, but not exclusively, the 30 or so MPs in the Campaign Group). This group was nothing new; they'd been rebelling against the government since 1997. But they'd now been joined by two new groups: the *dis*appointed – those who thought they ought to have a job in government but didn't – and the *dis*missed, those who had been in government but were no longer.

By 2001, there was a growing number of Labour backbenchers disappointed that their talents had not been recognised. In many cases, of course, their talents had been recognised – and that was precisely the reason why they remained on the back benches – but, curiously enough, most of them didn't see it like that. Few would admit publicly that their rebellions were motivated by bitterness at having failed to get into government, although some would privately. As one member of the 1997 intake put it,

> why the hell should I do anything for you? You've done nothing for me. Why should I stand up – like I did over lone parent benefit – and scrabble around for arguments, when frankly I thought the policy stank? It doesn't mean that I'm going to start trotting through the lobbies on every vote, but when there's something that I disagree with then the Chief Whip can bully till she's blue in the face, but I'm still going to do it.

The third group, the dismissed, numbered around 60 at the beginning of the Parliament, had reached 90 by its midpoint, and had climbed to over a hundred by the end. Not all of these ex-ministers had begun to vote against the government out of bitterness (although some were very bitter), but they were all liberated by their departure from government, which gave them a freedom that they had previously been denied. The whips estimated that these three groups collectively amounted to around a third of the PLP, or around half the backbenchers. As one whip put it, they constituted 'combustible material'.

\* \* \*

Immediately prior to 11 September 2001, there had been only very sporadic outbreaks of backbench revolt – six rebellions, five of them minor – but there was already plenty of legislation in the pipeline which the whips knew had the potential to cause them trouble.[9] They faced a rebellion over the abolition of community health councils in England and Wales (with 26 Labour MPs voting against the plans), although later modifications of the proposals prevented further rebellions over the issue. There was also trouble over the Enterprise Bill – 24 Labour MPs supported an amendment compelling the Office of Fair Trading to take into account damage to the public interest and employment levels when determining competition policy on mergers and acquisitions. There were much more serious problems over the Nationality, Immigration and Asylum Bill (seventeen rebellions in total, the largest seeing 43 Labour MPs defy their whips) and the Education Bill – in particular the government's proposals to expand the number of faith schools in England and Wales. This was an issue that had antecedents for the PLP. In January 1931, the MacDonald government had gone down to defeat over financial aid to voluntary schools, when 36 rebellious Labour backbenchers had voted against it; the somewhat battered Education (School Attendance) Bill then went to the Lords, where its subsequent failure led to the resignation of the Secretary of State for Education, Sir Charles Philip Trevelyan. Apart from the change in nomenclature (voluntary schools in the 1930s, faith schools in the 21st century), the key difference between the rebellions in the 1930s and those seventy years later was that the earlier rebellions were conducted by supporters of faith schools (the government being opposed), whereas those in 2002 were carried out by opponents (the government supporting). The largest revolt in 2002 saw 46 Labour backbenchers support a new clause moved by Frank Dobson that required religious schools to admit 25 per cent of their pupils from outside that religion, and that would have made it illegal for new faith schools to require children or parents to attend religious services as part of their admissions procedures. This time, the Bill – and the Secretary of State – survived.

But the most serious problems came with opposition to the government's proposals to deal with terrorism after 11 September. In the first session alone, this provoked 25 separate backbench rebellions, of which 22 came during the passage of one Bill: the Anti-Terrorism, Crime and Security Bill.

★ ★ ★

When the details of the Anti-Terrorism, Crime and Security Bill were announced, it was clear that the Home Office had prioritised neither brevity nor focus. Instead of a short, targeted Bill, making one or two emergency changes to the law, the Home Secretary instead proposed a large catch-all Bill, amounting to a whopping 128 paragraphs. As well as legislation essential to combat terrorism, the Bill contained, as David Blunkett was later to concede, a range of measures that the Home Office had been trying to achieve for years, but for which they had never managed to find the appropriate legislative vehicle.[10] The Bill gave law enforcement agencies sweeping powers to access information, in relation to not only suspected terrorists but also those suspected of criminal offences. It amended the immigration laws to ensure that those suspected of committing terrorist offences abroad were not able to seek asylum in the United Kingdom, and instead could be detained without trial, subject only to a right of appeal to a Special Immigration Appeals Tribunal (SIAC). To do this, the government was proposing to derogate from (opt out of) Article 5.1 of the European Convention on Human Rights, which prohibits detention without trial. And – equally controversially – the Bill also proposed to widen the law on incitement to include religious as well as racial hatred.

As soon as the Home Secretary had finished announcing the proposals, he came under attack from Labour MPs worried both about the civil liberties implications of the proposals and about the haste with which they were being introduced: the measures were announced in October, with the Home Secretary aiming to have the Bill on the statute book before the Christmas recess. Chris Mullin, the chair of the Home Affairs Select Committee, spoke for many Labour MPs when he pointed to the 'long history of anti-terrorism legislation being introduced in haste and repented at leisure'.

Thanks to support from the Conservatives, the government was assured of victory on the Bill's second reading in November. But theirs was conditional and partial support: the Conservatives were prepared to lend their support at second reading but wanted a series of 'sunset clauses' added to the Bill, to force the government to revisit aspects of the legislation at a later date. They also wanted to narrow the focus of the Bill, restricting it to terrorist offences only, and were opposed to the extension of incitement laws to include religious hatred. The easy margin of victory in the second reading vote – by 458 votes to just five, with four Labour MPs voting against – masked a pretty torrid time for the Home Secretary. Of the eleven Labour MPs who intervened during his speech, only one was supportive. Kevin Hughes, the Labour MP for Doncaster North, asked Blunkett whether he found it 'bizarre – as I do – that the yoghurt- and muesli-eating, *Guardian*-reading fraternity are only too happy to protect the human rights of people engaged in terrorist acts, but never once do they talk about the human rights of those who are affected by them?' The intervention was not particularly helpful – especially when it was later revealed that Hughes himself had a penchant for Greek yoghurt, had (horror of horrors!) tried muesli, and in fact bore an uncanny resemblance to the caricature bearded leftie which he had been mocking.

The following day's press reports wrote of the Home Secretary being 'under fire', facing a 'barrage of hostile questions' during a 'stormy' six-hour debate. But Frank Johnson's sketch of the debate in the *Daily Telegraph* was more accurate.

> Mr Blunkett's performance was awesome. Behind him, on the Labour backbenches, was every independent-minded libertarian in his party. Bearing in mind the size of the parliamentary Labour party, this is a tiny number. There are probably more Taliban in Tel Aviv. But when they are all together, and constantly inter-rupting the Home Secretary with their high-minded questions and observations, they seem to be a seething mass of rebellion.[11]

There were some Labour MPs who were fiercely opposed to the whole Bill, or at least to the majority of its contents. Brian Sedgemore – later to defect to the Liberal Democrats in the run-up to the 2005 election – was the most vociferous, describing the legislation as 'a rag bag of the most coercive measures that the best mandarin minds from the Home Office can produce'. 'Not since the panic and hysteria that overcame the British establishment in the aftermath of the French Revolution', he said, 'has the House considered such draconian legislation.' But other Labour MPs – even those critical of some of the proposals – were more balanced. There was a fairly widespread scepticism about the prohibition of incitement to religious hatred (and, more generally, a belief that whatever its merits, it did not belong in the Bill), and there was also concern about derogating from the European Convention on Human Rights. Yet despite such mutterings, many of the rebellions were relatively small; the revolt over derogation, for example, saw just fifteen Labour MPs vote against the party line.[12]

Blunkett approached the Bill, claimed his biographer, as if it was a game of chess, being willing to give way on minor matters in order to achieve his main objectives.[13] He'd sacrificed his first pawns even before the second reading vote, announcing two concessions from his original proposals, and he gave a more significant concession when the Bill reached its committee stage, giving in to Mullin's request for a sunset clause for the section of the Bill dealing with detention without trial, meaning that after five years the measure would lapse and Parliament would have to vote to approve it. This concession was enough to persuade several previously unconvinced Labour MPs to vote for the measure.[14] He then also announced that he would make three other changes to the Bill, changes that had been suggested to him during his appearance before the Joint Committee on Human Rights. Jean Corston and Vera Baird QC, both members of the committee, had tabled an amendment to the Bill, which they then withdrew following Blunkett's announcement.

This string of fairly low-level concessions failed to mollify the more hard-line critics of the Bill, several of whom found Blunkett's chess-playing just a little too obvious, and more than a little reminiscent of tactics used in the previous Parliament.

Diane Abbott made a telling comment on the process of granting concessions that was being used by Blunkett and had been used to such effect by his predecessor, Jack Straw. She accepted that the sunset clause was a positive step, but she called on MPs to cast their mind back to when Straw had been Home Secretary:

> He was a past master at the art of the carefully calibrated concession – just enough to get people voting with the government but not enough to alter the substance of the legislation. I hope that in this parliament we will not get caught up with such concessions, because, a few years on, no one can remember what the concessions were but we know that we are lumbered with thoroughly bad legislation.

Despite Abbott's misgivings, Blunkett's 'carefully calibrated concessions' were enough to persuade many previously unsure Labour MPs to back the Bill. The Bill's first day in committee, 21 November, had produced seven separate Labour rebellions, but most had been relatively small. The largest – it turned out to be the largest on the Bill – saw 32 Labour MPs vote against allowing judicial review of the Home Secretary's decisions to detain suspects without trial, but the rest ranged between just six and fifteen MPs.

The Bill's second day in committee and its report stage, on 26 November, were similar. There were six more rebellions, most of which concerned attempts to restrict the scope of the Bill to those offences that might reasonably be assumed to relate to terrorism. But again, most were fairly small, ranging between three and eleven MPs. Slightly more difficulty came with the proposals on religious hatred. The two-hour debate on the religious hatred clause revealed plenty of Labour MPs who had concerns about the proposal. When the House divided, the government won comfortably by 328 votes to 209, but 21 Labour MPs voted against the government.[15]

Finally, at midnight, after a three-minute speech by Blunkett on third reading, the Bill's strict timetable ran out. When the House divided, just seventeen Labour backbenchers voted against the third reading, with the government winning easily. Having been battered by the coverage of the earlier select committee votes and the Paul Marsden affair (see below, pp. 101–105), the whips believed that they had managed to contain what potentially could have been a far more serious revolt. Although there were some relatively large rebellions during the Bill's passage, most of the revolts were fairly small (the average rebellion over the Bill was just eleven), with the concessions enough to placate most backbench critics. 'We well contained it,' said one whip. It was the first big test of the 2001 Parliament and the Whips' Office believed they had done a good job. The Bill then went to the Lords – at which point the real trouble began.

★ ★ ★

Labour's reforms of the House of Lords – and in particular, the removal of most of the hereditary peers – used to be a central part of complaints about the Blair government's marginalisation of Parliament. The government, so its critics said, was emasculating the one remaining check on its parliamentary dominance. Of the first 53 defeats the government suffered in the Lords after 1997, all but six occurred as a result of the votes of the hereditary peers. And so, the argument went, remove the hereditary peers and you remove any effective opposition.

In fact, as was clear within a year or two of the House of Lords Act 1999 coming into effect, the exact opposite occurred. The pre-reform House of Lords – conscious that its legitimacy was limited by the presence of so many hereditary peers – frequently practised a self-denying ordinance, pulling back from many confrontations with the government. But with the hereditaries largely gone, the remaining peers saw themselves as more legitimate, and – as a result – became far more assertive than before. If the government had hoped to create a poodle of an upper chamber, then it was very much mistaken.

This became increasingly clear during Tony Blair's second term; the 2001–05 Parliament saw the government defeated in the Lords on 245 separate occasions, more than double the number of defeats in the first Blair term (108).[16] The average (mean) number of Lords defeats per session during the extended period of Conservative government between 1979 and 1997 was just over thirteen. The equivalent figure for the 2001 Parliament was just over 61. In other words, the Lords defeated the Labour government of 2001–05 more than four times as often as they had defeated the Thatcher and Major governments, and more than twice as often as they had defeated the first Blair government.

The extra problems which the government faced in the Lords are sometimes ascribed to the greater sagacity of peers, their great wisdom, and their increased independence of thought. In fact, research has shown that the parliamentary parties in the Lords are no less cohesive than those in the Commons.[17] The real difference – and it is the crucial one – is that no one party holds a majority in the Lords. Despite Labour increasing its membership in the Lords throughout the Blair years, they remain in a minority position. The process of Lords reform since 1999 has created a second chamber which is permanently hung, and one which is increasingly willing to stand up to, and regularly defeat, the government of the day. Predictions that stage one of Lords reform would produce a feeble legislature, packed with acquiescent legislators, now look very silly indeed.

In the first session of the 2001 Parliament, the Lords caused the government serious problems during the Animal Health Bill and the Nationality, Immigration and Asylum Bill (both of which were passed only after last-minute concessions from the government), but its continued power to stand up to the government was best illustrated during the passage of the Anti-Terrorism Bill, with the Lords inflicting no fewer than thirteen defeats on the government and with the Home Secretary forced to make a humiliatingly large number of concessions in order to secure the passage of the Bill. Most of the defeats concerned their Lordships' desire to restrict disclosures of information to law enforcement agencies to cases of suspected terrorism rather than criminal activity, but peers also opposed the derogation from Article 5.1 and insisted on the right of judicial review of the Home Secretary's powers of detention and deportation of suspected terrorists, arguing that the right to appeal to the SIAC was insufficient.

The government's initial reaction was to come out fighting. Downing Street and the Home Secretary both issued statements indicating that they would ask the Commons to overturn the Lords' amendments, accusing opponents of the legislation of being 'naïve' in the face of 'the continuing terrorist threat'. The statements variously accused the Lords of 'deliberate sabotage' and of 'disembowelling' the Bill. But reality kicked in fairly quickly, and Blunkett began the process of offering concessions to the Lords in order to safeguard the Bill. In advance of the Lords debate on religious hatred, due on Monday, 10 December, the Home Secretary announced that amendments would be introduced which would refer matters of religious hatred to the Attorney General, Lord Goldsmith. It would then be the Attorney General's job to establish guidelines, defining what constituted incitement to religious hatred. A second amendment introduced yet another sunset clause, limiting the period in which Europe-wide anti-terrorism measures could be introduced using secondary legislation. Peers took little notice, and continued to shred the Bill, inflicting two further defeats. Crucially, they backed an amendment removing the laws on religious hatred, and then introduced an even wider range of sunset clauses. By now, the press was describing the defeats as 'a crushing blow' to the Bill, creating 'renewed chaos' to Blunkett's plans to have the Bill on the statute book by that Thursday.

When the Bill returned to the Commons, Blunkett made another attempt to reverse the Lords' defeats. The Lords' amendments on confining disclosure of information by public authorities only to terrorist cases were comfortably overturned, with just twelve Labour MPs voting against the government. The Home Secretary faced more difficulty over detention without trial, despite offering yet another concession, upgrading the status of the SIAC into 'a superior court of record', thus providing what he argued was the equivalent of judicial review.[18] When the issue came to a vote, 21 Labour backbenchers voted against the government concessions, fewer than the 32 who had defied the government on the previous vote in committee.

But later that evening, Beverley Hughes, a parliamentary under-secretary of state at the Home Office, faced a wretched time from her own backbenchers as she attempted to defend the continued inclusion of the incitement to religious hatred provisions in the Bill. She was ridiculed for promising to publish guidance from the Attorney General on what the government regarded as 'a legitimate religious belief' – with backbenchers complaining that they were being asked to accept a clause to the Bill without seeing the guidance to be published. The minister was almost friendless in the debate, and although the clause was subsequently approved by 307 votes to 236, the government's majority fell to 71, with 27 Labour backbenchers voting against the Bill, and many others absenting themselves.

★ ★ ★

Just before 10 p.m. on 13 December 2001, the Home Secretary had an encounter with political reality from which he came off distinctly second best. When the Bill had first returned to the Commons, the Prime Minister's official spokesperson had told reporters, 'What the government is not prepared to do is to gut the Bill.' That was, however, precisely what it was to end up doing.

The Bill had returned to the Lords – at which point their Lordships dug their heels in, again throwing out the proposals to make incitement to religious hatred a criminal offence. Blunkett was now faced with little choice: if he wanted his Bill on the statute book by Christmas, he had to give way on religious hatred. He did so with bad grace, losing his temper in the Commons after being heckled by opposition MPs. He was also forced to compromise on the disclosure of information by public authorities to law enforcement agencies, restricting such disclosure to those cases involving terrorism, and elevated the status of the SIAC, giving suspected terrorists the right to a full appeal, although not to a full court of law. The power would, however, have to be renewed by Parliament after fifteen months. He refused to accept sunset clauses on every part of the Bill, which would have meant Parliament revisiting each part of the Act, but did instead accept that a Privy Council committee of 'wise people' would review the measures within two years, with their report to be debated by the Commons.

Blunkett was to claim that the government had reached agreement with the Lords on 98 per cent of the Bill – a calculation that reveals a frighteningly high level of innumeracy for such a senior minister – and his biographer, Stephen Pollard, describes the Bill's passage as a 'triumph'. One would not like to see one of Mr Pollard's defeats.[19] Pollard's argument is that Blunkett had piloted all the key parts of the legislation onto the statute book, only failing on 'that one clause, put in as a sop to the Muslim Council of Great Britain and Labour activists, and about which Blunkett had no strong feelings'. The reality, as Pollard admits, was that 'outlawing incitement to religious hatred had nothing to do with the central purpose of the bill: fighting terror'.[20] But that, of course, was exactly the problem. True, the Home Secretary had got the key anti-terrorism legislation through Parliament, but he would have achieved that anyway, given the atmosphere after 11 September. What caused problems – surely more than they were worth – was the attempt to sneak through large amounts of other legislation on the back of an emergency Bill. Blunkett was later to complain about 'our stupid constitution' – which prevented him from railroading the Bill through. But if anyone or anything is to be blamed for stupidity, it is those who tried to push so much legislation through in the first place.

When he announced his climb down in the Commons, Blunkett said, 'Coming from Sheffield, I am familiar with the old nursery rhyme about the Grand Old Duke of York. So I have marched myself up to the top of the hill, and I am about to march them down again.' The solution to which is: don't march yourself up to the top of the hill unnecessarily in the first place.

\* \* \*

At the same time as the House of Lords was giving Blunkett such headaches, the wider question of what to do with the upper chamber was causing the government difficulties with its backbenchers.

Labour's proposals for the second stage of House of Lords reform had been published in November 2001 in the White Paper *Completing the Reform*.[21] The document did not generate widespread joy amongst the PLP – with the most vociferous opposition being reserved for the proposal that only 120 members of the reformed Lords, around 20 per cent, were to be elected.[22] The rest were to be appointed. Within a month, over a hundred Labour MPs had signed an EDM, put down by Fiona Mactaggart, the MP for Slough, supporting 'the democratic principle that any revised Second Chamber of Parliament should be wholly or substantially elected'.[23]

The proposal pitted two of the government's big hitters against one another. The 20 per cent proposal was the work of Lord (Derry) Irvine, the Lord Chancellor and the Prime Minister's former employer and mentor. Leading the opposition within government was Robin Cook, the Leader of the Commons, who as early as a day after the launch of Irvine's White Paper, was commenting to journalists: 'There is still room for us to find a consensus on the proportion of elected members. Having asked people to take part in the consultation we should be willing to listen to the answers.' In January 2002, as part of that consultation, Irvine was invited to address a meeting of the PLP. The idea for his invitation came from Meg Russell, one of Cook's special advisers, and, wrote Cook in his diary, it 'worked beyond our wildest dreams'.[24] Just as they had hoped, the result was that the PLP gave the Lord Chancellor a good duffing up. All but one Labour MP who spoke attacked the Lord Chancellor and his plans – generally in fairly brutal fashion. At the end of the meeting, Irvine declared, 'This is fun.' But it was only fun if you were the sort of person who liked being locked in a room whilst people shouted at you. The idea of the meeting had been to expose Irvine to the strength of feeling on the Labour benches in the Commons, which it certainly did, but it also had the effect of exposing the Labour benches to Irvine – and they didn't like what they saw. One MP described Irvine's performance as 'patronising, infantile and self-defeating'. Looking back, another said, 'What killed Derry's Bill was Derry's performance at the PLP.'

During an adjournment debate the following day, the vast majority of Labour backbenchers who spoke left the government in no doubt that Irvine's White Paper was unacceptable to them. 'Let us consign the White Paper to the dustbin and start again with something that is more legitimate,' said one. Responding to the debate, Cook announced a period of consultation: 'In the period of reflection that will follow, we will see where we can find the centre of gravity in order to move forward with reform.' But in private, to his diary, he was more candid, noting,

> By the end of the debate the White Paper was firmly skewered to the floor with the printer's ink fading from every page. There is simply nobody left who can believe that a bill based on this White Paper will get through the House. It is as dead as Monty Python's famous parrot.[25]

The Chief Whip had also come to the same conclusion, agreeing with Cook four days later that there was no way of piloting Irvine's proposals through the Commons. There was, however, much less agreement on what the proportion of elected peers should be – what Cook had called a 'centre of gravity' within the

PLP. In an attempt to maintain the pressure on the government to abandon its scheme, a group of Labour MPs canvassed the entire back bench – achieving a response rate of 91 per cent, which would put most academic surveys to shame – and found that the average percentage favoured by Labour backbenchers was 58 per cent, almost three times that proposed by Irvine.[26] Their findings were further strengthened by the publication of a Public Administration Committee report, headed by Dr Tony Wright, the MP for Cannock Chase, which called for 60 per cent of peers to be directly elected. Even the government's own consultation process revealed that 89 per cent of those replying favoured a second chamber in which the majority of its members were elected.

By 13 February 2002, the number of Labour signatories to Mactaggart's EDM had climbed to 140. They were joined by the majority of Conservative MPs, after the shadow Cabinet came out in support of an elected second chamber in January 2002. The government's proposals were increasingly untenable. The problem was that a significant group within the Cabinet were opposed to a second chamber with a large elected element. The difficulties that the government was already having getting legislation through the Lords made it extremely wary of anything – like election – that might give the upper chamber any more of a mandate, any more legitimacy, and thus make it even more of a hurdle. Behind the scenes, Cabinet members were trying to find a way out of the impasse, with Cook forced to ask for patience among the most vociferous of the opponents of the White Paper. Then, on 13 May 2002, in the biggest policy U-turn since Labour came to power in 1997, the plan was dropped entirely. In place of the White Paper, Cook announced the establishment of a 24-member joint committee, drawn equally from both Houses. The committee was to draw up a range of options for reform, particularly on the thorny question of composition, with these options then being subject to free votes. The government would then introduce legislation in the light of these free votes. This got the government off the hook, passing the responsibility to Parliament. As it turned out, Parliament – and in particular the Commons – proved spectacularly incapable of dealing with that responsibility (see pp. 34–36) but it was given it nonetheless.

Mactaggart subsequently congratulated the government on ditching the White Paper, 'with its scandalous accusations that elections would be a bad thing for the second chamber. They have accepted the weight of public and parliamentary opinion that that solution would not be acceptable and would stick in our throats.' She added, 'The grown-up aspect of what the government are doing – it is unusual for a government, and worthy of praise – is to say, "We were wrong; we are prepared to look again and think again on this matter."'

★ ★ ★

The first session of the 2001 Parliament saw a total of 76 rebellions by Labour MPs, more than in the first session of any previous Labour government, and more than in any session of the preceding Parliament. The fears of the whips that they were facing a more troublesome group of backbenchers had come to pass. The retreats seen over Lords reform and the Anti-Terrorism Bill would become commonplace throughout the rest of the Parliament, as the government was forced to give ground on items of policy in the face of resistance from either its backbench rebels in the Commons or the House of Lords (and frequently both). As the session grew to a close, though, the Labour whips were not especially concerned about what had happened in the first session. Their concern was the looming issue of Iraq, an issue which one whip dryly said represented 'a very profound challenge to party management'. It was, as Clive Soley, the former PLP chair, put it, an issue that could cause 'mega-problems' within the PLP. They were mega-problems of which those in government – and especially the whips – were well aware.

# Paul Marsden and Hilary Armstrong

The Labour MP for Shrewsbury and Atcham did not begin the 2001 Parliament with a reputation for rebelliousness. Paul Marsden captured the seat in the landslide of 1997, and during the next four years he didn't cast a single vote against the party line. After his re-election in 2001, however, he underwent a rapid change in behaviour. Between the 2001 election and his defection to the Liberal Democrats in December 2001, he voted against the party line on eleven occasions, including over the bombing of Afghanistan and over the Anti-Terrorism, Crime and Security Bill. That was a rebellion in almost 11 per cent of votes, a percentage rate of rebellion that was roughly equal to that of John McDonnell.

Higher profile, however, was his very public falling out with the government Whips' Office. After being called in to see Hilary Armstrong, the Chief Whip, to discuss his opposition to military action in Afghanistan, Marsden released what he claimed were verbatim transcripts of their conversation to the *Mail on Sunday*. Armstrong did not come out of Marsden's version of events terribly well. She began by asking for a guarantee that the MP would not talk to the media unless he had cleared it with her first; he refused. She then criticised his attendance record, claiming that he was a very inexperienced MP; Marsden responded that his absences in the first half of the 1997 Parliament had been because his wife had been seriously ill and he had been given time away from the Commons to look after her. His absences in the second half had been because he had been campaigning in the impending election ('We were fighting a general election and you lot told us to go home and campaign to win it.'). The conversation became progressively more heated: Marsden accused the Chief Whip of 'losing it', with Armstrong responding in kind ('You wait until I really do lose it') by accusing Marsden of being an appeaser ('It was people like you who appeased Hitler in 1938').

Perhaps the most bizarre part of the conversation came when the Chief Whip pleaded geographically induced dimness in her defence: 'The trouble with people like you', she was alleged to have said, 'is that you are so clever with words that us up North can't argue back.' Marsden's response? 'Do you mind? I'm a northerner myself. I was born in Cheshire. I spent four years at Teesside Polytechnic, near where you come from.' There was also a supposedly revealing exchange over whether any vote on military action in Afghanistan would be whipped or not, in which Armstrong was alleged to have said, 'War is not a matter of conscience. Abortion and embryo research are matters of conscience, but not wars.'

Marsden's publication of this conversation caught the Whips' Office by surprise. They had never thought that any Labour MP would give out accounts of private conversations between themselves and the Chief Whip (and certainly not to the *Mail on Sunday*, the *bête noire* of most Labour MPs). 'We got', one whip recalled, 'a slating across the media.' Marsden was almost universally portrayed as Shrewsbury's answer to Luke Skywalker, the plucky underdog, to be applauded for standing up for his rights against the nasty whips. As a letter to the *Guardian* – one of many on the subject – put it, 'so that's how MPs are bullied into losing their balls . . . Well done, Paul. Please continue to speak for me and for everyone I know.' The winner of the Award for the Most Ludicrous Hyperbole Used in a *Guardian* Letter (an award for which there is stiff competition) went to one correspondent who wondered whether Armstrong wore jackboots, and was appalled at the 'Hitlerian way she spoke to Paul Marsden'. 'What kind of a democracy are we living in when MPs and cabinet ministers are being coerced to speak in unison?' The writer concluded by observing that he had the misfortune of living in Holland during five years of Nazi occupation, and 'I must confess that at times I feel as uneasy as I did then.'[27]

This was then followed by an encounter between Marsden and some Labour MPs (often, but erroneously, described as all being whips) in a Commons bar at 3 a.m., during which Marsden claimed he was physically and verbally assaulted, a story which again was initially reported exclusively in the *Mail on Sunday*.[28] The paper's coverage included a rogues' gallery of those said to have been involved, including (the nicknames are the *Mail*'s) John 'Knuckles' Heppell, Gerry 'Fingers' Sutcliffe and Ivan 'Shorty' Henderson. According to Marsden's account, Henderson, then a PPS, approached him in the bar, saying, 'You are a fucking traitor. You're a fucking disgrace. I just want to say this to your face. You're a fucking arsehole.' Sutcliffe was then said to have grabbed his arm and leg. Marsden claimed, 'He put his arm across my throat on my windpipe. My head was pinned against the wall. It hurt. His face was inches from mine. His behaviour was appalling.'

No one disputes that there was an altercation between Marsden and some other Labour MPs in the bar that night, although the MPs concerned both dispute the words used and deny that there was any physical assault. Similarly, although Marsden's account of his discussion with Armstrong was almost universally accepted as if it was verbatim, he never produced a tape recording of the conversation (although you will often see it referred to as 'taped'), claiming to have written it from memory. For her part, Armstrong was mortified by the incident, both that it had happened at all, and, more specifically, that people accepted Marsden's account of events so unquestioningly. None of the hundreds of articles which appeared afterwards, all fulminating about the despicable way in which the whips treated dissenters, appeared even to acknowledge the possibility that the account might be somewhat one sided, and might – just might – be spun to the advantage of the person recounting it. The Chief Whip explicitly denied it was an accurate account of their conversation – especially the bit about northern thickos not being able to understand sophisticated southerners. 'We knew then that he wanted to go to the Liberals', she claimed, 'but he needed to be able to justify it, both to others and to himself. I was his justification.'

Moreover, even if every word of it was true, what horrors did it reveal? That the Chief Whip used some not very sophisticated and slightly crass arguments to try to persuade him to vote with the party and (Armstrong's initial complaint) not to be so critical of the leadership when talking to the media. If this really counted as 'bullying', then Armstrong's critics must have gone to some very soft schools. The 'Hitlerian' comparisons just revealed a feeble (if not downright offensive) understanding of history. The exchange over whether a free vote would be granted on military action in Afghanistan – which prompted Marsden to exclaim, 'Are you seriously saying that blowing people up and killing people is not a moral issue?' – revealed a certain naïveté on both his part and that of many of those who saw it as so outrageous. Almost all issues – aside from the most abstractly technical – have some element of 'conscience' involved in them, involving some debate about morals. The point made by the Chief Whip was that since military action in Afghanistan was government policy, there was no way it could sensibly be described as an 'issue of conscience', the phrase used at Westminster to describe policies on which the front bench takes no stance and where it issues no instructions to its backbenchers. It was bizarre to expect a government – any government – to allow a free vote on whether or not to go to war. A more nuanced criticism of the Chief Whip tended to come from some within the PLP, who wondered whether there might have been a better way of dealing with Marsden –

whether kid gloves might perhaps have been more effective than a formal talking to. But that was a matter of tactics rather than principle.

Marsden's subsequent defection to the Liberal Democrats (calling the Prime Minister 'lousy and arrogant' as he went) somewhat lessened the effect of his criticisms. They were further lessened by his later behaviour. He began, for example, to publish (not very good) poetry on his website. His poem about the First World War – which included the couplet 'Fear lay behind each pair of eyes | Answers were rarely found for their whys' – was described by one newspaper columnist as so 'utterly terrible a sin that the only appropriate punishment is a public apology to the now thoroughly vindicated Hilary Armstrong'.[29] His 'romantic' poetry – 'Tongue rippling across teeth so white | Breasts rising as I feel the urge to bite' – wasn't considered much better. There then followed an incident involving a female intern who had to be moved from his office. Then, just before the 2005 election, having only recently described his defection from Labour as his greatest achievement, he announced that he was leaving the Liberal Democrats and applying to rejoin Labour. By this point, he didn't have much credibility left, and the incident at the beginning of the Parliament looked somewhat different in hindsight. He was, unsurprisingly, never accepted back into the PLP.

# 5

# The Mother of All Rebellions

*Iraq*

> Do you support regime change in Baghdad or Downing Street?
> – Labour whips, March 2003

At 10 p.m. on 18 March 2003, a grand total of 139 Labour MPs took part in the largest rebellion by government backbenchers since the beginning of modern British party politics. In turn, that rebellion was breaking the record set only the previous month, when 121 Labour MPs – many, though not all, the same ones – had voted in then record numbers against their whip.

The two rebellions shattered all previous modern records: the 93 Liberals who had voted against Gladstone's proposals for Home Rule in June 1886; the 95 Conservatives who had defied the Major government over its post-Dunblane firearms legislation; or the 110 Labour MPs who had rebelled in July 1976, during the passage of the long-forgotten Rent (Agriculture) Bill, to back an amendment moved by Joan Maynard – the woman routinely described in *Private Eye* as 'Stalin's Granny' – that would have applied statutory tenancy rights to the Crown, the government and the City of London.

At one point, it looked possible that a government with a

nominal majority of over 160 would require the support of opposition MPs to get its way in the House of Commons. There was talk that the Prime Minister could be forced to resign if he could not gain sufficient support from his MPs; it was said that he had already written his resignation letter in the event that the vote went against him. The challenge from the Labour whips to any wavering MP was simple and to the point: Do you support regime change in Baghdad or Downing Street? For the first time since he entered Downing Street, and in a way that should have been inconceivable for a Prime Minister with a majority of over 160, Tony Blair's future seemed to hang on the outcome of a vote in the House of Commons.

★ ★ ★

Ever since President Bush's famous 'axis of evil' speech in January 2002 there had been deep concern and unease amongst many Labour MPs about the possibility of an invasion of Iraq – especially one without a UN resolution specifically authorising an attack. The first public manifestation of this came in March 2002, with an EDM put forward by Alice Mahon, the Labour MP for Halifax, which expressed 'deep unease . . . at the prospect that Her Majesty's Government might support United States military action against Iraq'. Mahon's EDM was signed by 133 Labour MPs – the same number as had rebelled during the whole of the 1997 parliament.

Their first challenge, though, was just to debate the issue. Throughout the summer of 2002, the pressure grew for Parliament to be recalled from its break so that MPs could discuss the growing crisis. The government was initially resistant, arguing publicly that no decisions had been taken and that there was therefore nothing to debate, whilst privately being very keen not to give a platform for the divisions within the party. The Labour backbencher Graham Allen decided to take matters into his own hands and arranged an alternative ad hoc 'House of Commons', solely for the purpose of discussing Iraq. Allen had been a whip during the 1997 Parliament, a job he'd not especially enjoyed, and he had made it clear to the Prime Minister before the 2001 election that he wanted to move on, either to a policy-related job or to the back benches. The Prime Minister, in his wisdom, had decided that the latter would suffice. Allen was a good example of the sort of former minister now knocking around outside of government and able to cause trouble – not corrosively bitter, not voting against the government out of spite, but emboldened by his time on the payroll and liberated by his exit from it. In a remarkable feat of ingenuity and planning, he hired Church House for his *faux* Parliament's meeting place, Lord Weatherill agreed to dig out his wig and reprise his former role as Speaker for the day, and the BBC agreed to provide coverage. Less than 36 hours before Allen's shadow Parliament began meeting, the government relented, and agreed to a formal recall. When Robin Cook phoned Allen to let him know, he was delighted, until he remembered one vital detail: 'My problem is that I have committed myself to four thousand vol-au-vents which I will now have to eat on my own.'[1]

There was no substantive motion for MPs to vote on at the end of the recall debate, so 56 Labour MPs instead defied their whips on a motion for the adjournment in order to register their protest.[2] The real surprise, though, was not how many rebels there were, but how few. With only a handful of exceptions, most of the speeches made by Labour's backbenchers during the debate were extremely sceptical, cautious and tentative, opposing military action unless it was backed by a fresh UN mandate, and in some cases even then. The media made much of the presence in the no lobby of some ex-ministers (such as Tony Banks and Glenda Jackson), but the absentees were far more noticeable. Gerald Kaufman, Donald Anderson, Chris Smith, Gavin Strang, Peter Kilfoyle, Doug Henderson, and Tony Lloyd – mostly ex-ministers, all senior members of the PLP – all made critical speeches, although none went on to rebel. That vote was just the warm-up act – as the powers that be knew full well. The real problems would come when (or if) the UN route to which the Prime Minister was committed failed, and when (or if) military action against Iraq went ahead regardless.

★ ★ ★

It's not difficult to explain why the Iraq votes were so problematic for the government; the reasons that led many Labour MPs to be so unhappy about the issue were exactly those that worried much of the rest of the population. They didn't understand the rationale or justification for war (especially the issue of 'why now?'), they didn't like the lack of any obvious post-conflict exit strategy, and they had a strong dislike and distrust of President Bush and US foreign policy. Brian White, normally a Labour loyalist, expressed the views of many Labour backbenchers during one session of Foreign Office Questions. He asked whether the Foreign Secretary was

> aware of the perception in many parts of the world that US foreign policy is based on double standards, because America is prepared to rip up the ABM Treaty [1972], reject the Kyoto agreement [on reducing the emission of greenhouse gases], ignore the World Trade Organization ruling [on steel tariffs], blockade Cuba and so on. Is it not up to us as the closest ally of the US to make it aware of the dangers of that approach?

In private, Labour backbenchers were much ruder – especially about George W. Bush. 'Just awful,' one Labour MP said. 'I just hate the man.' As Clive Soley put it,

> the real problem for Tony was that it was George Bush. If it had been Clinton or *anybody* else, then it wouldn't have been anywhere near as bad. But it was Bush and Rumsfeld and that bunch of idiots. If you'd designed an issue to alienate everyone to the left of Ken Clarke, this was the way to do it.

'In this', as one whip observed, 'MPs were not behaving in a way that was different from the rest of the liberal intelligentsia.'

But what made the rebellions so large was the lack of any widespread and significant international support for the war, and most obviously the lack of any fresh UN resolution explicitly sanctioning war.[3] The whips had been praying for a fresh UN resolution, and its eventual absence – as one of them put it – 'totally fucked us up'. There would still have been unhappiness amongst the PLP had military action gone ahead with a fresh UN resolution – they wouldn't have skipped through the division lobbies singing joyful songs as the bombs rained down on Baghdad – but any revolt would have been much smaller; it would, said one whip, 'have been a different world'. Although the whips would sometimes mock would-be rebels as 'peace-niks', a claim that triggered more than one confrontation between backbencher and whip ('You call me that again and I'll clout you'), the number of out-and-out pacifists on Labour's benches was almost non-existent. Previous rebellions against the Blair government's military engagements had been minor: just 22 Labour MPs voted against military action against Iraq in February 1998; a mere eleven voted against military involvement in Afghanistan in November 2001. But it's simplistic to claim that it was the lack of the UN mandate per se that caused so much trouble and magnified the size of the revolt. In April 1999 just thirteen Labour MPs had voted against the bombing of Kosovo, bombing that was – like Iraq – carried out without UN authorisation. But Kosovo had at least been carried out by NATO, and for reasons that many in the PLP – including many on the left of the PLP – understood and supported.[4] With Iraq it was the serious doubts about the wisdom of the policy, combined with the lack of widespread international support, that caused problems. The lack of the UN mandate was the most obvious manifestation of this, rather than being the problem itself.

These doubts about the wisdom and motivation of the policy were magnified by the political circumstances of the votes. As already made clear, the Iraq rebellions came on the back of a growing restlessness amongst the PLP; they were at least in part evidence of the growing rebelliousness on the back benches, rather than its cause.[5] The nature of the issue also made it very difficult for the government to enter into deals with its back-benchers. For those who had seen him wheeling and dealing his way out of trouble during the first term, it was an irony that the minister to oversee the largest backbench revolt for over a hundred years was the new Foreign Secretary, Jack Straw. His normal tactic of negotiating the rebellion away – offering concessions here, amendments there – wouldn't work with Iraq; you couldn't offer only to invade bits of it, or to phase in the killing, or give rebates to the dead. 'You can't negotiate between peace and war, or between people's attitudes to Bush,' said one whip. There was no 'third way' to construct here.

The electoral and parliamentary politics were also unhelpful for the whips. Because the Conservative front bench was supporting the government, Labour MPs knew they could vote against the government without any real risk of defeating it. By contrast, Labour MPs who voted for war would be entering the same division lobbies as the Conservatives – something that most of them dislike doing at the best of times. Labour MPs were also well aware of the way the issue was playing with the electorate – with most polls showing the majority of voters opposed, and with the largest demonstrations the UK had ever seen against the war. MPs varied hugely in how much post they received over the issue – some reporting masses, others very little (although most going to inordinate lengths to deal with what they got) – but it was the types of letter that they were receiving that caused some of them to worry.[6] One normally loyal Labour MP's thinking on the issue was influenced when he started to receive what he called letters from 'fair-minded people, quite different from the usual anti-war letters', which argued that UN approval should be required before military action took place. MPs will ignore demonstrations if they believe they are doing something that is right: most Labour MPs were almost completely unmoved by the size of the Countryside Alliance's marches. But when they are not so certain about the wisdom of a policy, then marches and demonstrations and piles of post feed their doubts.

Of greater concern to some was pressure from their selectors. Plenty of Labour MPs reported getting Grade A grief from their local party workers over Iraq, and the threat of war coincided with Labour MPs' reselection meetings, the moment in every Parliament when party members wield their most power. Only a handful of 'pro-war' MPs faced any formal discussion of deselection, but for some it was an unsaid threat. Even those MPs safe from deselection had reason to be worried. Few – especially those in marginal seats – could afford to alienate further those party workers needed to campaign at election time, and who were already deserting the party in droves. The pressure was reported to be especially intense for those MPs with large Muslim populations in their constituency. Labour's former deputy leader Roy Hattersley estimated the number of Labour backbenchers affected in this way to be as high as 50.[7] Joe Ashton, another former Labour MP, claimed that the size of the rebellion could be explained by the quantity of Labour MPs who had substantial numbers of Muslim voters – along with well-organised Muslim party members.[8] This, though, was to overstate the case. The rebellion would have been huge whenever in the parliamentary cycle it had taken place – and whilst the rebellion's ranks were swollen by MPs with large Muslim populations in their constituency, there were plenty of Labour rebels for whom this was not true. For every Roger Godsiff (Birmingham, Small Heath), Jim Marshall (Leicester South) or Khalid Mahmood (Birmingham, Perry Barr), there were two or three like Joan Humble (Blackpool North & Fleetwood), Martin Caton (Gower), Bob Blizzard (Waveney) or John Grogan (Selby), Labour MPs whose seats contained almost no sizeable Muslim population but who were still to be found amongst the ranks of the rebels.

★ ★ ★

After much diplomatic wrangling, on 8 November 2002 the United Nations Security Council unanimously agreed the now famous Resolution 1441. It was welcomed on the back benches, but was not sufficient to persuade many of the government's critics. When Parliament resumed for its second session in November 2002, the first Labour rebellion came over Iraq. The Speaker, Michael Martin, unusually selected a critical Liberal Democrat amendment to a government motion on Iraq, rather than a supportive Conservative one. As Robin Cook noted in his diary, the 'result was to leave both Labour and Conservative whips in a state of equal consternation, but with the entirely democratic outcome that there was now a genuine choice for those rebels who wished to take it'.[9]

In an attempt to placate Labour doubters, Jack Straw announced that any decision to take military action would be put to a vote, on a substantive motion in the House of Commons.[10] This was something he had long been advocating behind the scenes, but it was not sufficient for the 30 Labour MPs who supported the Liberal Democrat amendment, which would have required both a vote in the House of Commons and a UN mandate for military action.[11] Nonetheless, it was an important shift by the government, and one which was not entirely welcomed by the whips. They already knew that they faced severe problems of party management, but because the royal prerogative allowed the government to declare war without Parliament's explicit approval, they had initially been hoping to avoid any substantive votes on the issue. 'My heart sank,' recalled one member of the Whips' Office.

Early in the new year, January 2003, there was yet another rebellion, with 44 Labour backbenchers using an adjournment debate entitled 'Defence in the World' to express their opposition to the government's policy on Iraq.[12] Worryingly for the government, these three early Iraq revolts did not involve the same people, and combined they had already involved 71 different Labour MPs, who were to provide the core of the government's future problems over Iraq. Even more worryingly, the whips knew that there were plenty of MPs who had voiced opposition to the possibility of war – but who had yet to vote against. In addition to Alice Mahon's EDM (mentioned above), 84 Labour MPs signed a later EDM put down by the former Conservative Cabinet minister Douglas Hogg. A total of 55 Labour MPs had signed at least one of these two EDMs without (yet) rebelling. Even excluding all those harbouring private doubts (a group which included plenty of members of the government, at all levels), this brought the number of Labour MPs who had publicly protested about Iraq – by vote or signature – to 148, even before the record-breaking votes of February and March.[13]

\* \* \*

The first of those record-breaking votes came on Wednesday, 26 February 2003, during a government-initiated debate on Iraq.

Both the government's motion for discussion and the rebel amendment were carefully framed. The government motion supported UN efforts to disarm Saddam Hussein without even mentioning the possibility of war, in order to rally support from as many pro-UN and anti-war MPs as possible. The rebel amendment was deliberately cast in such a way as to generate the maximum possible cross-party support, not just from those opposed to war outright, but also from those in the 'not yet' camp. It was broad based, fronted by people respected across the House (Chris Smith for Labour and Hogg for the Conservatives), and signed by members of all parties. The precise wording was negotiated at length. Peter Kilfoyle, a former Labour defence minister, was responsible for coming up with the argument that the case for military action against Iraq was 'as yet unproven', echoing the Scottish legal verdict of 'not proven'. As one of the leading rebels explained, 'it was terse, simple, consensual and using a legal concept. The government was not guilty, but not yet innocent either. It appealed to our Scottish colleagues, including the Speaker . . . he was the one after all who had the power to call the amendment . . . It was the right common denominator.'

The previous weekend the Chief Whip had warned the Prime Minister that the rebellion over Smith's amendment could involve as many as a hundred Labour MPs. Armed with the amendment, it had taken Kilfoyle just an hour to gather 60 signatures in support of it. By the Tuesday morning, the day before the vote, more than 110 Labour backbenchers had already signed it, with every indication that the numbers could rise yet further.

Foreign Office ministers were deployed to the House of Commons in an effort to change minds. Mike O'Brien, the minister of state, set himself up in Room W4, just off Westminster Hall, and paged doubters to ask if they would like 'a briefing' from the Foreign Office on any 'outstanding issues'. At 10 a.m. on the morning of the vote, Straw addressed a meeting of the PLP in Committee Room 14. At Prime Minister's Question Time later that day, Tony Blair made a deliberate point of saying that he wanted several more votes in the Commons on the issue of Iraq – that this would not be MPs' last chance to voice concerns – and he later invited groups of wavering MPs into his Commons office in a further effort to change minds. But up until lunchtime on the day of the vote the Labour whips were still expecting 145 Labour MPs to back Smith's amendment.[14]

During the six-hour Commons debate, Smith told the House that he was speaking against the government with a heavy heart, but that 'we must say here that now is not the time, that the case has yet to be fully made, and that war and all its consequences cannot be the present answer.'[15] As the vote grew nearer, Fraser Kemp, a Labour whip, scribbled a note to the Chief Whip: '122 MPs against'. He was spot on: 122 Labour MPs went through the lobbies in support of the anti-war amendment. (One of these, Andy Reed, the MP for Loughborough, had also voted in the government lobby, in order to register an abstention. So technically there were 121 MPs voting against the government.)[16]

Reed was one of just over 20 Labour MPs to abstain, the others doing so by absenting themselves or by ostentatiously remaining seated in the chamber during the vote. Smith's amendment was defeated by 393 votes to 199. The government motion backing UN efforts to disarm Saddam was then carried by 434 votes to 124. Many of the Labour MPs who had voted for the amendment then abstained on the substantive motion, with the number of Labour cross-voters falling to a still sizeable 60.

There had been a gasp of disbelief in the chamber when the result had been announced. It was not that the vote was particularly close – the support of the Conservative front bench meant that the government won both votes easily – but the size of the Labour rebellion stunned many observers. After the vote, Smith told reporters that the scale of the vote went 'beyond my wildest imaginings'. It could have been worse. The Prime Minister arrived so late for the 7 p.m. vote that the doors of the lobby were already closing. One of his whips shoved Blair through, urging, 'Come *on*, Prime Minister!' Blair just made it, avoiding yet more embarrassment.[17]

One of the rebel organisers claimed that if the government failed to change policy there would be worse to follow, which would make the rebellion seem like a 'tea-party'. Many of those who had abstained had told their whips that they were prepared to vote against the government in any future vote authorising conflict. A survey for the BBC's *The Politics Show* asked all Labour backbenchers whether they would support the government without a further Security Council resolution. Of the 129 who responded, 95 said no – and of these sixteen were new converts to the rebel camp. Doug Henderson, another leading rebel, predicted that upwards of 150 Labour MPs would rebel unless there was a new UN resolution explicitly authorising war. One newspaper report even suggested that Blair might face a rebellion of up to 200 Labour MPs and the resignation of ten members of the government if he failed to secure a second UN resolution.[18] The doubts reached up to the Cabinet. The rebels received high-level backing when Clare Short, the international development secretary, claimed on *The Westminster Hour* on Sunday, 9 March that the Prime Minister had been 'extraordinarily reckless' with the future of the government, and that unless UN authority was gained for military action, or for the reconstruction of Iraq, she would be voting against war.

Three days later, at PMQs, Blair promised to work 'flat out' for that much-sought-after fresh UN resolution. But the following day (13 March), Robin Cook effectively told the Cabinet that he would resign if no fresh UN resolution was forthcoming. The Leader of the House sounded even more intent on leaving the government later that day at Business Questions, noting publicly that 'collective responsibility applies to all those who are in Cabinet at the time of the debate' – the clear implication being that he would no longer be in government when that came about.

★ ★ ★

For the government Whips' Office, Iraq represented a ratcheting up of their operation. For the first time, every vote really mattered. There had, of course, been large rebellions before, with the whips working hard to keep them to a minimum. But none had been as important as the Iraq rebellions; of necessity the level of information-gathering stepped up a gear. It established a *modus operandi* that the whips would use for all major rebellions throughout the Parliament. The basic tactics, though, were the same as they always had been, and would have been recognised by any graduate of the Whips' Office for over a hundred years.

They focus on their own. Opposition MPs are largely ignored, with the whips assuming a worst-case scenario as regards all non-Labour MPs – on the basis that you should never rely on the other parties to get you out of a hole. They start by gathering basic information on the views of every Labour MP. Will they support the government or not? If not, why not? This information-gathering – called a 'ring-round' (although it isn't necessarily done by phone) – is conducted by the regional whips, each one gathering the views of his or her flock, with the data then collated in the Whips' Office. One of the myths about the whips is that they are all identikit characters, produced on some assembly line somewhere. In reality, they have very different styles and abilities. Some whips quickly gain a reputation for being spot on at understanding their colleagues' intentions and doubts; others are less perceptive, with the result that their MPs might need to be contacted more than once. The initial ring-round also tends to throw up too many MPs who say they are undecided ('That's no good,' said one, 'we can't do anything with that.') so they too require more probing.

MPs are placed into one of four columns on a master grid: aye, no, abstain or authorised absence. And then the whips begin the process of trying to move people from no to abstain and from abstain to aye. Right from the start over Iraq, the whips knew that they faced a large group of utter irreconcilables, those Labour MPs who would not be persuaded whatever the government said or did. Although some MPs found the Iraq votes very difficult – some voting in tears, others drinking themselves stupid before going through the division lobby – for many, especially some of the diehard opponents, it was a remarkably easy decision. 'I was so convinced I was right,' said one. 'It's when you're not sure, when you've got doubts, that it's tough.' 'On something like that', recalled another, 'I just thought it was so wrong. On some matters you think, "I've done my bit, and there's no point in getting more votes against the government than you need." But this wasn't one of them.' Or as another put it, 'the issue is so enormous, and the rebellion is so big, that essentially it's a free vote.' This group were largely left alone by the whips. One Labour MP firmly in the anti-war camp went up to his whip and asked, 'Why aren't you bothering me? I'm feeling ignored.' He received a two-word answer. Jeremy Corbyn was approached by his regional whip, who simply said, 'I've got you down in the anti-war camp.' Corbyn replied,

'Well, your intelligence does you credit.' So ended the lobbying of J. Corbyn MP.

Instead, the pressure went onto those who were felt to be wavering, to be 'wobbly'. 'They sense weakness,' one rebel said of the whips. From the very first rebellion, it had been clear how intense the pressure placed on the wobbly was going to be. As Labour MPs exited the rebel division lobby in September 2002, they found government whips ostentatiously writing down their names. 'There was no need to do that,' said one MP. 'You knew that the pressure was going to build after that.' Even in the last few hours before March's key vote there were still 50 MPs believed to be undecided.[19] 'The pressures', one whip recalled, 'went on to the good guys.' Do whips get flashbacks, like Vietnam vets? 'If I have flashbacks,' he said, 'it will be trying to persuade people like Dave Wright or Rob Marris . . . It was the good guys, the nice guys, who we submitted to the most pressure. I'm not saying it was a pleasant experience for them.'

The whips worked out which ministers would be best to talk to which MPs, matching up friends with friends, those with similar interests, and those who had worked together in the past. Individual ministers were asked to act as a 'friend' to the rebels, and over the weekend before the key vote in March they telephoned many of the 121 Labour rebels from the February vote to try to persuade them into abstaining or voting against the amendment. Another 50 potential rebels were also contacted in this way. They also tried to work out which MPs would be swayed by which argument; it was, one official said, 'à la carte reassurance'.[20] The whips also made use of others in the PLP, backbenchers who were supportive of the government's position and could apply pressure on friends and colleagues. 'For the first time', said one whip, 'we were seeking to identify who their friends were – and encouraging those pressures.' One whip singled out George Mudie, the MP for Leeds East and a former Deputy Chief Whip, as an 'absolutely outstanding' example of this. 'He was absolutely essential,' the whip said. 'And what was important', he added, 'was that none of his work was official.'

The golden rule, however, utilised for the Iraq votes and then afterwards, was that an MP had to be seen by a whip before intelligence on that person would be accepted. 'You've got to look in their eyes,' said one whip. 'You can't just trust what people are saying – and you've got to double-check it.' It didn't matter who the information had come from; even information from Cabinet ministers or the Prime Minister would be double-checked by whips before an MP would be moved from one category to another on their spreadsheet.

★ ★ ★

The very earliest meetings of parliamentary parties – those held in the eighteenth century – were designed essentially for one-way communication: from party leaders to followers. 'The leaders, who summoned the meetings, attended to inform their supporters of decisions already taken, not to seek their advice or invite discussion.'[21] It would be an exaggeration to say that the weekly meeting of the PLP has now regained this role – but only just. Meetings of the PLP can occasionally be useful for putting pressure onto ministers – as over Lords' reform, for example – and some MPs say that they find the meetings valuable, at least to hear the views of frontbenchers, and occasionally for a more general discussion. But the full meeting of the PLP suffers from two flaws. The first is that it leaks like a sieve, with detailed accounts of any arguments appearing almost verbatim in the next day's newspapers. And second, whenever there is a difficult issue to be debated, particularly something current and controversial, the meeting tends to be orchestrated by the whips and others in the party hierarchy. 'People gang up on anyone who's trying to question what the government's doing,' said one MP. Other MPs described it as 'a lynch mob', 'a charade', 'sycophantic', 'a Nuremberg Rally', 'a job interview – with the people who are potentially going to employ you up on the top table', and said it was full of 'prima donnas' and 'people who stick their noses up ministers' backsides'.[22] One MP compared the pressure to 'sledging' – the cricketing term for intimidating opponents through verbal abuse – although such sledging was more likely to come from those freelancing on behalf of the whips than from the whips themselves. On Wednesday, 12 March, more than 250 Labour MPs packed into Committee Room 14 to hear Jack Straw. The meeting was stuffed full of Labour MPs in marginal seats who began warning of the need to back the Prime Minister. Tam Dalyell sat shaking his head with rage, before storming out. The day before the vote for war, the Prime Minister spoke at another packed (and hastily arranged) meeting of the PLP; his eighteen-minute address was met with thunderous applause. As one ex-whip put it, 'If you can't organise an intimidatory meeting at the PLP, you're not worth being in the Whips' Office.'

The day before March's key vote, seven members of the Cabinet trawled the Commons tearoom. 'It was an extraordinary sight; ministers and whips out-numbered backbenchers by two to one . . . There was a lot of tea and jobs on offer,' commented one leading rebel. Some Labour MPs had meetings with four Cabinet ministers in a day, and right up until the vote, the whips were feeding Labour MPs into meetings with the Foreign Secretary. Meanwhile, Tony Blair set up camp in the Commons tearoom (an extremely rare event), seeing waverers in groups of between three and five. Blair would argue calmly and reasonably, stressing the reasons for his actions ('if you knew what I knew') and arguing that they could not withdraw now ('Do you really think we can pull the troops out now?'). He would end with a straightforward plea: 'I need your support.' It was enough for some. One MP – until then adamant that he would vote against war – came out of a meeting with the Prime Minister having agreed to back the government. 'Why did you do that?' asked another anti-war MP. 'The Prime Minister pleaded with me,' said the switcher. 'What was I supposed to do?' To which the anti-war MP replied, 'Tell him to fuck off.' But there were still enough Labour MPs for whom a direct plea from the Prime

Minister carried weight – and who were not prepared to tell him where to go. 'If he had pleaded with me', said one, 'I don't know what I could have done. If the Prime Minister is asking you to support him, you've got to do it really.'

As the Prime Minister flew off to the Azores for his war summit with President Bush and Prime Minister Aznar of Spain, one Cabinet minister gloomily predicted at least 30 resignations by junior ministers and ministerial aides. On the eve of the substantive vote (17 March), Robin Cook resigned from the government, claiming that he was unable to support a war with 'neither international agreement nor domestic support', and accusing the British government of 'a diplomatic miscalculation that will astonish history'.[23] When Cook sat down after giving his resignation speech in the House of Commons, he was rewarded with a round of applause – Labour MPs clapping – rather than the customary farmyard ''ear, 'ear'.

★ ★ ★

The government's motion for the main Iraq debate on 18 March offered support to the troops in the Gulf, blamed the French for blocking moves to a new UN resolution, cited legal advice authorising war, and stated that the government should 'use all means necessary' to disarm Saddam Hussein. Again, the rebel amendment moved by Chris Smith was a cross-party affair, arguing that 'the case for war against Iraq has not yet been established, especially given the absence of specific United Nations authorisation,' but nonetheless pledging 'total support for the British forces engaged in the Middle East'.

Opening the debate, in what is widely agreed to be one of his finest speeches in the Commons, Blair argued that it was not the time for the international community to falter in the face of twelve years of non-compliance from Saddam; and in an effort to limit the revolt, he offered two assurances – that he would press Bush to call for further progress to be made on the Middle East peace process (the so-called road-map) and that humanitarian aid and a proper programme of reconstruction would be delivered to Iraq in the post-conflict period. After he sat down, the Prime Minister did not repeat his mistake of the previous month (when he had been criticised for only staying in the Commons to listen to Straw's opening speech, preferring to record a television programme instead), staying in the chamber for three hours. The debate lasted ten hours, and included passionate pleas for and against military action. One of the leading rebels, Peter Kilfoyle, focused on what he termed 'the idiocy of fighting the wrong war, in the wrong place, against the wrong people'.

At 10 p.m., the rebel Labour amendment was defeated by 396 votes to 217, a government majority of 179. A record-breaking 139 Labour MPs backed the rebel amendment, eighteen more than in February. Having tried and failed to carry an amendment to stop war, many of the Labour rebels then abstained on the government motion, although 84 still voted against the government's own motion, which the government then won by 412 to 149.[24] Many of those abstaining in the second vote did not want to vote against a motion which declared support for British troops. 'What about people in my constituency?' said one. 'Will they think I'm letting their sons and daughters down?' As one of the rebels put it,

> a few of us took the view that, to be consistent, you had to follow that logic through on every single vote. But some of us took the view that the crucial vote was the amendment, and once that had been lost, then it was fine to abstain on the main motion, because there was a lot of things in the main motion that we would all agree with. You couldn't vote for it, because of war, but abstaining was OK. And once the decision had been made, you wanted to get behind the troops who were going to be at risk.

Although it was the largest rebellion by government back-benchers against the whip for over 150 years, it could so easily have been much worse. There were 30 MPs who voted for the anti-war amendment in March who had not done so in February. Eighteen of these were casting their first votes against the Blair government. They included Cook and John Denham, the minister of state in the Home Office (marked down by many as future Cabinet material), who resigned from the government on the morning of the vote. The government lost one further minister – the health minister Lord Hunt of Kings Heath (although John Prescott dismissively claimed not even to know that Hunt was a member of the government). Nine PPSs also left the government. If all those who had voted against the government in February had stayed with the rebellion the total revolt would have exceeded 150. They were saved from this fate by twelve Labour MPs who rebelled in February but who either switched to vote with the government (four) or did not vote (eight) in March. They were: Anne Begg (although she then did vote against on the main motion), Colin Challen, Jim Cunningham, Brian Donohoe, Jeff Ennis, Paul Farrelly, Khalid Mahmood, David Marshall, Chris Mole, Paul Stinchcombe, Brian White and Dennis Skinner (who was then seriously ill).[25]

There were also a further 28 Labour MPs who had signed one or more of the Iraq EDMs but who did not then go on to vote against the whip. Had they had joined in as well, the rebellion would have reached almost 180. Add in those within government who considered but ultimately rejected resignation – including Clare Short, who, despite her public agonising, chose to stay in the government, only to resign anyway two months later with her credibility shredded – and the revolt could have hit the 200 mark. Compared with that, or with several of the predictions made just a few days before, a rebellion by 139 government MPs seemed almost a triumph of party unity. At least that was the way the result was spun in a carefully coordinated media offensive by the party leadership (who were not necessarily all that unhappy about the earlier predictions of a much larger revolt). 'It is ironic,' admitted a whip. 'The biggest ever rebellion and a triumph for the whips!'

★ ★ ★

So, why the 'triumph'? Given the unhappiness on the Labour benches, why was it 'only' 139 Labour MPs who rebelled?

For some the issue became a vote of confidence in Blair's leadership; or, as Peter Mandelson put it to one rebel, 'it's not about the war, it's about Tony.'[26] Iraq was to be the first time that Blair would put his leadership on the line over a vote, a tactic that he would later reprise over foundation hospitals and top-up fees. Or, to be more accurate, it was to be the first time that the Prime Minister would *appear* to put his reputation on the line over a vote. As the prospect of a second resolution at the UN diminished, so he let it be known that he would resign if the vote went against him, and rumours swept Westminster that he had already written his letter of resignation just in case. It was this that allowed the Labour whips to use the line 'Do you support regime change in Baghdad or Downing Street?'. But since he could rely on the votes of the Conservatives (who were largely, but not wholly, in support of the government), this was extremely unlikely to happen; with the ballast of the Tory front bench in support of the government, the rebellion by Labour MPs would have needed to reach around 250 before a defeat became likely.

This, though, was no constraint on would-be Labour rebels. So several other hurdles – lower, more likely, more dangerous – began to be mentioned. The Prime Minister would resign if he had to rely on the Conservatives to win the vote. The Prime Minister would resign if more than half of his MPs voted against the government. The Prime Minister would resign if more than half of his backbenchers voted against the government. As Austin Mitchell recalled,

> in the lobby Tommy MacAvoy [sic] grabbed me warmly by the throat and took me into the Whips' Office where he gently explained that the media, not him I had to understand, were saying that Tony would step down if more Labour MPs voted

against than for him . . . Did I want to be personally responsible for bringing down the most successful election winner Labour had ever had?[27]

Mitchell didn't – and he went on to abstain. Other Labour MPs had the same arguments made to them, by whips and colleagues. In the event, most of these hurdles were cleared – although on the Smith amendment, more Labour backbenchers voted against the government than for it. But Blair had been careful never to go on the record about any of these other hurdles anyway. Whilst lobbying MPs he had mentioned that he did not want to win only because of the Tories – but he had not committed himself to resigning if that had happened. It would certainly have been very damaging had more than half the PLP voted against. It may well have been difficult to carry on as Prime Minister for long had he only carried the measure with the support of the Conservatives (although the idea that, if the Commons had voted for war, a Prime Minister – *any* Prime Minister – would resign on the eve of a military conflict on the grounds that the result wasn't quite good enough must be considered implausible in the extreme). But no statement made by the Prime Minister tied him to any of these outcomes. They were rumours put about in order to increase the pressure on those who were contemplating rebellion.

They were helped in this by the self-defeating actions of some of Labour MPs, who began to talk openly of a change in the leadership of the party. On 24 February, Alice Mahon, a leading opponent of war, had declared, 'It's our party. Leaders come and go, but it's our party'; and on 11 March, some Labour left-wingers tried to arrange a special conference to unseat Blair, arguing, 'It is time for the Prime Minister to consider his position. If he is not prepared to stand up to George Bush, he must make way for those that will.'[28] This represented a step too far for many Labour backbenchers, especially those who may have been anti-war but who remained pro-Blair. Most of the anti-war rebels were desperate to stamp on such talk as soon as possible, because they knew exactly how it would play with the bulk of the PLP, exactly how the whips would be able to use it. At the PLP meeting on 12 March, a fellow left-winger, Lynne Jones, attacked Diane Abbott for her 'stupid tactical error' in trying to undermine Blair's leadership in this way. Tom Harris, an MP from the 2001 intake, said that he had come close to joining the rebels, 'but when I heard some of my colleagues talking about leadership challenges to Tony Blair, I thought this was ridiculous'.

The second factor which prevented the rebellion growing yet further was the actions of the French government, which came riding (inadvertently) to Blair's aid on 10 March when President Chirac indicated that France would vote against a fresh UN resolution, 'whatever the circumstances'. Jack Straw took Chirac's remarks to mean that the French were abandoning enforcement of UN Resolution 1441, and Downing Street accused the French of 'poisoning' the diplomatic process. The French (and others) protested that that was a distorted reading of Chirac's statement – pointing out the phrase '*ce soir*' in Chirac's remarks, and arguing that this meant the French would vote against any UN resolution as things stood on 10 March, but not necessarily later – but this gave the Labour whips (and some newspapers) the opportunity to engage in a bout of good old-fashioned French-bashing. Labour MPs were now asked a different question: Do you support Jacques Chirac or Tony Blair? A number of MPs – one estimate puts the figure at 20 – were persuaded to stay in post and/or to support the government in the lobbies due to what they regarded as the French use of an 'unreasonable veto'.[29] Among these MPs were one or two PPSs who had earlier said they might vote against the government without a second UN resolution. At the very least, Chirac's comments gave wavering Labour MPs an argument (however flimsy it was in reality) with which to justify support for the government; as Mary Ann Sieghart argued in *The Times*: 'This allowed the Prime Minister to portray himself as the one desperate to follow the UN route, while the French President acted as a wrecker. Chirac's behaviour gave those MPs who had impaled themselves on a second resolution an excuse to get off the hook'.[30] Or, as a whip put it, Chirac's comments meant that it was 'possible for people to have a UN justification for both lines of action'.

And third, the government had effectively given the House of Commons the opportunity to decide whether British forces went to war. This had been one of the initial demands of many of the anti-war rebels. Although the formal prerogative power to declare war remained with the Crown, there had still been an important de facto change: had the vote gone against war, the Prime Minister would have resigned and British soldiers would not have gone into battle. The government's decision to concede a substantive vote on war – although largely a reflection of its weakness – did therefore have the effect of satisfying one of the basic demands of many Labour MPs: that the House of Commons should decide the matter. The Commons may not have taken its chance to stop war – but it was given it. Military action began 28 hours after the vote.

# Jeff Ennis and John Grogan

Shortly after the Iraq rebellions, I received an e-mail from a very well-qualified observer of the PLP, someone with decades of experience of backbench revolts and their consequences. In it, he queried the then conventional view that those who had taken part in the Iraq rebellions would inevitably go on to rebel again. His argument was that there was something unique about the Iraq revolts, something with the potential to make otherwise solidly loyal Labour MPs defy their whip – but that once normal politics resumed, so MPs would revert to their normal behaviour. The rebels would go on rebelling. The loyalists would go back to being loyal. The e-mail concluded with the words 'I mean . . . Jeff Ennis, for God's sake!'

The subject of his valedictory ejaculation was the Labour MP for Barnsley East and Mexborough – and a party loyalist to his substantial core. A former primary school teacher, Ennis was first elected in a by-election in 1996, for what was then simply called Barnsley East (Mexborough being added to the nomenclature from 1997 onwards, as part of the Boundary Commission's ongoing mission to extend the names of all parliamentary constituencies beyond the point at which anyone can sensibly use them). Ennis has two dominant characteristics. First, he is Yorkshire born and bred – he was born in Grimethorpe, the setting for the film *Brassed Off* – and doesn't let you forget it. And second, he is the sort of MP who finds it extremely difficult to contemplate voting against their party. On a spectrum that starts at one end with Jeremy Corbyn and ends at the other with Siôn Simon, Ennis is – at least in terms of his deep-felt loyalism – much nearer to the latter.

And yet in February 2003, and for the first time in his life, he found himself in a rebel division lobby, one of the hundred-plus Labour MPs who voted against the government over Iraq. His loyalism was still strongly in evidence – he admitted to feeling 'terrible' for defying the whip – and he was then one of just four Labour MPs who switched and supported the government in March's Iraq votes, having been persuaded by the Prime Minister's stressing of the Middle East peace process.

The claim that *some* of those who defied the whips over Iraq would never go on to do so again was certainly correct. There were 63 Labour MPs who voted against their whip for the first time during the 2001 Parliament over Iraq, although 18 of these had rebelled during the preceding Parliament. That leaves 45 for whom their vote over Iraq was the first one they cast against the Blair government. Of these, 17 – listed in the left-hand column of the table on page 131 – did not then go on to rebel over any other subject during the rest of the Parliament. After Iraq, they went back to toeing the party line. Inclusion in this list should not be taken as indicating that the MPs concerned were slavishly or unthinkingly loyal post-Iraq. Several of those listed may not have voted against the government after the Iraq votes, but were still willing to challenge it over issues close to their hearts (most obviously Alan Whitehead over higher education, see pp. 174–205, and Kevin Brennan over pensions, pp. 219–220).

This leaves 28 Labour MPs: those who rebelled for the first time against the Blair government over Iraq, and who went on to rebel over other issues later in the Parliament. They are listed in the right-hand column of the table, and, *pace* the correspondent's expectations with which this discussion began, they do include Ennis, who was later also to defy the government whips over the issue of university top-up fees. (Although here, too, his fundamental party loyalty kicked in: he abstained rather than voting against the party in the key second reading vote – sitting in the chamber throughout, in order to register his abstention publicly – and then voted against on the much less dangerous vote at the report stage.) For the majority of those who rebelled for the first time over Iraq, then, it was *not* to be a one-off, never-to-be-repeated, experience. The majority of first-time rebels went on to rebel over other issues as well. Iraq was the first of their rebellions, not the last.

## Labour MPs who defied the party whip for the first time over Iraq

| MPs who did not go on to rebel over other issues | MPs who went on to rebel over other issues (including dissenting votes on other topics) |
| --- | --- |
| Anne Begg | John Battle (6) |
| Bob Blizzard | Anne Campbell (3) |
| Keith Bradley | Helen Clark (7) |
| Kevin Brennan | Robin Cook (5) |
| John Denham | Tom Cox (6) |
| Parmjit Dhanda | Jim Cunningham (4) |
| Frank Doran | Huw Edwards (2) |
| Hywel Francis | Jeff Ennis (1) |
| Stephen Hepburn | Paul Farrelly (2) |
| Helen Jackson | Roger Godsiff (9) |
| Mark Lazarowicz | John Grogan (14) |
| Khalid Mahmood | David Heyes (4) |
| Ann McKechin | Joan Humble (2) |
| Chris Mole | Martyn Jones (2) |
| Graham Stringer | Ian Lucas (1) |
| Alan Whitehead | John Lyons (5) |
| David Wright | Eddie O'Hara (3) |
| | Albert Owen (7) |
| | Peter Pike (1) |
| | Ken Purchase (5) |
| | John Robertson (2) |
| | Joan Ruddock (2) |
| | Mohammad Sarwar (3) |
| | Malcolm Savidge (3) |
| | Paul Stinchcombe (3) |
| | Paul Truswell (1) |
| | Bill Tynan (3) |
| | Brian White (2) |

The most rebellious of this group was John Grogan, another Yorkshire MP (although a supporter of Bradford City, rather than Ennis's beloved Barnsley). Grogan had become the first Labour MP for the North Yorkshire constituency of Selby in 1997, winning the seat at his third attempt, but he did not vote against the party during his first four years in the Commons. After Iraq, however, he was to vote against the party line fourteen times by the 2005 election, with rebellions over the Higher Education Bill, the Gambling Bill, the Railways Bill, the Serious Organised Crime and Police Bill and the Prevention of Terrorism Bill. He carried on rebelling when the 2005 Parliament resumed. Grogan was the exception, however. No other first-time Iraq rebel made it into double figures, and the median number of votes cast against the whip after Iraq by this group of MPs was just three.

It would be going too far to assume that Iraq was what *caused* this later rebellious behaviour. It is quite possible that even if Iraq had not happened something else would have triggered their discontent. Those who rebelled over, say, foundation hospitals might have done so anyway; those who objected to the government's anti-terrorism legislation might have found it objectionable irrespective of their vote over Iraq. But there was a clear difference in the later behaviour of MPs depending on whether or not they rebelled over Iraq. Of the 45 who rebelled over Iraq for the first time, just seventeen (that is, 38 per cent) did not rebel later. Of the 96 other backbenchers who had not previously voted against their government, and then who did not do so over Iraq, 64 (or 67 per cent) did not go on to rebel later either. In other words, those who rebelled for the first time over Iraq were almost twice as likely to go on to rebel later in the Parliament than those who remained loyal over Iraq.

Rebelling for the first time is routinely compared to a loss of virginity. The comparison's not perfect (not least because each division in the House of Commons takes between twelve and fifteen minutes) but the whips are well aware that once an MP has rebelled for the first time, they are more likely to do so again. Recidivism is a very real risk. And so, with each rebellion, the number of potential rebels for the next grows ever greater. In this, Iraq was similar to any other issue. The only difference was that it was responsible for adding more new names to the ranks of the rebels than any other issue in the Parliament.[31]

During the war itself, Labour discontent was subdued. Only two Labour MPs spoke out in vociferous terms. George Galloway allegedly incited foreign forces to rise up against British troops on Abu Dhabi television on 28 March, comments that led to his suspension from the party on 6 May and his expulsion by Labour's National Constitutional Committee on 23 October. Tam Dalyell flirted with a similar fate when he wrote that Tony Blair should be 'branded as a war criminal and sent to The Hague'.[32] Once the war ended, dissent continued, but on a much lower scale, with a handful of small rebellions on various opposition day motions.[33] The largest postwar Iraq revolt came on 20 July 2004, when 32 Labour MPs voted in favour of a closure motion at the end of an adjournment debate on the Butler report, into the prewar use of intelligence on weapons of mass destruction.

None of these rebellions were sizeable – most Labour MPs had no desire to revisit the issue – but the real damage caused by Iraq lay not in the numbers. It was more qualitative than quantitative. It wasn't just that it created a new band of backbench rebels; after all, it was hardly as if most of them became desperadoes. The problem came in the effect that the issue had on the rest of the PLP. Immediately following March's record-breaking rebellion, one whip was definite: 'Once CNN start beaming up the pictures of Saddam Hussein's torture chambers and the stockpiles of chemical weapons that he claims he does not have, you won't be able to find anyone who remembers voting against Tony Blair.' But although the torture chambers and mass graves were found, the stockpiles never appeared – and it was because of the stockpiles that many in the PLP thought they had voted for war. For some, those who had already been critics of the government before, this was the factor that destroyed their already weakened faith in the government's judgement and direction. For others – especially those who had stuck to the party line, in many cases against their better judgement, because they had put their faith in Blair and his arguments – this was a defining moment. They felt let down, betrayed even, by what had happened. As one concerned minister put it immediately after March's rebellion, 'we're not only facing the danger that Iraq will give some MPs a rebellion habit, it's also that they are not giving us the benefit of the doubt any more. People are asking us questions about where quite ordinary policies are going as if we have a hidden agenda.'

Just as with much of the electorate outside the Palace of Westminster, so too inside: Iraq was the moment when many Labour MPs stopped trusting Tony Blair.

# 6

# Sedgefield privatisers and Darlington money-changers

*Foundation hospitals – The view from the Whips' Office*

Until now, we have had a consensus on the National Health Service – just about – and it has been a Labour consensus. However, we are now in danger of setting out to establish a consensus that is basically Tory. I cannot see how the present proposals will lead to anything other than a two-tier health service, with one group of hospitals permanently doing better than the other. – Frank Dobson MP, former Secretary of State for Health, 2003

Anthony King once described British politics as 'over-the-shoulder politics'. The phrase conveys the extent to which what matters to a government minister is not the opposition of the people sitting across the chamber from him or her. What matters is the opposition from those who sit behind. 'One discounts the disapproval of the other party,' he wrote; 'the disapproval of one's own is harder to bear'.[1] Douglas Hurd, the former British Foreign Secretary, once said that he never lost the 'wholesome respect, even fear, of the House of Commons. I felt it was always there behind my shoulder.' But the Commons was not just behind his shoulder; the Commons was all around him. Behind his shoulder – and what was really responsible for causing him concern – were his own backbenchers.[2]

A good example of this came in July 2003 during the report stage of the government's Health and Social Care Bill, the Bill that introduced foundation hospitals. The minister, John Hutton, was winding up for the government – making the government's final speech – and he was taking repeated interventions, as Labour MP after Labour MP sought assurances about the Bill's contents. In mid-flow, Hutton was interrupted and then mildly rebuked by the Deputy Speaker:

Deputy Speaker: Order. I am sorry to interrupt the minister, but it would be helpful if he addressed his remarks to the chair, not behind him.

Mr Hutton: I am sorry, Mr Deputy Speaker. It is always nice to look into the eyes of my Hon. Friends when trying to be reassuring and tell them how it is. My only other choice is to look at that lot over there. [Interruption] Well, one or two of them are not bad, but some of them really do suck.

Leave aside Hutton's aesthetic judgement (it's hardly as if the PLP is full of lookers), and instead see this as over-the-shoulder politics *par excellence*. By July 2003, the government's proposals for foundation hospitals had run into real difficulties with its backbenchers, and Hutton's role that day was as Mr Reassurance, reminding Labour MPs exactly how far the government had backed down in the face of their concerns, and showering the PLP with comfort and kisses. 'The government have listened to the concerns that have been expressed about that part of the Bill,' he said, referring to foundation hospitals, 'and we have acted on those concerns . . . These are all significant movements.' They were indeed; by July 2003, the Bill that Hutton was defending looked very different from the Bill first unveiled as one of the government's flagship policies less than a year before.

★ ★ ★

Prior to 9/11, few people had expected foreign affairs to be the source of much backbench discontent during Tony Blair's second term. Friction between leaders and led in the first term had come over domestic legislation – especially issues of social security reform and the reform of the public services – and most observers expected something similar second time round. As the focus shifted, after Iraq, back onto domestic matters, it became clear that this was precisely what was going to happen for the remainder of the parliament. The middle two sessions of the 2001 parliament saw the whips scurrying around trying to dampen down rebellions over a range of domestic issues, including the fire-fighters' dispute (the largest of which saw 41 MPs rebel), legal reform (33 rebels), the asylum and immigration laws (34 rebels), energy efficiency targets (26 rebels) and the smacking of children (49 rebels). But their biggest problems came with NHS reform in the 2002/3 session and higher education reform in the 2003/4 session.

Although it was not apparent at the time, the dispute over foundation hospitals turned out to be merely the rehearsal for the later fight over top-up fees. Both issues involved similar complaints from backbenchers, both about the policies themselves (especially objections to what Labour MPs saw as the 'marketisation' of public policy) and to the way the policies were being introduced (emerging fully formed out of Downing Street and then dropped onto the PLP, rather than out of the party's policy apparatus). Both issues saw the government whips concerned that a Bill might be lost because of backbench dissent. Both issues produced claims that the Prime Minister's authority was on the line over the issue – with widely discussed rumours that he would step down if defeated. Both saw the government give repeated concessions to their backbench critics – the cause of John Hutton's crick in the neck in July 2003 – altering the Bill substantially in the process; and both showed the importance of the 'narrative' that accompanies policy, the way policies are sold, explained, and justified. Both issues also included a Gordon-versus-Tony subplot.

* * *

Launching the government's proposals for the establishment of foundation hospital trusts in May 2002, Alan Milburn, the then health secretary, portrayed the reforms as embracing 'devolution, diversity and choice'. The trusts, which would opt out of government control, becoming independent not-for-profit organisations, would act as beacons, spreading reform across the NHS.[3] The policy was a central part of the government's desire to end the 'one size fits all' approach to the provision of public services in the UK, and introduce 'choice'. In party management terms, however, the difficulty was that plenty of Blair's backbenchers rather liked the 'one size fits all' approach, distrusted the concept of 'choice' in the provision of public service, and didn't trust those who were pushing for reform. Their fundamental objection was that the proposals reintroduced competition into the NHS, and would thus create a two-tier health service. David Hinchliffe, the chairman of the Health Select Committee, commented on BBC Radio 4's *The World at One*, 'This is the internal market all over again. This is the competitive ethos that I thought we had been elected to get rid of.' Des Turner, the MP for Brighton, Kemptown, was equally vehement in his fundamental ideological opposition to the proposals: 'Tony Blair is proposing something which even Maggie Thatcher did not have the bottle to do and that is to partially privatise the health service. We regard the foundation trust idea as a betrayal of the NHS ethos that we have all fought for.' As Blair's first Secretary of State for Health, Frank Dobson had been responsible for abolishing the internal market created by the Conservatives, and he objected to any proposals to reintroduce it. Foundation hospitals, he argued, 'represent part of a reintroduction of competition into the NHS, deliberately setting hospital against hospital in a way that, sadly, reflects the lamentable and failed policy of the Conservatives, who introduced division and expense into the health service'. He went on:

> Until now, we have had a consensus on the National Health Service – just about – and it has been a Labour consensus. However, we are now in danger of setting out to establish a consensus that is basically Tory. I cannot see how the present proposals will lead to anything other than a two-tier health service, with one group of hospitals permanently doing better than the other.

Some of the scheme's critics feared that this was merely the first stage in a process of full-blown privatisation: that once foundation hospitals were established, it would be easier to break up the health service entirely. But others had more immediate, short-term, criticisms or fears – not least that trusts would poach staff from other local hospitals, as they would be in a position to pay higher wages. At the Bill's second reading, Hinchliffe argued that just as school league tables had resulted in middle-class parents moving their children to schools with better exam results, so the best staff would be attracted to the best foundation hospitals, meaning a loss of income and services for non-foundation hospitals. Other MPs feared having to explain to their constituents why they could not use as good a hospital as the one with foundation status in the neighbouring constituency, or why one hospital in the constituency received all the resources at the expense of the other.

As the rebellion over foundation hospitals came to the boil in the spring of 2003, Turner commented:

> This could get very serious indeed if there is not some rethink on

the part of the government. It is something that could cause the biggest crisis that we have had in the Labour government with the Labour Party, even greater than the difficulty over whether to go to war with Iraq.

That the issue had the potential to top Iraq seemed unlikely even then, but the whips were well aware that they faced real difficulties – significant enough to have the potential to cost them the Bill. For the first time since Labour came to power, the whips were forced to consult the parliamentary authorities about the procedure for dealing with a government defeat. 'What on earth do you do if you lose?' asked one whip. This was uncharted territory.

\* \* \*

Labour MPs also objected to how the policy had been produced, claiming that there had been nothing in the 2001 Labour manifesto about foundation hospitals, and that the policy had been presented to the PLP as a *fait accompli*. (Labour's manifesto had contained a vague reference to giving patients 'more choice', and promising to engage in 'greater decentralisation to frontline services and to the staff who run them', but nothing that opponents of the policy claimed justified foundation hospitals.) This was part of a more widespread feeling that the policy had been dreamt up by advisers at No. 10. 'People are fed up,' complained one MP, 'with proposals being produced by kids in Number Ten and that MPs are not involved earlier.' Dobson voiced similar concerns, calling on Milburn to 'ignore the anonymous advisers who have an obsession with continuous change. They are like a collection of Maoists driven by the concept of continuous revolution.'

The irony with such complaints is that, since its establishment in 1906, the PLP has had the most developed internal structures of any of the parliamentary parties.[4] It was established with whips, written rules, weekly meetings and elected officers. Ever since it first entered government in 1924, it has had a liaison committee consisting of backbenchers and ministers. By the 1920s it had also acquired other ad hoc backbench groupings, including a union group, a miners' group, an Independent Labour Party group, and a temperance group; in 1945 these were superseded by a formal and elaborate structure of backbench subject groups. In theory, all of these bodies fulfilled two basic functions. The first was top down: to enable the leadership to communicate its desires to the backbenchers. The second, though, was bottom up: to help communicate the thoughts and concerns of the backbenchers to the leadership. Not the least of the motivations for the latter was the internalisation of dissent: by ensuring the leadership was aware of backbenchers' views, it should be able to contain and mediate discontent within private forums, preventing it becoming public.

The history of the PLP suggests that the practice has never lived up to the theory. The problems with the PLP meeting have already been discussed (pp. 120–121). The subject committees have likewise never lived up to their potential. In 1976 a PLP committee set up to investigate communications between the PLP and the government noted that the numbers attending subject committees 'are often small, sometimes embarrassingly so'. Little appears to have changed in the intervening years. Since 1997, and despite several attempts to reinvigorate them, attendance has remained pitiful for the most part, except when a topic of current controversy is being discussed. The whips used this feeble attendance at backbench committees as a refutation of the claim that backbenchers weren't being sufficiently consulted. One pointed out that the backbench committees were 'horrendously expensive' to run and yet 'hardly any of them turn up'. 'They are always going on about how they want to be involved in policy-making but it's mostly rubbish. What they usually mean is: you should develop policy that I want. Or: I want to be involved in policy-making only when it's controversial.' Similarly, another whip said, 'We offer a level of consultation that no previous backbenchers have enjoyed. And the buggers never come.'

For their part, the buggers responded that there was little point in them turning up to such meetings, because their views weren't properly listened to, and the most important policy decisions – like foundation hospitals – were taken elsewhere. As one put it,

> we're having all these meetings to discuss detailed bits of policy, to try to involve us in all these forward plans, and then the Prime Minister goes and makes these grand announcements, which completely change [policy]. It's clearly more important than what we're discussing, and so it's difficult to persuade people that their views are being taken seriously.

There is an important distinction between access to ministers and influence on ministers. Most Labour MPs think the former is relatively good. 'There's hundreds of ways of making your views known,' said one of the 2001 intake. 'All the PPSs do all day is organise consultations, and hardly anybody gets involved. We've got backbench committees that nobody ever goes to. It's ridiculously easy to get hold of a minister.' But few think much of the influence that such contacts would have – although there was also a clear distinction between the influence MPs could have on policy before it was announced (relatively poor) and the influence they could have after it had been announced (much better). As one long-serving MP pointed out, 'ministers have said that they'd like backbenchers more involved in the making of policy. But there's a gap in terms of the way that policy is being generated.' With both foundation hospitals in 2003 and top-up fees in 2004, MPs enjoyed almost no influence while significant areas of government policy were being developed. They were then, however, able to achieve significant changes once the proposals had been published.

This, though, is a recipe for conflict, for exactly the sort of public battles between front- and backbenchers which party managers claim they wish to avoid.[5] Consulting the PLP *before* the policy is launched, getting as many MPs on board as possible, is the stuff of Politics 101. But on key pieces of policy like this, it's an approach that can't be used because of the fundamental disjuncture between the views of some of those in and around No. 10 and those of the PLP (or, more accurately, the views in No. 10 and what they perceive to be the views in the PLP). One ex-Downing Street adviser said, 'If you're not careful you get the demands of impossiblism. I mean, if Diane Abbott was leading the party, then we'd never win an election ever again. What's the point of listening to that?' Or as one Blairite whip put it, 'the only concession some people want is to roll back the history of the Labour Party 20 years. And that's not a concession we should be giving.' The problem in terms of party management, however, is that it wasn't just the Diane Abbotts who were unhappy with the types of proposal coming from No. 10, nor were those who felt ignored confined to the tiny band of MPs who saw 1983 as the high point of Labour's history. Complaints about their exclusion from decision-making extended deep into the heartland of the PLP.

\* \* \*

One of the biggest Labour rebels over foundation hospitals was the Chancellor of the Exchequer. Both Alan Milburn and Gordon Brown supported greater autonomy for provision of the public services, but they disagreed profoundly over the extent of that autonomy. Milburn favoured hospitals being given constitutional autonomy as self-governing 'public interest' foundations. In order to be able to grow speedily, they needed the power to borrow cash from the private sector without Treasury approval. Brown argued that the Treasury would have to pick up the bill if they borrowed unwisely. He supported autonomy but firmly within the NHS, fearing the Balkanisation of the public sector, and the possible loss of Treasury control over public spending.[6] In the summer of 2002, Brown and Milburn fought a highly publicised battle over the borrowing powers to be enjoyed by the new foundation trusts. In the end, Millburn was forced to back down: foundation hospitals could borrow, but if their collective borrowings exceeded Treasury expectations, then the excess would be deducted from the Department of Health's hospital budget. In itself, this removed a central part of the original proposal, and – at a stroke – removed one of the objections that some of the scheme's backbench critics had with the policy.

But not all. Backbench opposition had mobilised around an EDM, tabled by George Stevenson, the MP for Stoke-on-Trent South. It noted 'with concern the intention by the government to introduce foundation hospitals', believing that this would 'create a two-tier NHS system', and urged the government 'to ensure that all NHS services are brought up to the best possible standards'. By the time MPs had returned to the Commons in the New Year, the number of Labour signatories to Stevenson's EDM had risen to 105. Around 50 Labour MPs then abstained on a motion on foundation hospitals in January 2003, and in March Milburn received a rough ride when he appeared before the Commons Health Select Committee. One committee member, the Labour MP for South Swindon, Julia Drown, commented:

> The policy does not seem to have been explained and has not been backed up. Questions remain unanswered and most Labour MPs feel uncomfortable about giving one set of hospitals advantages over others. We want fairness across the board and we do not see how foundation hospitals fit into that.

After Easter, on 29 April 2003, Labour backbench anger spilled over into Health Questions. David Taylor wondered whether foundation hospitals were 'a Trojan horse for Sedgefield privatisers and Darlington money-changers', Sedgefield being the constituency of the Prime Minister, Darlington that of the health secretary. And the next day, the Prime Minister addressed the PLP to stress that foundation hospitals were merely a way of driving up standards, and not what he called a 'Clause Four issue'. The very same day, however, saw the Chancellor evading questions from the Treasury Select Committee, refusing to deny a suggestion that non-foundation hospitals would lose out financially because the new trusts would have fund-raising powers. 'I am not getting into this,' Brown replied.[7] Afterwards, one Treasury Select Committee member even speculated that the number of likely rebels would come close to the 139 who had voted against the government over Iraq earlier in the year. George Mudie, who had transformed from the Helpful Friend of the Iraq Votes to a leading critic of the hospital proposals, warned, 'This is going to be the hottest issue in Parliament since Iraq with maybe even a bigger revolt.' That night, the *Evening Standard* ran with the front-page headline 'Massive Labour revolt on NHS: 100 MPs to vote against foundation hospitals'. Milburn meanwhile gave a speech to the Social Market Foundation think-tank, in which he denounced the 'conservatism' of those who were opposing reform, and called upon the government to keep the foot firmly 'on the accelerator, not the brake'.

By 1 May 2003, a week before the second reading of the Health and Social Care (Community Health and Standards) Bill, the number of Labour signatories to Stevenson's EDM had risen to 124. The government's difficulties intensified when the Conservatives indicated that they might abstain, or even oppose the Bill. The Conservatives had previously supported the policy – something which hardly encouraged Labour doubters that it was the correct one – and so the government had initially assumed that, just like Iraq, they would have Tory votes to ensure safety. But this wasn't Iraq – and the Tories sensed a chance to put the boot in. Liam Fox, the shadow Health Secretary, commented, 'We voted with them on Iraq because it was in the national interest. But the government cannot take it for granted that we will support it over this Bill.' He added, 'Although we believe in the principle of foundation hospitals, we also think that the government's Bill is a dog's breakfast.' Few people were fooled. The government were in a hole, and the Tories did not intend to do anything to make getting out of it any easier.

On 7 May 2003, the day of the second reading debate, the Prime Minister warned his party that to turn their backs on the reform of the public services 'would be a collective mistake of historic proportions'. But with deliberate timing, the same day saw the Health Select Committee produce a highly critical report on foundation hospitals, calling for stronger safeguards to protect other parts of the NHS from staff poaching, and warning that foundation trusts could face extra bureaucracy.[8]

★ ★ ★

The standard tactic of backbench rebels during the first Blair term (and, indeed, beforehand) had been to use a Bill's second reading debate as a chance to raise issues of concern, but only very rarely to try to vote against or to defeat the entire Bill. The aim was to demonstrate unhappiness, in the hope that the government would alter the Bill before any later votes. For the most part, this was just sensible politics. Few pieces of legislation are entirely without merit (even the Murder of the First Born Bill would have something in it for any second siblings) and attempting to defeat an entire Bill was therefore difficult; would-be rebels are always susceptible to arguments not to throw out the positive policy contained in some obscure subclause of the Bill. The tactic therefore at second reading was to mutter, moan and gripe (Labour MPs being quite good at all three), and then to focus a rebellion on the Bill's later stages, targeting particular pieces of a Bill. Eschewing the nuclear strike in favour of the scalpel was also sensible because rebellions can lose momentum once they have been unsuccessful; rebels therefore hold back from striking until the most advantageous moment. As one whip (a whip who really believed in mixing her metaphors) put it, 'if you go big at second reading, then you've fired your gun. And if you can't beat it with your best shot, then the game's over.'

But by 2003 the nuclear option was looking increasingly attractive to many of Labour's backbenchers. This was partly just frustration; having seen so many pieces of legislation reach the statute book as a result of carefully calibrated concessions that placated just enough backbench opinion to get through the Commons, plenty of Labour MPs began to think that it was better to stop legislation as early as possible. There was also a feeling that the changes to the Commons procedures introduced as part of the government's package of 'modernisation' – especially the automatic programming of government legislation – squeezed out backbenchers from the later stages of Bills. Programming, many backbenchers began to complain, divided the time up between the front benches, but meant there was no guarantee that backbench amendments would be chosen for debate (or, if they were chosen, there was no guarantee that they would be the right amendments, the ones with most chance of maximising backbench support). Therefore, increasingly, the view on the back benches was that when faced with objectionable legislation, the thing to do was to stop it outright. 'All the committee meetings in the world won't alter anything,' said one, 'so I take the view, let's get in there and kill it.'

Over foundation hospitals, the rebels gathered around a 'reasoned amendment' at second reading – an amendment which declines to give a second reading to a Bill, and explains why (the 'reasoned' bit). The amendment was organised by David Hinchliffe, and his co-signatories were at this stage not seen as natural rebels; they were hand picked in order to show the government that all kinds of Labour backbenchers, from all parts of the country, had problems with the proposals: Helen Jones was from the north-west and had been pro-government on the Iraq war; Kevan Jones was from the north-east, and had also voted with the government on Iraq; George Mudie, from a Yorkshire constituency, had likewise been pro-government on the war; Desmond Turner represented a south-east constituency, and had also voted for war, as had Julia Drown, representing a seat in the south-west. The Conservatives had agreed to abstain on the rebel amendment (thereby maximising the number of rebels on the Labour side), but would then vote against the government on second reading. When the House divided on Hinchliffe's amendment, 65 Labour MPs voted against the government, but because the Conservatives abstained, the government comfortably survived.[9] On the second reading vote that followed immediately afterwards, 31 Labour backbenchers again defied the government, with many more abstaining, including Clare Short, technically still then the international development secretary but clearly halfway through the exit, having also failed to attend Cabinet earlier in the day. Tory opposition to the principle of the Bill boosted the numbers in the no lobby, but the government still won by 74 votes.

Several media accounts of the rebellion portrayed it as a damp squib, as a revolt that had 'melted away' or 'fizzled out'. The leader in the *Independent* commented, 'As backbench rebellions go, this was one of the less spectacular.' And yet the government had just survived the second largest rebellion on a domestic issue since Labour came to power in 1997, only marginally fewer than the 67 Labour MPs who had voted against the cuts in incapacity benefit in May 1999. One positive consequence from the mammoth Iraq revolts was that almost everything seemed small by comparison. *The Times*'s editorial was more accurate, grasping the rebellion's significance:

> The willingness of an ad hoc coalition of Labour MPs – the fringe, the freelance and the fired – to obstruct ministers at this early stage of legislative proceedings is a warning shot, albeit one fired from a loose cannon. It cannot be dismissed as an isolated incident of no wider importance.[10]

★ ★ ★

In his entertaining book *The Rise of Political Lying*, Peter Oborne examines how the meaning of the word 'narrative' has changed in recent years.[11] Oborne is, unsurprisingly, not a fan of its new post-modern usage. 'New Labour', he writes, 'has always felt liberated from this boring reliance on mere facts. From the very beginning it believed that reality was capable of being created afresh. It imported the postmodernist notion of "narrative", and the associated proposition that the truth is something that can be artfully "constructed" into the British political system.' Whether or not you accept Oborne's overall thesis – and however entertaining it is at times, I've got my doubts – he's certainly right that 'narrative' has become one of the vogue political words. Everyone uses it. Everyone has one. To be without a narrative in modern British politics is the equivalent of those dreams in which you are walking down the street without having put on your trousers.

Whatever you think about the word itself, the *idea* of a narrative is important. Explaining where you are heading (which is an important dynamic aspect of a narrative) and why (also key) are hardly peripheral parts of politics. In June 2003, the dynamics of the foundation hospital issue changed with the appointment of John Reid as the new Secretary of State for Health, following Alan Milburn's decision (as it turned out, a temporary one) to spend more time with his family. This was Reid's fifth Cabinet appointment in four years; 'I have had more titles than Muhammad Ali,' he joked. As it happens, Reid shares Oborne's dislike for the modern use of 'narrative' – but nonetheless his appointment did help change the narrative around the Bill.

Reid was able to appeal to backbench MPs, talking a language that they understood, and arguing the case for reform with arguments with which they felt comfortable.[12] His conference speech that year, in which he tried to win over unhappy delegates, was a good example; he called on them to become 'pioneers in our time', and prayed in aid Nye Bevan, the founding father of the NHS, asking delegates to have the same open mind about developing healthcare as Bevan had had nearly 60 years before. One commentator teased, 'It was a speech that would have made Citizen Smith proud – the concept of giving power back to the people, giving the poor a taste of what the rich have taken as their right for decades.'[13] On the day of one vote during the Bill's passage, he took head on Roy Hattersley's argument that 'every time the right to choose is extended, the poor get second best', by pointing out that the past 50 years of attempting uniformity of healthcare provision had not created equality, and arguing that to deny the need for reform was to deny working people the right to choose to go somewhere else if their local hospital had a long waiting list and they could be treated quicker elsewhere.[14] Reid turned Hattersley's argument around: 'The question on choice is not whether working people want it, but whether it is the job of the Labour government to deny them choice.'[15] Similarly, several Co-op MPs were won over by the government's argument that behind the reforms was a new form of social ownership, 'like your friendly Co-op store around the corner' (although this argument infuriated some of the Bill's opponents). As one whip commented, Reid was great at changing the tone, 'talking Labour language'. He argued that such a change in tone was arguably more important in winning over doubters than the many concessions agreed to the legislation. Or, as another whip argued,

> no amount of managerial concessions will make Labour members vote for something that they think will kick their constituents in the shins. Without the language you could have concessioned it out of existence, and still no one would vote for it . . . You can't excite Labour politicians by talking about process.

When some MPs say that Reid created a 'Labour narrative' to accompany the reforms, that's all they mean.

Reid used the Labour Party conference to hone his formidable persuasive skills. In an attempt to try to win over Labour's unhappy rank and file, the teetotal Secretary of State sat in his conference room, armed only with a two-litre bottle of Coke, meeting Labour activist after Labour activist, arguing the toss. Some he'd win, some he'd lose (and the leadership eventually still lost the conference vote), but the effort that he put into arguing his case – the sheer graft of it all – certainly impressed the whips. Reid was similarly relentless in his pursuit of wavering Labour MPs. One Scottish Labour MP was hunted down for two weeks prior to a key Commons vote. He tried to hide because he knew that Reid had the best chance of persuading him not to vote against, describing him as 'a good communicator'. 'He argues at your level. It's disheartening. I cannae beat him in an argument. He knows all the detail.' Eventually he couldn't put it off any longer but told Reid that there was no way he was going to move on the subject, that there was simply no way he could be persuaded, that there was no way he was going to back the government. But by the time the MP had left the room Reid had asked for and received a promise that he would abstain instead of voting against.

★ ★ ★

When the Bill came back from committee to the floor of the Commons for its report stage in July 2003 the rebels were armed with an amendment that would have removed all mention of foundation hospitals, whilst leaving the rest of the legislation intact. This time, 62 Labour MPs voted against the government, but more abstentions than before meant the government's majority was cut to 35.[16] This was then the lowest majority caused by backbench dissent since 1997, and – more importantly – it was a majority that was shrinking, down by more than half from just a few months before. Things were even worse than the headline figures suggested. There had been some sympathy for the fact that Reid had inherited the policy from his predecessor, and some Labour MPs thought it unfair to undermine Reid's authority by voting against the government at report stage just three weeks after he had taken up his post. As one MP put it, 'I did not want to give him a bloody nose so early on in the job.' But these MPs hadn't been converted to the cause, and if the Bill was later to return from the Lords to the Commons, they'd be less forgiving at the next time of asking. Even worse for the government – and not reported at the time – the real reason it won the vote was simply because not enough opposition MPs turned up. The government whips had been taken by surprise by the size of the revolt, having taken their eye off the ball slightly. 'We didn't realise how much hostility there still was to the issue,' said one. Even with a poor Tory turnout, they were saved (and mightily relieved) by the fact that so many Labour MPs decided to abstain rather than vote against. But even so, if opposition MPs had turned up in sufficient numbers the government would have gone down to defeat.

When the House of Commons returned for its short two-week September session Frank Dobson and David Hinchliffe circulated a memorandum to Labour and crossbench peers explaining how the proposals would destroy the fundamental values of the NHS. The memorandum, sent in advance of the Bill's second reading in the Lords, asked peers not to feel constrained by the convention that the Lords did not defy the will of the elected chamber. It argued:

> The proposal for foundation hospitals was not in our 2001 general election manifesto. It was not the subject of a green paper or a white paper. It is opposed by most people who work in the NHS and the level of discontent on the Labour benches is demonstrated by the fact that it scraped through by a majority of just 35 votes. We believe this proposal will harm both the NHS and the Labour party. We therefore urge you to consider withholding your support.

Peers did just that on 6 November, defeating the government by 150 votes to 100 in an attempt to remove all mention of foundation hospitals from the legislation, and setting up another battle between Labour rebels and the government when the Bill returned to the House of Commons on 19 November.

★ ★ ★

The government backed up any changes in narrative with substantive changes to the Bill. Movement had begun even before the Bill was published. Back in March 2003, in an attempt to deal with the two-tier argument, the Prime Minister indicated at PMQs that he wished to see all hospitals become foundation hospitals within four or five years (with Alan Milburn announcing just before second reading that an extra £200 million would be available to help hospitals achieve this). And on 13 March, when the Bill was published, the government gave three more concessions: it introduced a cap on the income that the new foundation hospitals could earn from private patients; it ensured that NHS pay arrangements applied to foundation hospitals (to try to alleviate the fear that they might unfairly poach staff from other non-foundation hospitals); and it announced that new trusts would be required to maintain NHS values, overseen by a regulator, who would be obliged to intervene if they did anything detrimental to the wider NHS. The new foundation hospitals were also referred to as 'public benefit corporations' rather than 'companies', as had been the case in earlier descriptions in the Bill. Not all the rebels were impressed – Frank Dobson wrote an article for the *Guardian* in which he claimed that foundation hospitals would still be better funded, and that poaching of staff would still occur because nobody could stop staff from neighbouring hospitals from applying for jobs there – but it was another sign that the government was willing to give ground.[17]

The government moved yet again when the Bill was in committee, tabling a series of amendments to strengthen the accountability of the independent regulator and tightening the audit rules to ensure greater financial transparency. And then, just before the report stage, even more concessions: in his response to the Health Select Committee, Reid indicated that pay arrangements in foundation hospitals would be bound 'by the results of any future collective bargaining'. The new Health Secretary also reiterated the government's earlier assurances that foundation trusts' income from private patients would be capped at the level it was in April 2003. The government also brought forward further concessions, particularly an amendment to ensure that local health authorities were to be given a seat on the board of foundation hospital trusts. They accepted amendments tabled by Adrian Bailey, a member of the Co-operative Party Group of MPs, and Stephen Pound, ensuring that the membership of foundation trusts was 'representative' in order to prevent small groups or cliques taking over trusts; and foundation hospitals were to have to report annually on the steps they were taking to ensure all parts of the local community were represented. Even Hinchliffe acknowledged that the government was 'working very hard, offering concessions right, left and centre'.

By the time Reid faced the Commons before November's crucial vote, he was quite open (indeed, almost boastful) about the extent to which the Bill had been amended as a result of backbench pressure:

> I want to illustrate just how far we have gone in our discussions on compromise. We will insist on reinserting the statutory limit on the proportion of private patients treated in NHS foundation trusts, removed by the opposition in another place. We have agreed to limit the borrowing powers, as explained earlier, of NHS foundation trusts through a prudential borrowing code. We have compromised on, and listened to, a number of concerns. Those are just a few examples.

He then threw in yet another major concession: agreeing to a review of the first wave of trusts after twelve months. This concession was so last minute that Department of Health officials later admitted they only found out about it when Reid announced the change in the Commons. The combination of Treasury pressure and backbench opposition had achieved major changes to what had been a flagship government Bill, leading some observers to argue that the rebels had effectively won, whatever the outcome of the vote.[18] There were so many government concessions that the central criticism – that the new hospitals would operate outside the state sector – had essentially been removed from the policy.

The government whips took November's vote much more seriously than they had July's, when they'd cocked up and almost seen the measure fall. Richard Caborn, the sports minister, was recalled from Australia on the junket of a lifetime – watching England play in the Rugby Union World Cup. When Caborn's spokesperson was asked to comment on how the minister felt, he replied, 'I can't tell you – it's before the watershed.' To rub salt into the wounds, Tessa Jowell, the culture secretary, then flew out on the Thursday morning after the vote, leaving Caborn stuck at home to watch the final on TV.

Meanwhile, the Conservatives issued what they (somewhat ridiculously) described as 'a four-line whip' to maximise their chance of defeating the government, even calling back one MP from a trip to China.[19] But the improved chances of Tory success also gave the Labour whips a fresh argument to deploy on recalcitrant MPs: that they would be handing a propaganda coup to the new Tory leader, Michael Howard. Two days before the big vote on 19 November, Reid sent a letter and accompanying briefing paper to wavering MPs calling for their support in the division lobbies. The Tories were, he claimed, not only trying to wound the government, they were also ultimately trying to privatise the NHS. 'They [the Conservatives] know that if we continue to improve the NHS then their health policy will lack all credibility.' He enclosed a copy of a *Daily Mirror* article, quoting remarks supposedly made by Liam Fox that 'if Labour fix the NHS we're fucked.' Reid's strongest argument, however, was that a government defeat would 'boost Michael Howard's Tory Party. Why should Labour MPs hand Michael Howard his political victory?'[20] It is difficult now – after the disastrous Conservative performance in the 2005 election – to understand why any Labour MP was particularly concerned about a reborn

Conservative Party in late 2003. But back then, the replacement of Iain Duncan Smith with Howard appeared to have re-energised the Conservative Party, boosting morale (if not their poll ratings), making them appear a more credible electoral threat, and thus making Labour MPs far more wary of presenting the Conservatives with victories. Graham Allen, for example, who had opposed the Bill at second reading, supported the government in the vote in November for what he called 'political rather than policy reasons': 'I refuse to help Michael Howard get off to a winning start just eighteen months before a general election,' he said. Another Labour MP abstained on the basis of this argument, having rebelled previously: 'It wasn't the issue, which I still felt the same about. But it was about giving the Tories a victory, when they'd just appointed a new leader.' She later reflected that the issue of Howard and a Conservative victory was one of those things that seemed very important at the time, but, in retrospect, seems less so. 'I mean, in ten years time', she said, 'no one will know about Michael Howard, but we'll be lumbered with foundation hospitals. But there you go.'

The government motion reversing the Lords amendments removing foundation hospitals from the Bill passed by 302 votes to 285, a majority of just seventeen. At the time, this was the lowest government majority since Tony Blair had come to power. Sixty-two Labour MPs had voted against the government, and around 30 to 35 had abstained. As the result was announced, the Prime Minister gave the Chief Whip a congratulatory pat on the back. Given the closeness of the vote, the government had prepared its response in the event of a defeat; the government would have accepted the loss of foundation hospitals from the Bill, but continued with the rest of the measure. There would have been no vote of confidence, as had been variously rumoured – 'We'd decided that, however important this was, it was not a vote of confidence,' said one of those involved in the Bill's passage – but the government would have promised to reintroduce foundation hospitals in the next

Queen's Speech. The House of Lords made one final attempt to strike out foundation hospitals from the Bill, defeating the government by 169 votes to 101, but this time around when the Bill came back to the Commons, the number of Labour rebels fell from 62 to 35, and the House of Commons voted against the Lords amendment with a more comfortable majority of 41. Some backbenchers remained implacably opposed to the Bill, but most others saw that the battle had been lost.

★ ★ ★

If the Bill's survival caused concern in the government Whips' Office, one other aspect of the Bill's passage caused concern elsewhere. Prior to devolution, its proponents were keen to argue that the so-called West Lothian question was not a genuine problem. Even if one accepted the theoretical problems of Scottish (and sometimes Welsh) MPs being able to vote on issues concerning the English, whilst English MPs were unable to reciprocate, its practical impact was – so we were told – limited. As one academic, William Miller, argued,

> there has never ever been any occasion on which the Conservatives have had a majority in 'England and Wales', but Labour has had a majority in parliament as a whole. In short the situation postulated in the West Lothian question, always unlikely because there are so few Scottish MPs, has never occurred in practice.[21]

We should therefore just stop worrying about it and get on with our lives. But arguments such as this assume that parliamentary parties are unitary actors – that all the MPs of one party would vote together. Instead, of course, political parties routinely split and splinter. Because of this it was quite possible for the West Lothian question to have a substantive impact, even when – as in the 2001–05 period – the government did not depend for its overall majority on the votes of Scottish (or Scottish and Welsh) MPs. This happened in November's foundation hospitals vote.[22]

The policy applied directly only to England, but the government got its way because of the votes of its Scottish (and Welsh) MPs. The government's majority was just seventeen, but there were 43 Scottish MPs voting with the government. From the opposition front bench Tim Yeo raised a point of order: 'The government's greatly reduced majority has been obtained through Scottish members of Parliament. What advice do you have for those of us whose constituents will regard this as a constitutional outrage?' Reid's reply did not engage on a particularly intellectual level with Yeo: 'The expression "pathetically bad losers" springs to mind.' Maybe it does, but the point still remains valid. Plenty of Scottish and Welsh Labour MPs justified their decision to vote on the issue (as they would later do over top-up fees), arguing that although the policy did not apply outside England, its implications would affect their constituencies – an argument they shared with the SNP and the Liberal Democrats, whose Scottish MPs also voted. But whatever the arguments, the vote remained the first example of the West Lothian question in practice. It is no longer merely a theoretical concern.

* * *

Writing in the *Independent* after the government had scraped through by seventeen votes, Simon Carr described the Labour rebels as 'a consistently disappointing lot'. 'They sense exactly the point at which they could do real damage then taken one decisive step back from it.'[23] He'd earlier described them as 'a relentless disappointment'. 'If they needed six votes to bring the government down, they'd get four. If they needed one, they wouldn't get it. They shrink to fit.' This was a slightly unfair observation, if only because it doesn't just apply to today's Labour MPs but to all MPs, Labour and Conservative, and throughout the entire postwar period (and quite possibly before too). Backbench rebellions didn't start fizzling out in 1997. But Carr's observation was only slightly unfair, because despite all the concessions and all the pressure, a total of 87 Labour MPs had still voted against their government over the issue of foundation hospitals at some point during the Bill's passage through the Commons. If all of those who were prepared to vote against their whips over the issue at any point had done so together, then the government would have been defeated. But they didn't, and so instead the number of cross-votes in any one rebellion never exceeded 65, and the legislation passed as a result.

A hard core of 40 Labour MPs voted against the government in each of the three main revolts. But this group alone was not large enough to bring about a government defeat. And the problem for those opposed to the government's plans was that the other 47 rebels – a majority of those who were prepared to vote against the government – were not as consistent in their opposition. Of the 80 Labour MPs who voted against the government over foundation hospitals in May or July, over a quarter (24) did not do so in November. There can, of course, be good reasons for such changes to the composition of a rebellion. MPs may have been persuaded to hold their fire at second reading – either voting with the government or abstaining – whilst making clear their demands for further concessions. And then, such concessions not having been sufficient, they would vote against at report stage. Other MPs, who rebelled during the Bill's early stages to indicate their unhappiness, might be satisfied by the concessions and come back on side. But this was exactly what the Whips' Office wanted. In the run-up to the second reading vote, the constant refrain from the whips was that MPs should not vote against the Bill at second reading, but allow it to go into committee, and thence to report, where they could make more detailed changes. The Whips were confident that if they could get past the second reading vote, they would then be able to win over enough of those who had rebelled to survive any subsequent vote, with the defections more than cancelling out any new rebels.

It is easy to blame the failure of these rebellions on the gargantuan size of the government's majority. But the foundation hospitals vote was the first indication that it was also due to the inability of Labour rebels to muster their forces at the right time. Even when there were enough backbench rebels to defeat the government, they didn't manage it.

★ ★ ★

At the Whips' Office summer drinks party in July 2003, Hilary Armstrong thanked her team for their hard work, acknowledging, 'It has been a difficult year.' But she reminded them of her father, Ernest Armstrong, who had served as one of Harold Wilson's whips in the late 1960s. She had recently reread some letters that he had written at the time, and she said, 'If we think we've got it bad, just remember what it was like then.' At which point, Charlotte Atkins, one of Armstrong's whips and herself also the daughter of an MP, the left-winger Ron Atkins, whispered, 'That's when my dad was rebelling!'

During Ernest Armstrong's time in the Whips' Office there were sizeable revolts over what J. R. Piper has described as 'virtually all of the major policy positions of the Labour government'.[24] In the face of backbench (and trade union) opposition, Wilson's government had been forced to scrap its industrial relations White Paper, *In Place of Strife*, as well as the Parliament (No. 2) Bill to reform the House of Lords (the latter facing opposition from a small but determined group of both Labour and Conservative MPs, including Michael Foot and Enoch Powell). There were also notable revolts against health policy (with rebellions against the reintroduction of prescription charges and charges for NHS false teeth and spectacles), immigration (with Labour MPs opposing changes to the immigration rules to curb the perceived problem of marriages of convenience) and employment law (over allowing children to work in the entertainment industry).[25] Wilson also faced backbench hostility over his handling of the Rhodesian situation and for allowing arms sales to the Nigerian government, as well as over policy towards Europe. And just as the issue of Iraq soured Blair's second term, so support for America's war in Vietnam took the gloss off Wilson's 1966–70 administration. The first significant Labour rebellion of the 1966 parliament, in April 1967, was over Vietnam, 59 Labour backbenchers supporting a motion calling for the cessation of the American bombing and a UN-backed peace initiative.[26] That Wilson's backing of the United States was limited to vocal support, rather than extending to troops as the US requested, is now often seen as one of his few achievements. Labour backbenchers didn't see it quite like that at the time.

Yet in some ways, Hilary Armstrong's team had faced a tougher time of it than had the Whips' Office in which Ernest had done his stint. By the whips' summer party in 2003, after just two years of the 2001 parliament, Blair's whips had already had to deal with more backbench revolts than Wilson's faced in the whole of the 1966 parliament. And whatever else they'd faced, Wilson's whips didn't have to cope with anything on the scale of the Iraq votes. The only way in which the Wilson era was more difficult for the whips was that the rebellions were – on average – slightly larger. By 2003, the pattern of backbench rebellion in the 2001 parliament was already pretty clear. There were certainly lots of revolts, but they were mostly pretty minor. The whoppers over Iraq or foundation hospitals (just like the forthcoming whoppers over top-up fees and the Prevention of Terrorism Bill) – were the exceptions, not the norm. The norm was smaller and more manageable; the majority consisted of fewer than ten Labour MPs, not the sort of thing to cause sleepless nights in even the most cautious of whips. The average rebellion involved 5 per cent of Blair's backbenchers. Between 1964 and 1970 the comparable figure was 8 per cent. The real stinker for Labour's whips came in the 1970s (by which time Ernest Armstrong had moved on to other posts in government, although Charlotte Atkins' dad was still causing trouble): the average revolt between 1974 and 1979 involved 11 per cent of Labour backbenchers; the figure for the short 1974 parliament was a stonking 19 per cent.

An exasperated Wilson, addressing the PLP on 2 March 1967, complained about the behaviour of his MPs and employed a famous canine metaphor: 'Every dog is allowed one bite,' he said, 'but a different view is taken of a dog that goes on biting all the time.' He warned them, 'He may not get his licence renewed when it falls due.' The allusion has lost something since the UK abolished its dog-licensing scheme, but anyway, there was little evidence that Wilson's threat did much good even then – the dogs just kept biting. Blair was similarly forced to appeal to the PLP during the middle of the foundation hospitals saga; the morning after the July rebellion, he warned a meeting of the PLP not to 'self-destruct' through division: 'If you look back at our history,' he said, 'we are better at putting ourselves out [of office] than the Tories. There's a tremendous prize. Let's take that prize, and not give it away to the Tories.' Blair's 2003 appeal lacks the wit of Wilson's dog licence analogy – although it had roughly the same impact.

Blair's frustrations were shared by many of his whips. They understood (and sometimes privately shared) the objections that MPs had to particular pieces of policy, but they struggled to understand the way that some MPs were beginning to articulate those objections. Particularly irritating were a small but vocal group of backbenchers who the whips felt had begun to rebel whenever they felt like it. If their views coincided with the views of the government, then fine. But when they didn't, so be it. 'They have no moral anguish about voting against the government, unlike the vast majority of Labour MPs,' complained one whip. Proof positive of this lack of 'moral anguish' was that some of them had begun to rebel on opposition day motions, motions put forward for discussion by the opposition parties but which have no substantive impact and for which most Labour MPs will not vote, almost whatever the subject, and whatever the motion's wording. As if to prove his point, on the night of the whips' summer party eight Labour MPs went through the lobbies to vote for a Conservative opposition day motion on Iraq. Cue much bemused shaking of heads and mild cursing by whips.

This group was an irritant but they were at least few in number. The real problems lay elsewhere, with the much larger group of Labour MPs who were increasingly disgruntled, albeit with suitable 'moral anguish'. A particular complaint from the whips was that too many MPs were going public with their opposition, nailing their colours to the mast before giving the government the chance to explain policy fully or to discuss possible changes or concessions. Sometimes this was done through EDMs, but equally constraining could be promises easily made, but less easily retracted, on local radio or TV or to their local party. As one whip put it,

> you get a nice letter from a nice constituent, asking you to support some inoffensive EDM, which seems to be sensible. And you think, 'I'm for good things and against bad things.' Most Labour MPs are. It's why they're in the Labour Party. And then it becomes clear that you've publicly committed to supporting something that will cost billions or whatever. You've got to think three steps – or two years – ahead.

Once MPs go public in their opposition, it is harder to talk them out of a rebellion, without this involving a loss of face. To back down then involves explaining, and almost inevitably attracting criticism for not having stood one's ground. 'It's not a nice thing to say,' said one whip in a reversal of the conventional cowardly/ heroic labels, 'but many of them aren't brave enough to do it.' A central role of the whips, from time immemorial, has been to identify issues with the potential to cause trouble, and then to defuse them. But with MPs flagging up their opposition so early in the process, one of the tasks of the whips became to provide 'opportunities for them to get off whatever hook they'd impaled themselves on'. Or, as another put it in strikingly similar language, 'they get themselves onto a hook, and you've got to get them off it. And any story that we can give them that will help them get off that hook is welcome.'

The whips are well aware what is driving much of this unease. As one whip noted, 'even Labour MPs are human.' They are, he added, 'subject to all the usual stresses and strains of the human condition, including sometimes a sense of injustice'. The combustible mix on the back benches – the rejected, the overlooked, the bitter – is well known to the whips; and, largely unnoticed outside of Westminster, they have made various attempts to ameliorate the problem in reshuffles. When the Prime Minister shuffled his ministerial pack, back into government would come a handful of ex-ministers, thus sending out a message that resurrection is possible. Into government would also come one or two of the 1997 loyalists who might otherwise have come to the conclusion that they had no chance of ever making it even slightly up the greasy pole. And third, a handful of MPs who had rebelled very occasionally would make it onto the payroll, in order to show that sporadic rebellion does not of itself result in an eternity in darkness. 'There's always redemption,' said one whip. 'There's always a way back.' The first batch of promotions after the Iraq votes saw loyalty to the government rewarded in a quite spectacular way: of the 21 promotions from the back benches, not one MP had rebelled over the war. But as the Parliament went on, Iraq rebels were no longer cast into outer darkness, with several making their way onto the payroll; by the beginning of Blair's third term, the Whips' Office itself included two former Iraq rebels. It was, as one whip put it, a way of 'sending a message that the slate has [been] wiped clean'. Blair's reshuffles have been routinely (and rightly) criticised for the cack-handed way they deal with the senior positions in government – but the changes at the lower levels have been more strategic and more thought through.

But there is a limit to how far this can be taken, and such tactics aren't without problems of their own. Promoting from among the longer-serving MPs has meant slower promotion for the 2001 intake – which has itself caused mutterings. Bringing ex-ministers back into government means fewer new ministers each reshuffle. Promoting rebels aggrieves the loyalists. The exemplar of this was Chris Mullin, the MP for Sunderland South, who had been a rebel before becoming a minister, then went back to being a rebel, before returning to being a minister (and who is now a backbencher again). Whereas other rebels have found themselves in almost permanent exclusion for a mere handful of rebellions, Mullin appeared to have his very own get-out-of-jail-free card, with licence to rebel much more often than other backbenchers and still be promoted, causing some resentment amongst some of the less rebellious, but still unpromoted, MPs. 'You can't blame them,' acknowledged one whip.

The extent to which backbench rebellion has become widespread is also causing the whips problems with those MPs who have stayed loyal and don't rebel – sometimes despite grave reservations on their part. 'Reasonable people', said one whip, 'get pissed off that the ranters and ravers are tolerated.' There is, as another put it, 'a huge and growing anger amongst those who don't rebel that there are no sanctions against those who do.' What makes it worse was that the rebels tend to be not just tolerated, but fêted. Those who rebel are seen as brave and upstanding and independent, whereas those who vote with the party are the gutless ones. As one whip put it, 'take Peter Kilfoyle, for example. He's all over the *Liverpool Echo*, whereas the loyalist MP – if he gets reported at all – gets reported as a toady, creep, careerist wanker.'

Yet all this, of course, is evidence of the weakness of the whips, not their mythical all-conquering power. They aren't able simply to bully or bribe the disgruntled out of existence. These are problems that they have to deal with, to manage, somehow.

# David Hamilton and John McDonnell

Shortly after the 2001 election a cross-party group of MPs set up an organisation called Parliament First, their first act being a motion stating that 'the role of Parliament has weakened, is weakening, and ought to be strengthened.' This was then followed, two years later, by a pamphlet, *Parliament's Last Chance,* which alongside a fairly routine set of proposals for reform – all fairly sensible, if not especially exciting – contained some observations on the regrettable decline of the independent-minded parliamentarian.[27] By 2003, when the pamphlet was published, and after the mammoth Iraq rebellions, it was a ludicrous claim. Yet launching the pamphlet on the *Today* programme Kenneth Clarke was still allowed to get away with the statement that party discipline was stronger than it had ever been before – when the truth was exactly the opposite.

*Parliament's Last Chance* combined its general whinge about the decline of independence with a more narrowly focused complaint – about the increasing centralisation of political parties. The argument was straightforward: the parties' head offices weed out any dissident voices from their aspiring candidates. All those who might think for themselves and cause the whips sleepless nights get blocked, with the result that only party apparatchiks make it to the Commons. There was nothing particularly novel in this complaint; it is heard every time the parties reform their selection procedures.[28]

The 2001 intake of Labour MPs – listed in the table below – was a good test case for the effects of Labour's new selection procedures.[29] In 1997 the scale of Labour's victory had meant that it had won fistfuls of seats that no one, including plenty of Labour's victorious candidates, had ever expected to win. The result was that Labour's 1997 intake included scores of MPs who had not been properly vetted by the party's HQ – a group that became known as the 'unlikely lads'. In 2001, by contrast, there were almost no unlikely lads or lasses; because there was so little change in the number of seats held by each party, nearly every new Labour MP inherited his or her seat from a retiring Labour incumbent. They had all been vetted properly and the party hierarchy had plenty of warning about who was about to sit on the government benches. Everyone knew what they were getting.

At each recent election there have been high-profile cases of (usually London-based) leadership-favoured candidates being parachuted into (usually northern heartland) seats at the last moment. These, though, draw attention away from the extent to which most new Labour candidates continue to have local connections. Around half of the 2001 intake had clear local connections, and around two-thirds had prior experience in local government, frequently in the same area. For every David Miliband or James Purnell, both swapping the No. 10 Policy Unit for a seat in the Commons, there were three or four like Iain Luke (Dundee East), John MacDougall (Central Fife), Meg Munn (Sheffield, Heeley) or David Wright (Telford). And far from them all being compliant clones, by the end of the Parliament most of them had revolted. Of the 38 new Labour MPs elected in 2001, 24 – or nearly two-thirds – had voted against their whip by the time the 2001 Parliament came to an end.[30] Compare that to the 1997 Parliament: between 1997 and 2001 just 28 per cent of the 1997 intake had rebelled. The highly vetted 2001 intake were therefore more than twice as rebellious as those elected four years before, many of whom had stumbled into the Commons almost by accident.

The most rebellious of the 2001 intake was David

Hamilton, the newly elected MP for Midlothian. When running for the Labour nomination, he was asked whether he had anything in his background that might embarrass the Labour Party; he replied that he had been in the Communist Party for ten years and had served two months in prison as a striking miner. The chairwoman's reaction? 'Medals, dear boy, medals.' After that, the nomination was his.

Hamilton voted against the whip eighteen times between 2001 and 2005, making him the most rebellious of the new intake by a long way. But, as with so many of the more rebellious MPs, he still saw himself fundamentally as a loyalist ('you disagree about 5 per cent') and he didn't particularly like rebelling. The top five new rebels all came from Scotland or Wales. This was partly because of the consequences of devolution, as those elected to both Westminster and a devolved body left to concentrate on devolved politics, leading to a high turnover in Scottish and Welsh seats (almost half of Labour's 2001 intake came from outside England). But only partly. The Scottish MPs were also just more rebellious (and tended to see themselves as distinct from many of the other members of the 2001 intake). The newly elected English MPs rebelled on an average of 1.6 occasions, the newly elected Welsh MPs an average of 3.3 times. The figure for Scottish MPs was 5.9.

Probe beneath the whipped votes and there was further evidence of deviance from the desires of the leadership. Despite having only recently been elected, in 2001 nine of the new intake voted for Donald Anderson or Gwyneth Dunwoody to remain on their select committees. When it came to a key vote on the modernisation of the Commons – on the reform of the process of selection in 2002 – the opposition of many in the Whips' Office to Robin Cook's proposals was well known, and was widely blamed for the defeat of the reform.[31] Yet of the new intake, 20, more than half, backed Cook's proposals. In 2003, when voting on reform of the House of Lords, the vote was similarly formally

## The behaviour of the 2001 intake

| Name | Constituency | Votes against the party whip, 2001–05 |
|---|---|---|
| David Hamilton | Midlothian | 18 |
| Albert Owen | Ynys Môn | 11 |
| John Lyons | Strathkelvin and Bearsden | 10 |
| Dai Havard | Merthyr Tydfil & Rhymney | 9 |
| *Iain Luke* | *Dundee East* | 7 |
| Vera Baird | Redcar | 6 |
| David Heyes | Ashton under Lyne | 6 |
| Colin Challen | Morley & Rothwell | 5 |
| Anne Picking | East Lothian | 5 |
| Paul Farrelly | Newcastle-under-Lyme | 3 |
| Hywel Francis | Aberavon | 3 |
| *Kevan Jones* | *North Durham* | 3 |
| Mark Lazarowicz | Edinburgh North & Leith | 3 |
| Rob Marris | Wolverhampton South West | 3 |
| Ann McKechin | Glasgow Maryhill | 3 |
| Jon Cruddas | Dagenham | 2 |
| Ian Lucas | Wrexham | 2 |
| James Sheridan | West Renfrewshire | 2 |
| Kevin Brennan | Cardiff West | 1 |
| Parmjit Dhanda | Gloucester | 1 |
| *John MacDougall* | *Central Fife* | 1 |
| *Khalid Mahmood* | *Birmingham, Perry Barr* | 1 |
| John Mann | Bassetlaw | 1 |
| David Wright | Telford | 1 |
| Chris Bryant | Rhondda | 0 |
| Andrew Burnham | Leigh | 0 |
| *David Cairns* | *Greenock & Inverclyde* | 0 |
| *Tony Cunningham* | *Workington* | 0 |
| Paul Daisley | Brent East | 0 |
| Wayne David | Caerphilly | 0 |
| Tom Harris | Glasgow Cathcart | 0 |
| Jim Knight | South Dorset | 0 |
| David Miliband | South Shields | 0 |
| Meg Munn | Sheffield, Heeley | 0 |
| *James Purnell* | *Stalybridge & Hyde* | 0 |
| *Siôn Simon* | *Birmingham, Erdington* | 0 |
| *Mark Tami* | *Alyn & Deeside* | 0 |
| *Tom Watson* | *West Bromwich East* | 0 |

## The Rebels

Note: italics indicate MPs loyal to the leadership's known preferences on key free votes, as explained in the text.

'free' but the Prime Minister's preference for a 100 per cent appointed chamber was well known. Of the 38, just sixteen of the new MPs – less than half – backed the PM's preferred outcome.

The 2001 cohort nearly all sat for safe seats; barring unfortunate encounters with their local constituency party, the Boundary Commission or God, they had a job in the Commons for 20 or 30 years if they choose – 'we are', as one of them said, 'going to be here for a while'.[32] They were also much more politically experienced than many of the 1997 intake. These were people who knew the system: the new intake included plenty of policy advisers, trade unionists and ex-councillors. There was little of the wide-eyed naïveté evident in some of the 1997 intake. The 2001 intake was packed to the gills with so-called 'career politicians', with a long future in the Commons ahead of them. But here's the irony. This worked in exactly the opposite way from all the supposed complaints about career politicians. Rather than enfeebling them, it emboldened them. The length of their potential career enabled some of them to take the long view, some clearly thinking of a post-Blair future, in which obedience to the party line under Blair would not necessarily be a positive attribute. Their previous political experience also enabled some of them to be more robust in dealing with ministers or the whips. So if the aim of Labour's selection process was to ensure that only Blairite clones made it to the Commons, then it failed dismally. By the second anniversary of their election over half had defied their whips; two-thirds had done so within four years of their election. On free votes, they similarly showed no inclination to do as either the Prime Minister or the Whips' Office desired. Just six – a mere 16 per cent – neither rebelled nor defied the whips or the Prime Minister. There is, in other words, absolutely no evidence that the recent changes to selection procedures have produced more compliant or acquiescent MPs.

Rebellious new MPs should, however, be under no illusions about the cost of this behaviour. Those who rebel early on in their time in Parliament do not tend to achieve rapid promotion up the ministerial ladder; rebel early on in your parliamentary career, and you are unlikely to be found clutching a ministerial red box in the near future. Of the fourteen newly elected MPs who rebelled over lone parent benefit in December 1997, only one later went on to serve in government – and even he only reached the giddy heights of PPS. Similarly, not a single one of the newly elected MPs who rebelled in the first session of the 2001 Parliament had made it into government by 2005. Compare that with the careers of those who did what they were told. Of the fourteen MPs who did not rebel during the Parliament, almost two-thirds had made it into government by the 2005 election. The six super-loyalists – those who followed the whip and the leadership's desire on free votes – had been even more successful. All but one had made it into government by 2005. This is unlikely to be entirely coincidental.

The flip side of this, though, is that the whips are also under no illusion about the future behaviour of those left on the back benches. Take these two groups again. All of the MPs who rebelled over lone parent benefit in December 1997 went on to rebel over something else later during the 1997 Parliament, and of those MPs who rebelled in the first session of the 2001 Parliament, all but one went on to rebel over other issues during the Parliament. Indeed, it is not just that most of the early rebels go on to rebel again, but that they rebel *more often* than other MPs from the same intake. There is a clear and positive relationship between the number of dissenting votes cast by an MP in their first session and the number they go on to cast in the rest of the Parliament. For the MPs elected in 2001, for example, the correlation between the number of dissenting votes cast in the first session of the Parliament and those in the final three sessions is 0.56.[33] The figures for those elected in 1997 are even more striking: the correlation between the number of dissenting votes in the 1997/8 session and the final three sessions of the 1997 parliament is 0.67.[34] And the correlation between the 1997/8 session and the 2001 Parliament is an astonishing 0.91.[35] That is, there is an almost perfect linear relationship between the number of votes that members of the 1997 intake cast against the whip in their first session in the Commons and the number they went on to cast in the 2001 Parliament.

In the first year of the 1997 Parliament, for example, the most rebellious of the 1997 intake was John McDonnell, the MP for Hayes and Harlington. In his first year in the Commons he voted against the party whip on nine occasions, almost double the number cast by the next most rebellious member of that intake. He was then the most rebellious member of that intake in the second session of the 1997 Parliament (fourteen votes against the party whip), and then also in the third (35 votes) and in the short fourth session (when he was the only member of the 1997 intake to rebel). He went on to begin the 2001 Parliament as the most rebellious member of his intake (45 votes against the whip in the first session alone), and then also in the second session (34), and the third (21), and the fourth (35).[36] He has begun the 2005 Parliament as – you've guessed it – the most rebellious member of his intake.

Stripped of the statistics, it boils down to this: MPs who rebel early rebel often.

# 7

# Not Mission Impossible but Mission Bloody Difficult

## Top-up fees

We will not introduce 'top up' fees, and have legislated to prevent them. – *Ambitions for Britain*, Labour's 2001 election manifesto

When John Prescott went on Radio 4's *Today* programme at 8 a.m. on 27 January 2004 to say that the government's flagship Higher Education Bill was heading for defeat later that day, he wasn't bluffing. Despite the Prime Minister's claim that the Bill's defeat would have been 'a complete betrayal of the proper interests of the country', despite rumours that the Prime Minister would step down if the Bill fell, and despite months of intense pressure by ministers and whips on those threatening to rebel, the tallies kept by the Whips' Office were that morning still predicting a defeat at second reading by a margin of more than 20.

Even right up to the vote, there was no confidence within the government that they had the bodies they needed to win. With just an hour to go, the whips' calculations were still pointing to a defeat. They 'went positive' 30 minutes before the seven o'clock vote, with the Prime Minister being told at 6.50 p.m. that he would have the Bill – albeit with what they were then predicting would be a majority of just three. In the event, the majority was five. In the largest rebellion on domestic legislation since Labour came to power in 1997 more than 90 Labour MPs refused to back the government's proposals, and the Bill got its second reading by 316 votes to 311. It was the lowest majority on a whipped vote since 1997, and for a government with a nominal majority of over 160, it was a truly remarkable state of affairs.

Yet the really remarkable feature of the vote was not how big the rebellion was, but how small. The rebellion involved just over 90 MPs, but almost 200 Labour MPs had declared publicly that they were opposed to the government's plans. And so it was not the narrowness of the government's majority that surprised most observers – but that they managed to get a majority at all.

★ ★ ★

Alarm bells had been ringing on the back benches since July 2002, when the then higher education minister, Margaret Hodge, had told the Education Select Committee that when it came to university funding 'nothing is ruled in and nothing is ruled out.' This was considerably too *laissez-faire* for most Labour MPs, who wanted variable – or so-called top-up fees – to be ruled out explicitly, and who were not slow to indicate their opposition to any policy which did not do so. Paul Farrelly's EDM, which noted that 'a number of elite universities are making contingency plans for top-up fees, which would create a two-tier university system,' and which urged the government 'to adhere to its policy of ruling out such charges in this and successive future parliaments', was soon signed by 138 Labour MPs – with Farrelly arguing that opposition to top-up fees 'runs wide and it runs deep'.

The government's White Paper *The Future of Higher Education*, published in January 2003, proposed that universities be allowed to vary tuition fees from zero to £3,000 a year from September 2006 onwards. Ian Gibson, chairman of the Commons Science and Technology Committee, claimed that Labour MPs were 'seething' at the contents of the White Paper, and a second EDM, put forward by John Grogan, arguing that top-up fees would be 'based on ability to pay not ability to learn' and urging the government to abandon them, attracted 93 Labour signatories, whilst Anne Campbell's later EDM, which supported most aspects of the White Paper but argued that 'differential fees will deter students from low-income backgrounds from applying to the top academic institutions,' attracted some 70 names. Between them, these three early day motions attracted 171 Labour signatories – more than 40 per cent of the PLP, and over half the government's backbenchers.

A *Financial Times* survey in early September 2003 revealed that 70 of the 103 Labour MPs interviewed would vote against the government unless it changed policy.[1] Even allowing for the bias inherent in such surveys (would-be rebels are always more willing to participate than would-be loyalists) it was clear that the government was in trouble. One minister greeted the Queen's Speech on 26 November, which contained the Higher Education Bill, with the prediction that its passage would be 'not Mission Impossible, but Mission Bloody Difficult'. He had good cause – by the morning of 1 December, 132 Labour MPs had signed yet another EDM, this time in Gibson's name:

That this House recognises the widespread concern about the effects of variable tuition fees and the perception of debt may have on access to universities, particularly among students from families on modest or lower incomes; notes that there are alternative models of funding higher education, which the Department for Education and Skills has considered and which do not involve variable top-up fees; and calls on the government, therefore, to publish full details of these alternatives to facilitate proper, informed debate and understanding before proceeding with legislation to reform the higher education funding system.

By the time of the Bill's second reading, Gibson's EDM had gathered a total of 155 Labour signatories. Of these, all but sixteen had already voted against the government during the parliament. Over top-up fees, therefore, the government faced just sixteen rebellion 'virgins', but 139 MPs who were battle hardened. A further 41 MPs had signed one of the three earlier EDMs but not Gibson's; that brought the total number of Labour MPs to have declared themselves opponents of top-up fees to 196, almost half the parliamentary party, two-thirds of back-benchers – and easily enough to bring the government crashing to its first defeat since 1997.

★ ★ ★

Labour MPs had four basic objections to top-up fees.[2] First, there were those Labour MPs who objected to the charging of *any* fees, whether up front or post-graduation, variable or fixed, believing that all education should be free of charge. This group was dismissed by one whip as living in 'cloud cuckoo land'. If so, it was a land inhabited by a sizeable group of Labour backbenchers. When Labour had first introduced tuition fees, following the Dearing report in 1997, the policy had been opposed by around 50 backbenchers.[3] And in May 2002, an EDM tabled by David Drew, which urged the government to 'introduce grants for low-income students and end the current system of tuition fees', had attracted 94 Labour signatures, around a third of all government backbenchers. The government could, of course, respond that the proposals in the White Paper did exactly that – both reintroducing grants and scrapping the 'current system' of up-front tuition fees – but that's not what most of those signing Drew's EDM were after.

Second, there were those who doubted that the government's proposals would raise sufficient revenue to solve university underfunding, claiming that the amount of money raised by top-up fees would be something in the order of £250 million out of a total higher education budget of £10 billion. 'Apart from anything else,' one said, 'it didn't produce anywhere near enough money for the universities. Was it really worth causing such a huge row for such small sums of money?' And concerns about the limited amount of additional revenue also led some MPs to doubt whether the government's £3,000 upper limit on fees would survive for long. Since the proposals raised too little money – so the argument went – then there would be immediate pressure to raise the cap, in order to generate the money that the universities required. Many of the rebels therefore saw the eventual lifting of the £3,000 cap as inevitable.[4]

Third, many Labour MPs were concerned with the levels of student debt that would result – and especially with the effect that this would have on working-class applications to university. As George Mudie put it to Alan Johnson, just after Johnson had been made the new Minister for Higher Education,

> is he really telling this House that working-class kids will be encouraged to go to university, when they are not encouraged by debts of £8,000 and £9,000 and we are now projecting a debt of £21,000? Do you think they will be queuing up to go to university in working class estates with this policy?

Eric Illsley, the MP for Barnsley Central, described the proposals as 'a betrayal of working people in my constituency'.

But the fourth – and probably the most fundamental– objection was to what many Labour MPs saw as the 'marketisation' of the public services that would be created by variability. 'If you have a marketplace in higher education', one of them argued, 'it will one day be money driven and if it is money driven then it will disadvantage those who don't have money.' Or as another put it, it was 'morally wrong for students from identical backgrounds who have equal ability and who study the same subjects at different universities to pay widely varying fees . . . That cannot be right – it is not fair.' In January 2003, after the government had outlined a series of changes to the Bill (see below), a series of Labour MPs stood up to explain that – whilst they welcomed the changes – their opposition remained, because their opposition was based on variability, what one called 'the big, big issue'. Robin Cook wrote in the *Independent*: 'Ministers still show no grasp that what worries backbenchers is the principle of the marketisation of higher education, and the inequity of variable fees in rewarding and entrenching the privilege of those elite universities who can charge a premium for prestige.'[5]

This concern was even greater if the MP doubted that the £3,000 cap would remain. Anne Campbell said, 'As one student put it to me, we would be letting the genie out of the bottle. Whether the cap goes up in 10 years' time or 12 years' time, or whenever it is, that will still lead to a far greater degree of variability between courses than exists at present.' Hence the proposal put forward by two Labour MPs, Alan Whitehead and Peter Bradley, which offered the government a 'Plan B' if their proposals fell. Their solution was to drop variable fees in favour of an across-the-board flat fee of £2,500.[6] This would have involved charging *every* student just £500 a year less than the government was proposing as a *maximum* – with almost identical increases in the levels of student debt to those which some MPs thought would deter applicants. But because it did not allow for variability, and thus marketisation, it was widely seen as far more acceptable by Labour MPs.

But it wasn't just the policy that caused so much discontent. Just as with foundation hospitals the year before, Labour backbenchers were as angry about the lack of prior consultation over the policy as about the policy itself. 'For a lot of people the problem wasn't the policy,' argued one whip. 'The problem was the process.' This was seen by most backbenchers as yet another example of Downing Street policy advisers imposing market-driven policy on the parliamentary party, without any prior discussion or debate. To do it once was bad enough. Twice was pushing the loyalties of a lot of MPs. As Steve Richards commented in the *Independent*, 'even some of Blair's most ardent supporters on the backbenches have complained that they feel neglected and taken for granted as controversial policies are rushed out from Downing Street.'[7] During his speech at the Bill's second reading, the former Chief Whip Nick Brown – and one of the key opponents of top-up fees – called for government policy to be developed through the Party's National Policy Forum:

> We would be in better shape – and so would the proposals – had we gone through that exercise first to test the ideas in front of our Hon. Friends and colleagues whom we expect to support us before rallying behind the agreed proposals. Instead, the proposals were presented to us first, there was a demand that we should agree with them and we put up a fight to try to amend them so that they could be agreed.

This feeling was compounded by the fact that the government appeared to be doing the exact opposite of what it had set out in its 2001 election manifesto, *Ambitions for Britain*, in which it had starkly claimed, 'We will not introduce "top up" fees, and have legislated to prevent them.'[8] 'The real problem', one Labour MP admitted, 'was we said we wouldn't do it.' The government had a number of ingenious explanations as to why the Higher Education Bill was not breaking this manifesto pledge. Since the legislation would not come into effect until after the next election, no extra fees would be levied during the Parliament to which the pledge applied. And the new fees would be variable, but since the Bill also abolished the existing up-front fees, these variable fees were not topping up anything, and they were therefore not top-up fees. None of this cut much ice with Labour MPs. As one said, 'technically they didn't break the manifesto, but you shouldn't need a degree in linguistics to argue that.' Even some in the Whips' Office thought they weren't terribly convincing arguments, and that the government would have been better off had it just owned up. 'We'd have been better saying, "Yes, OK, but it's because we need to do it."'

The whips divvied rebels up into different groups, based on their objection to the policy – and the 'manifesto group', whilst fairly small, was one of the hardest groups of MPs to crack. Some thought that reversing a manifesto pledge like this was an inherently wrong thing to be doing (John Grogan, for example, talked about 'the deal that we all solemnly made with the electorate at the last election'); others feared that it would cause them problems when it came to the next election (if the government had done a U-turn on this, then how could anyone trust a word in Labour's next manifesto?). But it also had a more practical, short-term, consideration: it emboldened *all* those with doubts about the policy, and made it harder to pressurise them into backing the government. If the presence of a manifesto pledge to do something dampens down dissent, then a manifesto commitment to do the opposite of what the government is doing inflames the situation. When the new Deputy Chief Whip, Bob Ainsworth, caught one rebel in the division lobby and complained that he was voting against party policy, the backbencher was able to reply, 'Not me. I'm loyal. I'm following the manifesto.'

And into this fairly toxic mix were added the assorted grievances that had built up since 1997, and especially over the preceding two years. For some of the rebels, the revolt over top-up fees wasn't about mechanisms for funding higher education, it was about Iraq or foundation hospitals or asylum legislation or whatever else they had disliked but had been unable to defeat. For some, this was politics by proxy. Discontent on the Labour benches, Martin Kettle noted in the *Guardian*, 'comes from a steaming brew of frustration about everything from Peter Mandelson to Iraq . . . It is about heart, gut and accumulated grievance coming together in an unplanned, illogical but visceral act of destructive defiance.'[9] Some of the rebels wanted rid of the Prime Minister and grabbed onto top-up fees – as good a lever as was ever likely to appear. 'There were some who were against it in principle', said one MP, 'but many of them just wanted to give him a kick.' As one Labour MP commented two weeks before the vote, 'even if Tony Blair offers £20,000 a year and free flights to the Bahamas to every poor student, I'll still vote against him. We've got to get the bastard out.'

★ ★ ★

A seemingly tiny rebellion, on 23 June 2003, in which just ten Labour backbenchers supported a Liberal Democrat motion against top-up fees did not fool anyone in the Whips' Office. Many Labour backbenchers were only willing to support the government's subsequent amendment because it had been carefully crafted to make no mention of fees, and even so, the large number of abstentions by Labour MPs – some estimates put the figure at over a hundred – more than halved the government's Commons majority, cutting it to 74. Most Labour opponents of top-up fees were choosing to hold their fire, preferring to wait for the real battle to commence once the government had introduced legislation.

The whips had known for months that they were in a real hole over the legislation – what one called 'deep doo-doo' – and the scale of that doo-doo was made worse by the failure of some of those within the Department for Education and Skills to wake up to the reality of those difficulties. In February 2003, almost a year before the Bill's second reading, two of the whips held a meeting with Margaret Hodge and her advisers to discuss the future passage of the Bill, during which they tried to point out just how difficult things were going to be. According to one of those present, 'Margaret was absolutely dismissive and went back to [Charles] Clarke and said, "They're panicking."' The whip added (equally dismissively), 'Shows what she knew!'

Privately, some of those in the Whips' Office had come to the conclusion that they were not going to be able to get the Bill through with Hodge still in post, and had begun to lobby for her removal. 'She had', one said, 'absolutely no connection with the PLP at all.' 'We'd have lost it with Hodgie,' said another. 'She just put people's backs up all the time.' The Whips' Office made a series of requests to the Prime Minister about what they wanted out of the 2003 reshuffle and top of their list was to move Hodge out of the higher education portfolio. In her place came Alan Johnson, the MP for Hull West and Hessle. After the dust had settled and the Bill had reached the statute book, Johnson was showered with accolades for the way he engaged with Labour backbenchers. But as well as his (undoubted) talents, Johnson had one other important, symbolic, quality. A former postman and general secretary of the Union of Communication Workers, he was one of a shrinkingly few Labour MPs who could justifiably describe himself as 'someone of working-class background, foreground and hinterland'.[10] Having left school at fifteen, he was the first higher education minister not to have gone to university. When his appointment was announced, one lobby journalist asked the Prime Minister's official spokesperson whether Johnson's background would be a handicap in the post. The exact opposite turned out to be true: he was the physical embodiment of exactly the sort of bright, talented, working-class kid that Labour backbenchers claimed to want to help, and he was therefore able to sell the message that by reintroducing grants and scrapping up-front fees the Bill would help working-class university applicants, in a way that few other ministers could have. He 'gelled with Labour backbenchers', said one whip, 'especially working-class backbenchers'. On his appointment, just before the summer recess, one whip told him, 'You're not just up to your eyeballs. You're in well over your head . . . Use the recess to win the argument. Or we'll come back after the recess to almost certain defeat.'

* * *

If a complaint from Labour MPs was that they were not consulted sufficiently before legislation was introduced into Parliament, few of them complained about a lack of consultation once the Higher Education Bill began its passage through the Commons. Education ministers began with a series of 'seminars', open to all Labour MPs. The aim was to try to explain exactly what was in the proposals – and why. Ministers felt that some of the details about the legislation, especially the measures to help those from low-income families, were not sufficiently understood by Labour MPs. There was frustration within the DfES that all the focus had been on the variability of fees, with not enough on the other parts of the proposals. As well as variable fees, the Bill restored grants for students from the poorest backgrounds and abolished up-front fees, to be replaced with fees payable after students graduated, through the tax system and linked to a student's ability to pay. The income threshold at which students had to start repaying fees and loans was raised from £10,000 to £15,000, and there would be a new access regulator, the Office for Fair Access (OFFA).

As with foundation hospitals a year before, the attempt to sell the policy to backbenchers involved changing the narrative, creating a left-of-centre case for the proposals. The original DfES line had been to push the Bill as something that the universities wanted (the DfES used to argue, 'The VCs [vice-chancellors] are with us'; to which the whips would respond, 'How many votes do the VCs have?'),[11] but the government later sensibly shifted ground, selling the policy instead as a way of getting more working-class students into university, and ending the existing de facto subsidisation of middle-class university students by working-class voters.[12] The ground shifted, as one whip put it, 'from helping universities to helping students'. At times, this wasn't exactly subtle. Ann Cryer, the MP for Keighley, was having a cup of tea when a whip approached her and started to mention – more in sorrow than anger – her impoverished sister and her ever-so-clever niece. 'My sister is a single parent', said the whip, 'and her daughter won't be able to go to university without these grants. If you vote against this, you'll be voting against my niece.' The effect of this was somewhat spoilt later the same day when another MP sat down beside Cryer, and began – also more in sorrow than anger – to tell her about her underprivileged single-parent sister and her aspiring daughter . . .

The first 'seminar' was attended by 45 Labour backbenchers and Charles Clarke and Johnson handed out a seven-page paper outlining why the graduate tax was not a better solution than top-up fees, and why fixed-rate fees – a key rebel demand – were not appropriate to every course at every institution. MPs who attended said they found the seminars useful and informative, although John Grogan later commented, 'I now appreciate a little better how Maoist re-education worked all those years ago.' In addition to the seminars, education ministers were regularly seeing individual MPs or small groups of MPs to explain the policy and listen to their concerns. Both Clarke and Johnson were praised by most MPs for the way they were prepared to meet with and listen to backbenchers: 'no bluster', 'superb', 'I can't fault them for the amount of discussion', 'a fantastic political operation'. Johnson himself used to describe how he and Clarke went on a charm offensive: 'I did the charming and he was offensive.'[13] As the votes approached, so the contacts increased – and also changed in nature. They began as educational and discursive, involving mainly just DfES ministers and the relevant whip. As the vote got nearer, the meetings became more about ensuring that the MP understood (or in some cases, misunderstood – see below) what would happen if the government lost the vote, as well as requesting, and sometimes pleading, for support. They also began to involve more than just the whips and education ministers. Anyone who was wavering came under a blitz of contacts from government ministers, in all departments and of all ranks.

The extent of this pressure is well demonstrated by Gwyn Prosser, the MP for Dover, who was brought back into the fold after almost a dozen different meetings with the Prime Minister, ministers and whips in just four days. The week before the second reading vote, Prosser had three ad hoc meetings with Bob Ainsworth on the Monday, setting out his concerns about the Bill. On the Tuesday, he had face-to-face talks with Johnson, met with his regional whip, and chatted with another whip. He then attended a seminar on top-up fees hosted by Clarke, after which Clarke stayed behind to have a further chat with him. On the Wednesday, a second session with Clarke was followed by a fifteen-minute one-to-one with the Prime Minister: 'I told him I was angry about the policy being imposed from the top down without consultation with the party, but that I was willing to swallow it if he could convince me that concessions would be part of the Bill.' On the Thursday he had another meeting with his regional whip and more talks with another whip. He then agreed to support the Bill, but was still contacted twice by anxious whips to see if he wanted another meeting with Johnson.[14] One Scottish MP was seen by seven people – including Gordon Brown, John Reid, Hilary Armstrong and Ainsworth – during the course of one day. Another MP described it as like 'walking around like in an eighteenth-century ball, with my dance card. If you didn't have your full set of ministers, something was wrong.'

★ ★ ★

Announced in the Queen's Speech in November 2003, the Higher Education Bill was originally due to have its second reading before Christmas. But the whips' calculations revealed that they would have gone down to defeat by a majority of more than 80 had they pushed ahead with it then. This provoked another stinging row between the DfES and the whips, with the Secretary of State, Charles Clarke, furious that the vote was being delayed. The DfES advisers had their own figures for levels of backbench support, figures which were much more positive than those produced by the whips, and which indicated that they could get the legislation through safely. The whips were scornful, but firm: 'We were going to be defeated.' But there were in fact doubts in the Whips' Office about the wisdom of delaying. Privately some of them were so convinced that the Bill was doomed to defeat – whatever they did and whenever they held the vote – that they wanted to get it over with as quickly as possible. 'There's something psychological about the New Year, isn't there?' said one. 'We felt that it'd be better to lose and then put it behind us. Better that than start the New Year with a defeat.' The Chief Whip, however, 'never gave up on it' (as one of her colleagues put it) and persuaded the Prime Minister that if they were to have any chance of getting the measure through, then a delay was necessary. Come the New Year, though, and things didn't look much better. As Peter Riddell commented in *The Times*, 'few senior MPs privately believe that the government will be defeated on Second Reading, but they cannot yet explain how it will win.'[15] The tallies kept by the whips still had the government short by over 50 MPs as late as 22 January, five days before the Bill's second reading. That represented a rebellion of over 90 cross-votes, along with around 30 Labour abstentions.

Given the government's enormous majorities since 1997, there has rarely been much doubt about the outcome of votes in the Commons, and the process of telling – that is, counting – the votes has been somewhat predictable. The votes are cast, counted – and then the government wins. But the Higher Education Bill's second reading was so close that there was – for the first time since 1997 – some real doubt about what to do right up to the vote. Joan Ryan, the MP for Enfield North, was the Labour whip counting the opposition vote: 311. 'I knew that 311 was enough to have defeated us, depending on the abstentions,' she recalled. She walked into the chamber, and up to the clerk, to tell him the figure. 'And then, for the first time, I didn't know where to stand, because I didn't know if I'd won or not.' As one of the whips over Iraq, she knew the importance of symbolism – 'I announced the Iraq vote. People in my constituency think I declared war' – and she knew how any TV footage of her having to change position when she heard the other score would have been constantly replayed as *the* moment when the Blair government lost its authority. Cue mild panic – and some uncomfortable indistinct loitering until the other Labour whip, Jim Fitzpatrick, came into the chamber, and they were able to whisper to each other, 'What have you got?' Fitzpatrick had 316. Some 72 Labour MPs had voted against the government, David Taylor had voted in both the aye and the no lobbies in order to register a de facto abstention, and another nineteen Labour MPs did not participate in the vote, nearly all of whom were deliberately abstaining.[16] It was the largest revolt by government MPs on domestic legislation since 1997 and the joint largest revolt against the second reading of a Bill since 1945. It tied for this latter record with the revolt against the second reading of the National Service Bill on 1 April 1947, when 72 Labour MPs voted against and between 30 and 40 abstained, and with the revolt on the second reading of the Shops Bill on 14 April 1986, when 72 Conservative MPs voted against and between 15 and 20 abstained. It was also precisely double what had until 2001 been the previous record rebellion by Labour MPs against their government's education policy – the 36 who had rebelled over voluntary schools in 1931. But for all that, the government had still won.

Nearly all opposition MPs voted against the government, including all the Liberal Democrat, Plaid Cymru and SNP MPs, as did all those from Northern Ireland, with the exception of the four Sinn Fein MPs, who have not taken their seats and who do not therefore vote.[17] And so did Richard Taylor, the Independent MP, and George Galloway and Andrew Hunter, 'Independent Labour' and 'Independent Conservative' respectively. But not all Conservative MPs voted against. The lone Scottish Conservative MP, Peter Duncan, refused to vote as part of his long-standing self-denying ordinance on devolved matters. And, more importantly, it was widely known that not all Conservative MPs agreed with their party's stance; one report claimed that up to ten were considering defying their party whip over the issue.[18] In the end, just two did so: Robert Jackson, a former minister for higher education, argued that MPs were 'duty bound' to address the funding gap in the universities, and he launched a scathing attack on what he saw as Michael Howard's opportunism in voting against the government; Jackson – who was later to defect to the Labour Party – voted with the government, whilst Ian Taylor, who said that it was 'inconceivable' that the Conservatives would enter the next election saying that students would not face any costs, abstained. The calculation is straightforward: Jackson's pro-government vote was worth two to the government's majority; Taylor and Duncan's abstentions added one each. In other words, had the Conservatives presented a united front, the government's majority would have been just one.

One problem with much of the commentary prior to the vote was that it did not allow for Labour abstentions – or if it did, it did not allow for enough abstentions. Analysis routinely talked of the number of 'rebels', without indicating exactly how the MPs would rebel. Yet the precise mixture of dissenting votes and abstentions amongst Labour MPs was crucial. This calculation was also straightforward: each dissenting vote lowered the government's majority by two; each abstention lowered it by one. As the vote approached, estimates routinely put the size of any potential revolt at around 100 Labour MPs. But the government could survive a rebellion by around 100 backbenchers – as long as enough of them abstained. If the 92 who rebelled had split 78:14, with 78 voting against and fourteen abstentions, then the government would have gone down to defeat. That just 72 voted against and 20 abstained saved the Bill.[19] Throughout most of January, the Whips' Office had identified at least 30 abstainers, far more than in any of the media calculations.

★ ★ ★

All this – the Labour abstainers, the Tory splits, and the non-voting Sinn Feiners – remains secondary to the main question: how did the government manage to persuade so many of its own MPs to vote with it? Of the 155 Labour MPs who had signed Ian Gibson's EDM (excluding those who signed but then removed their names), 69 voted against the government at second reading.[20] A further eighteen signatories abstained. But 68 Labour

MPs who had signed the EDM – that is, who had publicly said that they were opposed to the government's policy – went on to vote with the government for a policy that they had opposed.

As with so many Bills during the Parliament, part of the answer lay in the changes that the government was willing to make to the Bill in the face of backbench opposition. But here the government faced a problem. The central rebel objection to the Bill, the totemic issue of variability, had to remain in place – otherwise there would essentially be no Bill. The rebels' main demand was therefore the one bit of the Bill on which the government was not prepared to negotiate. As Robin Cook pointed out, 'the government's attempts to defuse the rebellion are therefore fundamentally flawed as they rely on concessions at the margins, while preserving intact the very issue of principle that has provoked the rebellion.'[21] The government's response was two-fold. First, it gave as many concessions as it could on other parts of the Bill (those dismissed by Cook as 'at the margins', but which were considered more important by others), and made it clear that if the Bill was lost these other concessions would be lost too. And then, second, it tried to address concerns about the *future* amount of variability, without giving way on the issue itself.

The government's White Paper was itself already partly a compromise, designed to placate opponents within the PLP and outside. The cap on fees of £3,000 per year was much lower than many of the leading universities had hoped for (nor did they much like the promise that the cap would not rise), and the restoration of grants for the poorest third of students and the establishment of the access regulator were both meant to appeal to backbench Labour opinion. In early January, to coincide with the publication of the Bill, the education secretary had outlined a number of further compromises designed to placate his backbench critics. He promised that the £3,000 cap would be fixed throughout the next Parliament (something else that the leading universities did not like), and that it could only be increased beyond inflation if approved by both Houses of Parliament. He also promised an independent review to examine the impact of variability of fees after the first three years, to be conducted by the access regulator. He then increased the proposed maintenance grant from £1,000 in £2004 to £1,500 from 2006, said that student loans would be increased to match the median cost of students' basic living costs, and that student debts would be written off altogether after 25 years. Charles Clarke argued that these measures stood together: 'This is a coherent package to be taken as a whole or not at all. If not supported by this House, none of those benefits will arise. It is not a pick-and-mix menu.' Stressing that the Bill stood or fell as a whole was essential to the government. It wanted would-be rebels to know that if they voted down the Bill they would lose the reintroduction of grants *and* OFFA *and* the abolition of up-front fees, all of which most of them supported.

As second reading approached the government gave yet further ground. The day before the second reading, Clarke gave further reassurance on the £3,000 cap and spelled out the details of the review in 2009 into the impact of fees. He commented, 'I think that gives the kind of reassurance people were looking for who have been worried whether there is some secret plan – which there never has been, of course – to increase fees earlier than 2006.' The government also promised an interim review into the impact that debt would have on students from modest incomes who wanted to go into public sector professions – such as teaching – which was a concern of some Labour MPs. And, importantly, it also agreed to convert the remission of fees for poorer students after graduation into an extra grant of £1,200 up front (which had been one of Peter Bradley and Alan Whitehead's proposals), meaning that the poorest students effectively received a grant of £3,000.

His second reading speech saw Clarke accept repeated interventions from wavering Labour MP anxious for assurance on particular issues. Andy King sought and gained assurances that variability would be considered in the review. Angela Eagle welcomed the government's willingness to listen 'to ways of screwing down that cap for the whole of the next parliament'. Richard Burden sought and gained an assurance that primary legislation would be required to lift the cap. Clarke kept on replying, 'I can give that assurance.' After each one, a chorus of Conservative MPs cried, 'Another one gone.' Two further concessions were produced in the run-up to the report stage. Clarke accepted an amendment from Peter Bradley and Alan Whitehead which ensured that a debate, as well as a vote, would have to be held in the Commons and the Lords before any future government could raise the maximum cap on fees after 2010. And he accepted an amendment from Anne Campbell that conferred a duty, rather than a power, on the secretary of state to maintain the cap if a university attempted to raise it in the future. Both concessions were designed – yet again – to placate those worried about the future extent of variability.

Taken together, these concessions were enough to persuade many Labour MPs that they had ended up with a very different measure from the one that they had started with. Bradley described it as a 'radically different Bill from the one I believe ministers originally envisaged'. 'I make no pretence about variability. A free market in higher education would indeed entrench privilege – that is why I originally opposed the concept.' However, what was now on offer was 'a firmly regulated market, if it is a market at all'. His partner in crime, Whitehead, claimed that the end result was effectively 'a fixed fee with discounts rather than a market variable fee'. Equally importantly, Labour MPs had accepted Clarke's argument that the Bill was a package. 'If we'd killed the Bill,' Whitehead said, 'we would have killed the grants . . . Ministers did listen.' Another, who had supported the White Paper '95 per cent', added, 'I didn't want to throw the baby out with the bathwater. I wanted a lot of the Bill to go through.' One MP reflected, 'There were some really good things in that Bill.' But she added, 'Mind you, I used to say to my whip, "Why are

these wonderful things in the Bill? To buy us off, that's why.'"
She wasn't wrong.

★ ★ ★

Nick Brown's involvement in the rebellion – along with that of
George Mudie – had been controversial from the beginning.
Their extremely close association with the Chancellor led to a
widespread suspicion that they were as interested in removing
the Prime Minister as in the intricacies of student finance. But the
involvement of a former Chief Whip and Deputy Chief Whip
meant that the rebellion was much better organised than many of
the previous revolts had been. 'George and Nick were the closest
thing to a proper rebel whipping operation that we've seen,' one
whip grudgingly admitted.

This, however, also helped to demonstrate another strategic
weakness of backbench opposition. After the *Sunday Times*
exposed the high level of whipping among the rebels, revealing
how well organised they were, the whips were able to use this to
accuse the rebels of disloyalty. Jack Cunningham, a former
Cabinet colleague of Brown's and a steadfast loyalist, claimed that
Brown had set up 'an alternative Whips' Office intent on
defeating the government in general and the Prime Minister in
particular'. He described them as 'rebels without a cause . . . just
a grudge'. They came under further attack when it was revealed
that Mudie had discussed tactics with Phil Willis, the Liberal
Democrat education spokesperson. On the day after the vote,
Cunningham (again) told the *Today* programme:

> I spent 18 years in opposition. We were fighting then in the
> Labour party on all sorts of fronts against, in particular, Militant
> Tendency and the hard left to stop the development of a party
> within a party . . . A former Chief Whip and a former Deputy
> Chief Whip openly, coherently, working and planning to bring
> defeat to their own government gets perilously close to that,
> doesn't it?

Similarly, there were discussions between some of the rebels and the Conservative whips at the Bill's report stage. Such discussions were essential if they were to have a chance of uniting all the MPs who were against top-up fees – Labour rebels and opposition MPs – behind one amendment and to have a serious chance of defeating the measure. But Labour MPs are well aware that consorting with the enemy is a serious charge that can be levelled against them. The organisational advantage, therefore, is firmly with the government. They can organise and lobby to their heart's content. They can have discussions with the opposition front bench. But if rebels start to do the same, it is presented as disloyal and unacceptable behaviour.

And then, on the morning of the second reading vote, Brown suddenly switched sides, claiming that he was doing so after long-running secret negotiations with the government had yielded extra concessions which persuaded him that he could support the Bill. He described the modified Bill as 'not perfect', but said that 'it is the best we are going to do.' There is no doubt that there were such negotiations, but it is much less clear that they yielded the extra concessions that Brown claimed. His switch led to widespread derision amongst both rebels and members of the government. The most common interpretation was that Brown had switched after being told to do so by the Chancellor, that this was part of Gordon Brown's 'calling off the dogs'.

In his biography of Tony Blair, Anthony Seldon claims that Nick Brown's switching (which he ascribes entirely to Gordon Brown's prompting) was 'more crucial' than the concessions given by Clarke.[22] Yet the opposite was true. What was most striking about Nick Brown's switch was not how many MPs went with him, but how few. The rebellion didn't crumble with Brown's defection. Mudie, whose opposition continued, estimated that only eight or so Labour MPs followed Brown's lead. The whips put the figure at fewer than that. Of course, in a vote this tight, even a handful of votes make the difference between defeat and victory; and the Brownites (Nick or Gordon) could be said to have secured victory. In a vote this tight, almost anything that makes a difference can convincingly be said to be crucial.[23] But if this was the Chancellor 'calling off the dogs', then he didn't control many dogs.

What makes measuring the impact of Nick Brown's conversion even more tricky is that Gordon Brown was already active in persuading MPs not to vote against the government. Critics of the Chancellor complained that he began to lobby MPs too late – hence suspicion that he was secretly hoping for a defeat – and only began to work for the government's cause once he realised that a defeat would also be damaging to him. Others dispute this, but no one doubts that as the key vote approached Gordon Brown was lobbying MPs, especially MPs thought to be supporters of his, to back the Bill. Supporters of the Chancellor claim that 'Gordon' won over '20 to 30 rebels', and that 'Brown delivered that vote'. Even if the figure of '20 to 30' is a typical piece of exaggeration, it is still certain that Gordon Brown's intervention dissuaded enough MPs from rebelling to have made the difference between victory and defeat. Brown's lobbying is frequently said to be more political, more straightforward than Blair's. As he put it to one so-called Brownite MP, who was intending to vote against, 'now, there's only an hour to go, so I'm not going to bother arguing with you – you know all the arguments already. But you are just going to fucking vote with us. I'm not fucking asking, I'm telling.' 'What did you say?' his colleagues asked. 'Well, I thought about it for a while,' said the MP, 'and weighed up the pros and cons, and then I said, "OK, Gordon."'

But Brown was not the only senior minister lobbying MPs for eleventh-hour conversions. Almost all ministers were doing so, and (for perfectly obvious reasons) they tended to lobby those MPs that the whips felt were most susceptible to their charms. Just as Tony Blair, Charles Clarke, John Reid, John Prescott, David Blunkett or Alan Johnson were considered the best person to try to persuade particular MPs to change their minds in the final few hours, so Brown held sway over certain other MPs. Lobbying like this was ministerial horses for courses. Given the narrowness of the vote, 'Gordon' did indeed 'deliver' it. But so too did Tony, Charles, John, John and David, not to mention Alan.

★ ★ ★

When it realised it was heading for a defeat, the government Whips' Office did not keep this information to itself. The whips adopted megaphone politics, telling everyone they could find – MPs and reporters alike – that they were going down to defeat unless a substantial number of MPs changed their minds and voted for the government. Immediately prior to the second reading, they distributed copies of their running totals around backbenchers (updating them during the day), to show that they were not bluffing and that defeat was likely. The aim was to show MPs that they couldn't be what one whip called 'heroes in safety': 'They were going to vote against but we were still going to get the Bill through. We needed to show them that they couldn't do that.' The Prime Minister took the same approach when he spoke to MPs, making it clear that defeat was likely. This approach was described by one Labour MP as 'threatening us with victory', but – however paradoxical it might seem – it was an effective way of dampening down the rebellion. The pressure on an MP to stick to the party line increases as the prospect of defeat becomes more likely, and as it becomes more likely that their vote will be the crucial one. But when defeat is very unlikely, MPs find it easier to vote against the party line. Similarly, once defeat becomes certain, the pressure to stick to the party line becomes less pronounced. But when a government defeat seems *probable*, the pressure not to be the swing voter, the one who made the difference between victory and defeat, is very strong.

All the more so since the consequences of a government defeat were discussed in an over-the-top, exaggerated way. Prior to the second reading vote in January 2005, a potential government defeat was routinely compared to looking into the abyss – and other suitably apocalyptic metaphors. The constitutional implications were in fact slight (see Appendix 6), and contrary to much of the discussion, had the government lost the Bill at the second reading there would have been no need for a vote of confidence or a general election. The twentieth century saw just three government Bills defeated at second reading, but none of them triggered a vote of confidence. The most recent example came in April 1986, when the Thatcher government became the only government with a secure majority in the entire twentieth century to lose a Bill at second reading. The downfall of Margaret Thatcher's Shops Bill did not trigger a vote of confidence.[24] Immediately after the defeat, and despite calling it 'a central piece of their legislative programme', the then Labour leader Neil Kinnock merely demanded an assurance that the government would not reintroduce the Bill – an assurance that the Leader of the House, John Biffen, reading from a prepared text, duly gave. To lose a Bill with a majority of over 160 therefore would have been a remarkable achievement – but it would not have caused a constitutional crisis.

However, as so often before, Blair appeared to have raised the stakes, linking the Bill with his own future as Prime Minister. At his monthly news conference on 2 December 2003 he had said that there would be 'absolutely no retreat' on the principles of the Higher Education Bill. Asked if he would resign if he lost the vote, he said, 'Of course my authority is on the line – it always is with issues like this.' The *Independent*'s headline, 'Blair puts his premiership on the line over top-up fees', was remarkably similar to *The Times*'s: 'Blair puts his job on the line for top-up fees'. The *Daily Telegraph* described the top-up fees vote as being 'make or break for Blair', whilst the *Daily Mail* depicted Blair as 'the gambler', staking his leadership on the vote. This was the tactic's third outing during the parliament – something similar having been used over both Iraq and foundation hospitals – and one

Labour left-winger felt that the 'vote for the PM or he'll go' trick was wearing thin after its previous use: 'It's like spraying for weeds. If you spray sparingly, the effectiveness of the spray is maximised. If you overspray, you just build up the resistance of most weeds'. Another said that 'the Prime Minister is playing the vote-of-confidence card. It has worked for him in the votes on Iraq and foundation hospitals. But it might be third time unlucky.' But for those MPs who believed it, the idea that Blair might go if the vote was lost meant that the issue ceased to be purely about top-up fees; it also became about Blair. For those who wanted to remove the Prime Minister, this was fine and dandy. But it appeared to present those who wanted the Prime Minister to remain but who had a beef with his education policy with a dilemma.

It has been variously claimed that the Prime Minister had gained the Cabinet's agreement to put down a motion of confidence the following week if the second reading vote had been lost, and that this motion would have included a sentence endorsing the government's proposals to reform higher education. The rationale was that this would have forced Labour MPs to choose between their opposition to variable fees and a general election. Yet passing a motion endorsing the policy would not have ensured the passage of the Bill and introduced top-up fees. That would have required a vote on the Bill itself, if the government had reintroduced it (as they would have been fully entitled to do). The government could have reintroduced the Bill, and made its passage a vote of confidence, but this is a risky tactic (for reasons explained further in Appendix 6) and it is much less likely that they would have done so. Given how tight the vote was, a form of words had been prepared to be read out at the despatch box in the event of a defeat – but it did not commit the government to reintroducing the Bill or to a vote of confidence. It was merely a holding statement, designed to allow ministers and the whips to confer before deciding how to proceed.

And just as over Iraq and foundation hospitals, the Prime Minister was careful never actually to say that he would resign if the Bill was lost. He gave the impression that he might, but not that he would. At one point during the press conference in December 2003, he was asked:

> In the past when there have been very tight votes in the Commons – Iraq, foundation hospitals – the whips have said that this amounts to a vote of confidence. Do you regard this, if you like, flagship Bill as worth a vote of confidence and could you really continue to have the authority, as leader, if you can't get a Bill through to which you have attached such importance?

The Prime Minister's reply is revealing: 'I think, as ever when I am asked questions like this, I never get drawn into great speculation as to what happens if you lose. It is not a very sensible basis on which to go forward, and I don't believe we will, incidentally.'

The real consequences of a government defeat at second reading were much less dramatic than they were being made out to be. The Bill would have been lost. There would have some disgruntled university vice-chancellors (never a pretty-looking bunch at the best of times), and the government and Prime Minister would have suffered some battered egos and damaged reputations. But that would have been all. For some, though, that was enough. Strip away the hyperbole and accept that a defeat would not have brought down the government or the Prime Minister; but a defeat on such a high-profile piece of legislation would still have been damaging to them both.[25] There were plenty of MPs who wanted to avoid those battered egos and damaged reputations if possible, believing that they would only damage the party and the government. Gordon Brown, for example, was said to share such concerns – believing, according to one of those close to him, that 'the moment a Labour government is defeated by its own side, it never recovers' and 'the divide in the Labour Party becomes the new media thesis.'[26] Such concerns were heightened both by the apparent rebirth of the Conservative opposition and by the forthcoming Hutton report.

At a PLP meeting in January 2004, Kevin Barron gained the loudest cheer of the day when he claimed that a victory for the rebels would be a victory for Michael Howard, adding, 'If he [Howard] is crowned, my fingerprints won't be on that crown.' Brian Iddon, who eventually decided to abstain, said that it was 'preying on my mind, that, if I vote against the government, I'll have to go in the same lobby as Michael Howard . . . It would hurt me to go into the same lobby as Michael Howard and I am very loyal to the Labour party and it would hurt me to damage it.' Labour MPs were therefore more susceptible than usual to the argument deployed by the whips: 'Are you really going to go into the lobbies with the Tories?'

It now seems strange that anyone was especially concerned about the publication of Lord Hutton's report into the death of the scientist Dr David Kelly, due out the day after the Bill's second reading – given that the report is now considered to be extremely (if not excessively) favourable towards the government. But without the benefit of hindsight, things looked more dangerous. The coincidence of the two issues triggered lots of media guff about '24 hours that will decide Blair's fate', which ministers and whips were able to turn to the government's advantage. They were able to argue that the Prime Minister's position was under threat, and that a defeat on top-up fees combined with a savaging from Hutton might be enough to bring Blair down. This point was made repeatedly to MPs in the run-up to the vote. What was crucial was not just that the two events were so close together, but that the top-up fees vote came before Hutton. Had their places been reversed, with the vote coming the day after Hutton, then some Labour MPs would have felt free to vote against the government, once they'd seen that Hutton did not criticise it. In the event, they had to vote on top-up fees not knowing what lay ahead. As one of the 2001 intake put it,

I came very close to voting against, and I voted for it holding my nose. If Hutton had been the day before, I'd have voted against. But with Hutton coming up the day after, and not knowing the damage that that could have done to the party, I just couldn't do it.

Marsha Singh shrugged off a broken ankle (and his doctor's advice) to vote for the government, arguing that 'because of Hutton the next day, I was afraid of a double whammy.' The night before the second reading vote, Derek Wyatt described the Bill as 'a dog's breakfast', but said that he would be voting for it, to 'save the government', adding that he would have voted against had it not been for the forthcoming Hutton report. Had Hutton decided to publish his report on 26 January instead of 28 January, Wyatt and Singh would probably have been in the opposite division lobby. They would not have been the only ones – and the Bill would have been lost.

\* \* \*

Just as over foundation hospitals, the government was also helped by the inability of rebel MPs to concentrate their forces – or, to put it in terms of credit rather than blame, by the ability of the Whips' Office to divide and conquer.

After the second reading, and a very small rebellion over the Bill's programming motion, the Bill went into committee, where the government closed down potential dissent by ensuring that few rebels were selected to scrutinise the Bill. Of the 72 MPs who voted against the second reading only George Mudie was appointed to the committee, along with Anne Campbell, who had abstained. The rest of the sixteen Labour nominees selected were loyalists, and the Bill emerged unscathed from its committee stage. But Labour rebels were still planning what they hoped would be another big rebellion at the Bill's report stage – this time focusing on their opposition to variability, but leaving the rest of the Bill intact. A proposed amendment from Campbell would have restricted top-up fees either to the present £1,200 or a fixed higher rate of £2,500, whilst a proposed amendment from Ian Gibson would have removed the clauses permitting universities to vary their fees. But Campbell's amendment was not chosen for debate, and Gibson's became embroiled in claims both that it was inadequately worded and that he had been liaising too closely with the Conservatives in the run-up to the vote. Charles Clarke threatened to withdraw the whole Bill if Gibson's amendment was passed, and accused him of preferring to 'deal with the Tories than to deal with the Bill seriously', adding that the effect of the amendment would be to allow universities to charge whatever they liked, removing the £3,000 cap.[27] He argued that it 'opens the door to sky-high fees across the university sector which the government will have no power to prevent. A vote for the amendment is a vote for a free-for-all.' Gibson's amendment split the opponents of top-up fees: Campbell described it as 'a wrecking amendment which takes a chunk out of the Bill. It would leave fees completely deregulated', whilst Jon Owen Jones said that he had been told by many government sources that if Gibson's amendment was agreed to, it would wreck the Bill. 'That', he said defiantly, 'is why I am supporting it'.

Gibson's amendment was supported by 57 Labour MPs, fifteen fewer than voted against the second reading. Instead of five, the government's majority was a more comfortable – although still relatively small – 28. The Bill's third reading, later that day, saw just eighteen Labour MPs vote against their whip, together with a mass abstention by most of the other rebels, and with the government winning much more comfortably, 309 to 248.[28] The explanation for the report stage rebellion being smaller, and the government's majority larger, lay primarily in the 21 Labour MPs who had voted against the government at the second reading but who then abstained (eighteen) or voted with the government (three) at the report stage. Some of the 21 MPs whose opposition faded or collapsed had been convinced by changes that the government had made to the Bill since the second reading, whilst others felt that, having lost at the second reading, they should now accept that the Bill was going to become law and stop causing trouble. As one of the second reading rebels recalled, 'the time to beat this Bill was second reading. By the time it came to report stage, I was not interested in grandstanding.'

Of more interest, though, are the MPs who joined the rebellion *after* the second reading. There were six MPs who voted against the government at the report stage who had not done so at the second reading. And the third reading rebellion then included another six MPs who had not rebelled at the report stage; of these, four had not cross-voted at the second reading either. As with foundation hospitals the year before, on one level this behaviour is perfectly understandable. But it allowed the whips to divide the measure's opponents, confident that if they could get past the second reading vote, they would then be able to win over enough of those who had rebelled to survive any subsequent vote, with the defections more than cancelling out any new rebels. Some of these votes were pre-arranged deals with the Whips' Office, with MPs agreeing to abstain or vote with the government on the second reading, if they were then given an easier time over later rebellions. It was also evidence of there being MPs who were prepared to vote against the government only when there was no chance of defeating it – as at the third reading and (to a lesser extent) the report stage. This allowed an MP who had previously expressed opposition to the policy publicly, but who did not want to run the risk of defeating the Bill and damaging the government, to retain some credibility, to provide some justification for their actions, so that they were able to argue that they had voted against variability. 'We're sharp bastards,' one said. Or, as one very experienced MP put it, 'they were voting in safety . . . They'll be able to go back to their constituency party and say, "I opposed top-up fees," and most of their party members won't have a clue about what all the votes mean.' Together, the Bill's three key votes saw a total of 82

Labour MPs vote against top-up fees at some point. Just as a year before, even when there were enough backbench rebels to defeat the government, they didn't do it.

★ ★ ★

The issue of student finance presented the clearest challenge to the government's majority since 1997. And its eventual victory – however narrow – can be seen as proof that however rebellious Labour MPs were becoming when it *didn't* matter, they still lacked the necessary will to inflict defeat when it *did*. Top-up fees produced yet another of Simon Carr's shrink-to-fit rebellions. There were enough Labour rebels to have defeated the government, but too many chose to abstain. There were even enough Labour MPs prepared to vote against the government to have defeated it, but they were not prepared to do so at the same time.

Austin Mitchell had pre-empted any attempts to pressurise him into backing the government, by offering himself up for sale. 'I will be bribed on this Bill,' he said. 'If they can give me something big for Grimsby, I will think Tony Blair is wonderful.' He later admitted that he traded his vote for two projects for his Great Grimsby constituency. 'I thought this was a bad Bill. If they're going to put up stupid proposals I won't be able to stop, well, why not? If they can help, let them help. I put a couple of proposals and hope they will be delivered. It's a legitimate tactic, the pork barrel is important.' Others reported the usual pressure – being told that they were throwing their career away, or being told that they might not get resources or ministerial support at the forthcoming election. But on the whole, what was striking about the top-up fees rebellion was the general lack of any strong-arm tactics to bring the rebels into line. There were, as one MP noted, just 'too many arms to be twisted'. Gwyn Prosser described all the attention he received from ministers and whips as not arm-twisting 'so much as hand-shaking'.

A key reason for the government's eventual victory was that it was prepared to give ground on the Bill. 'They listened,' said one MP. 'And then they moved.' The Bill may not have been defeated, but it was amended. The fundamental nature of the Bill didn't change, but the alterations were still important. The Bill that ended up on the statute book was very different from the one that the government had first proposed – and was even more different from what would have been put forward if they had not had to get it through the PLP in the first place. Had the government not given way, it would have been defeated. Whatever the result in the division lobbies, top-up fees can clearly be chalked down as another modern example of backbench influence.

But only up to a point. Because although top-up fees is a clear example of backbench influence, it is also a good demonstration of the limits of that influence. Strip away the concessions and the negotiations, and it is still clear that one of the key reasons – perhaps *the* key reason – why the Bill passed was that a group of Labour MPs were simply not prepared to vote against their leadership if they thought they would defeat it. At second reading, the government was helped by the proximity of the Hutton report. More generally, though, the government has been helped to remain undefeated by the very fact that (slightly tautologically) it has remained undefeated. This has enabled it to get away with exaggerating the risks of a defeat. Only a microscopic handful of Labour MPs (those elected before 1979) have any experience of defeating their own government in the division lobbies. As a result, whenever defeat looks likely, the government is able to produce a whole range of scare stories about the consequences of a defeat. This makes Labour MPs particularly susceptible to the sort of intense lobbying which inevitably takes place in the run-up to a vote. There's no doubt that Labour backbenchers exerted influence on the Bill; the question that remains – and which it's harder to answer – is whether it was enough influence. Was the Bill different enough after it had been through the Commons to justify its passage, given the extremely strong objections that most Labour MPs had to its basic premise? Or – to use a sporting phrase – did the rebels just choke? As one insightful MP noted, shortly after the Bill's passage,

the view in the PLP is this is a victory: it'll stop the worse excesses of the Blairite agenda. And they see all the talk about consultation as evidence of that. But I think this is a complete misunderstanding of what the thinking will be in Downing Street. After this, they'll be thinking, 'If we got that through, we can get anything through the Parliamentary Labour Party, as long as we get the processes right.' So now it's all about process rather than issues. They just need to factor in the concessions in the Bill from the beginning and they'll be alright.

# Kate Hoey and Robin Cook

John Major is credited with just nine entries in the *Oxford Dictionary of Political Quotations*, fewer than almost every other postwar premier.[29] One Majorism which the *ODPQ* somewhat curiously does not list is Major's supposedly off-the-record comment in April 1993 on the difficulties he was facing with his backbenchers. 'Where do you think most of this poison is coming from?' he asked rhetorically, before answering, 'From the dispossessed and the never possessed. You can think of ex-ministers who are going around causing all sorts of trouble. We don't want another three more of the bastards out there.'[30] A decade later, plenty of Labour whips had similar views about some of those causing problems for the Blair government. As one whip put it,

> it's nauseating to see people who, when they lose the ministerial car, lose any sense of collective decision-making. It's repulsive to see people who helped the Whips' Office to get Labour MPs to vote for things that were right but unpopular now taking considerable sums of money to appear in print or on television attacking the government that they served in so recently. They're not just dismissed, they're now discredited.

The biggest group of backbench rebels during the 2001 Parliament, however, were not new rebels – the dismissed or the disappointed – but the long-term disaffected, those who had rebelled during the 1997 Parliament as well as after 2001. They accounted for a hundred of the 218 Labour MPs who voted against the whip during the 2001 Parliament. This group was not homogenous, being far from equally rebellious, but from their ranks came the majority of the more persistent rebels. Of the 30 most rebellious Labour backbenchers (those listed on p. 53), all but three had been rebelling against the Blair government since it was first elected in 1997.

What concerned the whips about this group was the increasing frequency with which they were rebelling: 85 of the hundred rebelled more often after 2001 than they did before.[31] In some cases, such as Jeremy Corbyn or John McDonnell, these were MPs who had already been rebelling frequently doing so even more often – and there wasn't much that the whips could do about that. More worryingly, there was also a sizeable group whose rebellions in the 1997 Parliament had been pretty infrequent, but who began to rebel much more regularly after 2001.[32] They included people such as David Taylor (North West Leicestershire), whose five votes against the whip before the election increased to 39 after the election; Ian Gibson (Norwich North), five prior to 2001, 37 after; or David Drew (Stroud), whose lone dissenting vote during the 1997 Parliament increased to 29 during the 2001 Parliament.

Even so, if backbench dissent had been confined to this group of rebel veterans, things would not have been too bad. What caused problems for the whips were the various groups of reinforcements who joined the ranks of the rebels. The first, and the least important, group were those elected in 2001, new MPs and new rebels to boot. But this group was far too small to explain the rise in the PLP's rebelliousness. They effectively just cancelled out the 20 rebels who had left the Commons, through retirement or defeat, at the 2001 election. What really caused the problems for the government after 2001 was two other groups of new rebels – those that Major would have described as the never possessed and the dispossessed.

There were, for example, 48 Labour MPs who sat on the

back benches throughout the whole of the 1997 Parliament without rebelling once – but who began to rebel after 2001. Few of the 48 became especially rebellious. The list is headed by Barbara Follett (Stevenage) and John Grogan (Selby), who rebelled on nineteen and fourteen occasions respectively, followed by three MPs who rebelled on eleven – Clive Efford (Eltham), Roger Godsiff (Birmingham, Sparkbrook & Small Heath) and Paul Marsden (Shrewsbury & Atcham), along with three who rebelled on ten occasions – Helen Clark (Peterborough), Karen Buck (Regent's Park & Kensington North) and Tom Cox (Tooting). But the other 34 rebelled on fewer than ten occasions; and the median number of rebellions for this group was just five. By contrast, long-term disaffected MPs rebelled more than three times as often, a median number of dissenting votes of 16.5.

So relatively few of this group became regular rebels. It is also a little unfair to assume that all of these MPs were rebelling because they were disgruntled about their failure to get into government (what one journalist described as 'ex-would-be ministers'). Some were (and some would admit it, quite openly) – but others had simply become increasingly dissatisfied about the direction that the government was taking. They'd put up with things during the 1997 Parliament – biting their tongue, holding their nose, doing all the other things that MPs do when their party is doing something that they don't like – but various pieces of policy pushed them too far after 2001.

The final group was the one that attracted most attention: those MPs who had been in government and who had now begun to enjoy (?) the freedom of the back benches – what one whip sneeringly dismissed as the 'ex-ministers club'. There were 45 MPs who had been on the payroll and who stayed loyal during the 1997 Parliament, but began to rebel after 2001. They are listed in the table below. It includes all those who had been part of the payroll vote – at whatever level – and thus extends to ex-PPSs. Although there is a constitutional difference between ministers and PPSs, for the individuals concerned the difference is less important. They've had their chance on the payroll – and it's over. The table excludes former members of the payroll who had begun to rebel before the 2001 election. There were, for example, sixteen ex-members of the government amongst the a hundred MPs who rebelled before and after 2001, including people such as Mark Fisher (Stoke-on-Trent Central) – in government between 1997 and 1998, and who rebelled just fifteen times in the 1997 Parliament but 74 times after 2001 – and Peter Kilfoyle (Liverpool, Walton), a minister until 2000, and a man about whom one whip said, 'He could start an argument in an empty room.' Kilfoyle cast just one vote against the whip before the 2001 election but 38 after it. If we stretch the concept as far as it will go, this group could also include those who were PPSs early on in the 1997 Parliament, but who have been backbenchers for most of the Blair government. For example, both Neil Gerrard (Walthamstow) and Alice Mahon (Halifax) – both high up on any list of backbench rebels – were PPSs until they resigned over the changes to lone parent benefit in December 1997. Include these as well, and the rebellious exes number just over 60.

The most rebellious members of the ex-ministers club, by a long way, were Kate Hoey and Glenda Jackson. Hoey, the most rebellious of all, was the MP for Vauxhall, and had been a PPS and a minister throughout the 1997 Parliament, most notably as minister for sport from 1999 to 2001; after returning to the back benches she rebelled on 73 occasions. She'd given problems for the Labour whips before, though, having been sacked by John Smith as junior spokesperson on the Citizen's Charter and women for voting against the third reading of the Maastricht Bill (instead of following the party line and abstaining) in May 1993. She was also one of a handful of Labour MPs to support fox-hunting; during one of the Countryside Alliance's marches one banner read 'We love you, Kate Hoey' – it was adoration from a source few Labour MPs would have welcomed. Clare Short was the most rebellious ex-Cabinet minister, ranking third in the table, although given that she was in government until 2003, her rate of rebellion is on a par with Hoey's. She is followed by another former Cabinet minister, Frank Dobson, who voted against his whip on 27 occasions.

Yet what is striking about the list is not how rebellious these ex-members of the payroll are – but how overwhelmingly loyal they turned out to be. After the unholy trinity of Hoey, Jackson and Short, the number of rebellions falls away sharply. Only six of the 45 voted against the whip on ten or more occasions, and the median number of rebellions was just three. This is exactly the same median as the new MPs – and less than the group of previously loyal backbenchers.

Much more typical was Robin Cook. Few of the glowing tributes paid to Cook after his death in August 2005 noted that he had in fact begun his parliamentary career as a backbench rebel, casting his first dissenting vote within four months of being elected as an MP in 1974 – in favour of an amendment that would have prevented ministers from removing the absolute liability provisions in the Health and Safety at Work Etc. Bill.[33] He went on to vote against the whips on 88 occasions in five years, including over devolution (on six occasions) and on issues relating to European integration (on 22 occasions). He was also an opponent of the annual defence estimates, the Civil List and cuts in public expenditure, whilst he rebelled in favour of the introduction of import duties, higher rates of income tax for the better off and measures to protect the rents of the less well off. His last dissenting vote of the 1974–79 Parliament involved an attempt to annul the draft Prevention of Terrorism (Temporary Provisions) Act 1976 (Continuance) Order, one of a dozen separate votes he cast in that period opposing detention of terrorist suspects without trial.

## Ex-members of the government who began to rebel after 2001

| Name | Constituency | Votes against the whip, 2001–05 |
|---|---|---|
| Kate Hoey | Vauxhall | 73 |
| Glenda Jackson | Hampstead & Highgate | 64 |
| Clare Short | Birmingham, Ladywood | 38 |
| Frank Dobson | Holborn & St Pancras | 27 |
| Jon Trickett | Hemsworth | 16 |
| Richard Burden | Birmingham, Northfield | 10 |
| John Battle | Leeds West | 9 |
| Tony Colman | Putney | 9 |
| Doug Henderson | Newcastle upon Tyne North | 9 |
| Graham Allen | Nottingham North | 8 |
| Win Griffiths | Bridgend | 8 |
| Robin Cook | Livingston | 7 |
| Calum MacDonald | Western Isles | 7 |
| Ken Purchase | Wolverhampton North East | 6 |
| Chris Smith | Islington South & Finsbury | 6 |
| Tony Banks | West Ham | 5 |
| Anne Campbell | Cambridge | 5 |
| Geoffrey Robinson | Coventry North West | 5 |
| Frank Roy | Motherwell & Wishaw | 5 |
| Alan Meale | Mansfield | 4 |
| Joan Ruddock | Lewisham, Deptford | 4 |
| Rachel Squire | Dunfermline West | 3 |
| Keith Vaz | Leicester East | 3 |
| Bob Blizzard | Waveney | 2 |
| Keith Bradley | Manchester, Withington | 2 |
| John Denham | Southampton, Itchen | 2 |
| Frank Doran | Aberdeen Central | 2 |
| Angela Eagle | Wallasey | 2 |
| Jeff Ennis | Barnsley East & Mexborough | 2 |
| Helen Jackson | Sheffield, Hillsborough | 2 |
| Eric Martlew | Carlisle | 2 |

| | | |
|---|---|---|
| Michael Meacher | Oldham West & Royton | 2 |
| Lewis Moonie | Kirkcaldy | 2 |
| Sandra Osborne | Ayr | 2 |
| Greg Pope | Hyndburn | 2 |
| Joyce Quin | Gateshead East & Washington West | 2 |
| Andy Reed | Loughborough | 2 |
| Graham Stringer | Manchester, Blackley | 2 |
| Clive Betts | Sheffield, Attercliffe | 1 |
| David Clelland | Tyne Bridge | 1 |
| George Howarth | Knowsley North & Sefton East | 1 |
| Sally Keeble | Northampton North | 1 |
| John McFall | Dumbarton | 1 |
| Terry Rooney | Bradford North | 1 |
| Alan Whitehead | Southampton, Test | 1 |

His second period on the government back benches, between 2003 and 2005, saw much more selectivity in his rebellions. Although he was in the top half of the table, he was very careful about the targets he picked, and took care not to be seen as a serial member of the ex-ministers club. On key pieces of legislation, Cook did not vote against the government. In May 2003, for instance, he spoke in support of the government during the crucial second reading vote introducing foundation hospitals, claiming there was nothing in the Bill 'to cause trouble to our party, to undermine our principles or to be hostile to the values of the NHS'. In one of the tributes plaid to him after his death, Gerald Kaufman claimed that Cook's actions helped to prevent a government defeat. That is probably going too far, but the fact that some high-profile Iraq rebels such as Cook were backing the government certainly helped take the sting out of the issue.[34] Cook was also persuaded to abstain on the second reading of the Higher Education Bill introducing top-up fees, and on the second reading of the Identity Cards Bill (in December 2004), despite harbouring doubts about whether the scheme could be made to work.

The very rebellious ex-ministers therefore were atypical of most of their peers. Most of the members of the ex-ministers club were far more selective in their rebellion than their popular image suggested. The problems that this group caused were much more qualitative than quantitative. They provided rebellions with intellectual justification, some verve, some organisation and (occasionally) some gravitas. They gave the rebellions what old-school Conservatives call 'bottom', something much more important than their numbers.

# 8

# Pig-sticking, Lammyitis and the odour of dissolution

*Backbenchers' views of the whips – Pension funds and fox-hunting – The final session – Prevention of terrorism*

> May I suggest that if that is the calibre of the minister's interventions today, he would do better to remain seated? – Sir Gerald Kaufman to David Lammy, December 2004

Any complaints that the whips had about the behaviour of their backbenchers were as nothing compared to the complaints that most backbenchers had about their whips. Right across the political spectrum, Labour MPs' views about their whips were overwhelmingly negative. A loyalist described them as 'dreadful'. A rebel thought the Whips' Office was filled with 'twats' who were 'useless' and 'hopeless'. A long-term rebel thought they were 'grossly incompetent'. As one woman MP put it, the whips were 'hopeless', 'incompetent beyond belief and idle to boot'. They are, said one backbencher, 'like First World War generals. They don't need to think. They just throw numbers at the problem.' Another described them as 'the instrument of the government, not the voice of MPs'. The Chief Whip was a particular target of venom. She was widely regarded as 'useless'. One soon-to-be-promoted Blairite called her 'hopeless – if she's not sacked, I'll be gobsmacked.' Backbenchers particularly criticised her inability to stand up to the Prime Minister, to be anything more than a one-way conduit from the leaders to the led. 'She's not good at saying, "No, no" to No. 10.' Another was even blunter: she 'has difficulty counting'.

Yet none of the comments in the preceding paragraph come from the 2001 Parliament. They are all from interviews undertaken during the 1997 Parliament, when Labour MPs had an equally low view of the whips. All those vicious comments about the Chief Whip were said not about Hilary Armstrong, but about her predecessor, Ann Taylor. There was a view then that the Chief Whip was unable to say no to the Prime Minister. There was a view then that the whips didn't work as a two-way channel of communication but merely issued instructions to the troops. There was a view then that the whips were incompetent. None of this is new.

That, though, shouldn't detract from the fact that there were similar complaints about the whips throughout the 2001 Parliament. Sit down with most backbench Labour MPs and before you'd had time to put the sugar in your coffee, or done the hello-how-was-your-journey thing, they'd have gone off on one about the whips. This, from one of the 2001 intake, is pretty typical:

> The Whips' Office is absolute crap, to be honest. For me, the role of the whip is to understand and involve, and they don't do that. It's just assumed that people will nod things through. It's partly to do with the majority. But it's also the way we have a very centralised – I don't like the word 'presidential' – Prime Minister. We're not consulted. Where are these policies coming from? They are just dropping on us from out of the sky.

Much of this was attributed to the character of the Chief

Whip, and to her very close and long-standing link to the Prime Minister. One of her senior colleagues argued that Armstrong was 'the most loyal, most can-do, Chief Whip that any PM has had in recent history'. She 'has always seen her overwhelming duty as delivering for the Prime Minister'. In a piece published in the *Spectator* as the government struggled to get its higher education legislation through the Commons, Peter Oborne argued that one of the problems the government faced was that the Chief Whip was a mere cipher – 'telling Tony what he wants to hear'. Critics such as Oborne argued that what was needed was someone who would say no to the Prime Minister occasionally, to say 'we simply cannot get this through'. What such arguments overlook, however, is that on all the occasions when it mattered, the whips *did* get their legislation through (albeit dangerously narrowly on some occasions). They won every whipped vote in the Commons. They lost not a single Bill as a result of backbench dissent. The problem in terms of party discipline was not the handling of the issues once they got to the Commons, but their origins. It was not the Whips' Office that decided to invade Iraq or to introduce foundation hospitals or top-up fees. Once those decisions had been taken – and in many cases they were taken despite the whips reporting back to No. 10 the extent of the dissatisfaction on the back benches – the whips helped ministers to pilot the legislation onto the statute book.

Oborne's other criticisms ranged widely. Evicted from their traditional base in 12 Downing Street shortly after the 2001 election in order to make way for Alastair Campbell's media team, the whips had been forced to scour Whitehall for alternative accommodation – what Oborne described as 'a humiliating state of affairs which immediately sent the message round Whitehall that the Chief Whip no longer counted'. The Whips' Office was no longer used as a training ground for bright young talent, he complained, being filled instead with 'the dullards and plodders' – and it had also been stripped of its powers of patronage, powers which had been gobbled up by the ever-expanding No. 10

Empire. 'No. 10 has lost its political touch,' declared Oborne. 'It will not find it again till it regains proper contact with the parliamentary party'.[1]

Oborne's article – which irked the whips – was a mixture of the spot on and the wildly inaccurate. Whilst the whips did leave 12 Downing Street, he didn't mention where they ended up: 9 Downing Street. It was hardly the Elephant and Castle. The criticisms of the recruitment and future career prospects of the whips were also off beam (see below, pp. 236–239). Where he was more accurate was in noting some of the broader changes. The whips tended to be prickly when questions of their relationship to No. 10 were raised, and to challenge suggestions that they had become less powerful or influential as a result. Yet the rise of No. 10 as a separate, and important, power in the political world is difficult to doubt. 'Everyone recognises the growing importance of Number Ten,' admitted one member of the Whips' Office. 'Any institution is weakened by comparison.' Several MPs would, for example, spontaneously mention Baroness Morgan, then the Prime Minister's Director of Government Relations, as being at least as important as the whips. As one young MP said, 'if you cross the whips, I don't think it's the end of your career. But if you cross Sally Morgan, then that's that.' (Perhaps unsurprisingly, where the whips do agree with Oborne is that they don't think No. 10 is terribly effective at managing the parliamentary party. No. 10 'does not have particularly good access to the mood of the Parliamentary Labour Party', argued one whip.) The powerful role played by the Chancellor was also a factor. Whilst it was never the case that the whips determined all promotions and appointments within the government, there are now more alternative sources of power to take into account. When it comes to appointments, for example, as one whip put it, 'it's Gordon's list, and Tony's list, and Hilary's list, and so on you go.' Rather than being the one, Hilary's list is now one of several.

Regardless of the rise of No. 10, it is also fair to note that whips today do not control quite the patronage that they used to. Buried away in the papers of Lord Weatherill, the former Speaker of the Commons, is a document from his time as Conservative Deputy Chief Whip. Drawn up in 1978, it identifies what positions the whips then thought would be suitable for their MPs in the event that the Conservatives won the subsequent election – and it shows the amount of patronage available to a whip in the 1970s. It runs from those who were identified as secretaries of state, down through the ranks of the government, and on to those who were labelled as getting 'NOTHING'. The posts extend far wider than the payroll. They include select committee memberships, 'Europe', knighthoods, peerages, quangos, and even one MP who is identified as being a possible future Lord Mayor. (The Conservative whips clearly didn't know what to do with the recently arrived defector from Labour, Reg Prentice, since he was marked down as deserving merely of 'A ROLE'). Much of this patronage remains available to the modern whip – but not all. Positions on quangos, for example, are now no longer at the discretion of party managers, having been opened up to public scrutiny as a result of various reforms in the late 1990s. This undoubtedly weakened the whips but it is a change that pre-dated Labour – and, just like the rise of No. 10, will similarly weaken any future Conservative whips.

Labour whips also have one systemic weakness compared with the Conservatives. Traditionally, Labour has not given out knighthoods to its MPs in return for political service – whereas the promise of a 'K' was always a good way of keeping Tory MPs in check. As one Labour whip put it,

> they look after theirs, we don't. Tories could always be kept quiet with the promise of a knighthood. Don't cause trouble and it'll be Lady Bloggs. But with us, once someone's been out of government for a bit, along comes the *Daily Mail*, saying if you slag off the Prime Minister and the Chancellor in the same sentence, it's a pound a word.

Or as another whip put it, 'it really annoys me when I hear them going on about Tony's cronies and all that rubbish. One of our big problems is we don't have the patronage to give them the things that they want. So they sit and fester.' To some bemusement in the Whips' Office – 'I always thought that Labour MPs wouldn't be impressed by knighthoods, but it's clear that some of them really want one' – they began to put forward names for knighthoods, beginning with two in 2004 and thus opening up the possibility for more in the future.

★ ★ ★

There were some fights which the whips couldn't win – and where the government gave way completely. The first case was House of Lords reform in 2001/2 (see pp. 97–100). Another good example came with the Pensions Bill, introduced by the government in 2003. Amongst other things, the Bill established a pension protection fund, compensating employees whose companies had gone bust, taking their occupational pensions with them. Whilst welcome on the Labour benches, the Bill was not thought to go far enough, because it only covered future claims for compensation, and did nothing about the high-profile private pension schemes that had already collapsed.

An EDM on the subject, which argued that the government had 'a moral and possibly legal obligation to help those workers who have been stripped of their pensions through no fault of their own', quickly attracted 298 signatories – more than 200 of them Labour. The EDM's timing, coming so soon after the Higher Education Bill, could not have been better. The government was keen to avoid another bruising encounter with its backbenchers. One MP who had been called in to see the Prime Minister to ensure his support over top-up fees had used the opportunity to point out to Tony Blair that student fees were not the only issue that required his attention. 'Here is an issue you've got to get your head round,' the MP said.

The Conservatives approached those organising the campaign

to see if they were willing to head up an amendment to the Bill when it came to its report stage, but the organisers felt it would be more credible if any amendment was Labour led, and knew the risks of being seen as cooperating too closely with the Conservatives. 'I didn't want to be their useful idiot,' one said. Their strategy was to 'give the government enough room to do the right thing'. The response of Andrew Smith, the then Secretary of State for Work and Pensions, was later praised by one senior backbencher: 'Often it's the quiet, thinking, minister who saves the party lots of flak.' The government conceded and, in return for the backbench amendment being withdrawn, tabled an amendment to its own Bill, conceding the need for an assistance fund to deal with schemes that had already collapsed.

It was a near-perfect backbench rebellion. Although there were still doubters who wondered whether the sums promised would be sufficient to meet all the future demands to be made upon it, the key trade unions involved – principally the Iron and Steel Trades Confederation and Amicus – believed that the fund was a workable proposal. The change – carried out without a single dissenting vote being cast – benefited around 60,000 people and cost at least £40 million.[2]

★ ★ ★

But perhaps the most obvious example of backbench influence – albeit one that was routinely misunderstood – was the issue of fox-hunting. Since 1997, the issue had been a little like Groundhog Day for both MPs and peers, appearing on the parliamentary timetable with monotonous regularity. Ever since Labour MPs voted in record numbers for a private member's Bill brought forward by Michael Foster, the MP for Worcester, in November 1997, it had been clear that there was an overwhelming majority in the Commons – largely, but not exclusively, comprised of Labour backbenchers – for an outright ban. But it was also clear that this view was not shared by all of those at the top of the government – including the Prime Minister and his first two

Home Secretaries. As a result, the government kept attempting to wriggle out of an outright ban, hoping that backbenchers would eventually give up and let the issue die. But they didn't. Every time that the government tried to offer a compromise, or a delay, or some other concession to the hunting lobby, their backbenchers refused to concede.

The first Queen's Speech of the 2001 Parliament had promised MPs another yet free vote on whether or not to ban hunting with dogs – and by the autumn, 205 Labour MPs had put their names to an EDM which looked forward to the Commons taking 'the earliest possible opportunity to re-affirm its stand on the abolition of hunting'. But when the votes came in March 2002 they were merely on a series of three non-legislative motions: a complete ban, the preservation of the status quo and a compromise solution permitting licensed fox-hunting – the so-called middle way option. These 'indicative' votes indicated what everyone already knew: that the Commons wanted an outright ban (which they backed by 386 votes to 175) but the Lords did not (their Lordships' backing the middle way by 366 votes to 59).

The government then delayed things by a further six months, by announcing a consultation exercise, culminating with a series of public hearings in Portcullis House, chaired by the rural affairs minister, Alun Michael. The subsequent Hunting Bill, introduced in the next session, outlawed hare coursing and stag-hunting but allowed some fox-hunting with hounds to continue under a strict licensing system. Labour backbenchers were not impressed. Tony Banks warned: 'He [Michael] will be caught like piggy in the middle, and I suspect that Parliament will indulge in a bit of pig-sticking, which is a revolting pursuit when it involves either pigs or ministers.' After the failure of one procedural manoeuvre from the government in order to prevent discussion of a pro-ban amendment, and despite the minister's pleading, the Commons, on a free vote, voted for the new clause by 362 votes to 154 – the majority including 62 members of the government, including most members of the Whips' Office. The government retreated, and all references to the licensing system were stripped from the Bill. But it was only a temporary victory. The Bill then went to the Lords, where the Lords threw out the Commons' preference for a complete ban, and reinserted licensing for fox- and stag-hunting, as well as hare coursing.

So, in the Queen's Speech in November 2003, the government announced another Hunting Bill, this time incorporating a total ban from the beginning. But they then delayed for almost a year, taking no action until the following September, at which point MPs (again) voted overwhelmingly in favour of its second reading. This time around, the government's attempt at a compromise was a two-year delay before the ban came into force, claiming that this would allow people involved in hunting to diversify into other businesses (although pro-hunt critics suspected that the government was just trying to avoid pro-hunting demonstrations during the 2005 election campaign). As a result of backbench pressure, the two-year delay was reduced to 20 months. The Bill then went to the Lords, where a series of pro-hunting amendments were made, with peers then giving the heavily amended Bill a third reading. Astonishingly, No. 10 still thought it could engineer a compromise, this time by indicating that the Prime Minister would support licensed hunting. This option too was heavily voted down by the Commons, by 321 votes to 204, with just a handful of Labour MPs backing the Prime Minister's favoured option (see pp. 23–24). Michael then asked the Lords to accept the government's proposal to delay a ban until July 2006, but pro-hunt peers preferred the so-called kamikaze option of rejecting any delay so that MPs would have to vote for a ban to come into force in the run-up to a general election.

By rejecting the government's proposal for a delay, the House of Lords forced the government into a corner. Under the 1949 Parliament Act, an amended Bill can only have the Act applied to it if the amendment in question is agreed by both Houses of Parliament, and so MPs chose to vote for the original Bill introduced in the previous session (rejecting yet again the government motion attempting to delay a ban until 2007 by 345 votes to 46), and therefore for an immediate ban. By this stage, few MPs expected the government not to try yet another compromise and during the final debate in the Commons, Hilary Armstrong was reported to have had some heated arguments in the members' tearoom after tempers flared with some MPs suspicious that the government was preparing to avoid the use of the Parliament Act. No agreement having been reached with the Lords, Michael Martin, the Speaker of the House of Commons, ruled that the conditions of the Parliament Act had been met, and the Hunting Bill received Royal Assent on 18 November 2004.

The use of the Parliament Act in this way has since been challenged on two grounds. First, on the grounds of legality, the Countryside Alliance and others arguing that the 1949 Act itself was illegal because it was passed into law using the 1911 Parliament Act, and was therefore never approved by the House of Lords. It has more widely been criticised on the grounds that the government was somehow morally wrong to 'force' legislation through like this, especially on a so-called conscience issue, and one that did not require urgent implementation. Whatever one's views on hunting, these seem spurious objections. The three previous occasions on which the 1949 Parliament Act had been used were the 1991 War Crimes Act, the 1999 European Parliamentary Elections Act, introducing a system of proportional representation for European parliamentary elections, and the 2000 Sexual Offences Amendment Act, reducing the age of consent for homosexual sex from eighteen to sixteen. It is difficult to argue that it is wrong to use the Parliament Act on a so-called moral issue when two of the three previous uses of it have been on just such issues.[3]

More substantially, such complaints also fail to understand what was happening with the issue. It was not a dispute between the government and the Lords. It was, first and foremost, a dispute between the government and its own backbenchers. And it was a struggle which, in the end, the PLP won. The hunting ban is a policy which is on the statute book because Labour MPs refused to let it go. As one anti-hunting Labour MP remarked after the vote, 'I'm quite proud of the PLP for getting us here – shows what one can achieve by polite persistence.' Whatever one's views about the policy, and whether one thinks hunting should continue or not, that aspect of the process is striking. There was a curious paradox – as there often is – between those who perpetually complained about the weakness of Parliament and the overbearing dominance of the executive but who then complained when the lower House – after a repeated series of votes, and quite clearly against the wishes of the executive – insisted on getting its way. For all the talk about executive dominance, and the weakness of Parliament, this was a victory for the latter over the former.

★ ★ ★

An approaching general election normally calms things down in the Commons. Fewer MPs want to rock the boat. There is anyway usually less serious legislation to cause trouble. Why introduce controversial legislation knowing that an election will cause it to fall? Why cause unnecessary resentment amongst backbenchers? It all combines to produce what the Conservative MP and diarist 'Chips' Channon called the 'odour of dissolution'.

As a result, nearly all pre-election sessions since the war have seen only a handful of revolts – fewer than 20 in every pre-election session. Until 2001, the only exception was the session of 1978/9, right at the end of Callaghan's term in office, when the PLP was tearing itself apart, and when there were 40 separate rebellions. In 2004/5, however, the PLP went crashing through that postwar record with some style. The final session of the 2001 Parliament saw 61 rebellions, beating the postwar record by more than 50 per cent.

Paradoxically, one reason for this was the impending election.

Whereas this normally works to restrain rebels, on this occasion it seemed to have the opposite effect with some MPs. There was widespread concern in the Whips' Office that some Labour MPs were beginning to rebel in order to distance themselves from the government, hoping that by displaying independence in the division lobbies they would retain the support of disgruntled Labour voters – and thus save themselves in the process. Geraldine Smith, the MP for Morecambe and Lunesdale, was frequently cited as the highest-profile example of this. As one MP put it, 'Geraldine Smith believes the people of Morecambe will vote for her. They won't vote for Tony Blair, they don't trust or like Tony Blair. But they trust and like her. She thinks that by being seen as an independent spirit, she'll save herself.' Unsurprisingly, this was a view that the whips were keen to stamp on. In a series of conversations with rebels, they put it like this: 'If you tell your voters that the government's crap all the time, and that Tony Blair must go, then when it comes to the election, they may well follow your lead. The only problem is that they can't vote against Tony Blair, or against the government, without also voting against you'. As another whip put it, 'people who don't understand politics see it as a reason to rebel – they think it'll make them look different. Those who understand politics see it as a reason to stick together. The old saying's true: you either hang together, or you hang apart.' In the event, the election results revealed almost no effect – with rebels and loyalists treated almost identically.[4] In 2005, voters exercised a judgement on the government as a whole, not on individual MPs. Voters frequently say that they like more independent MPs, but they don't then reward them at the polls.

★ ★ ★

But it wasn't just the forthcoming election that was causing so much trouble. It was also the sort of legislation that the government chose to push forward in the final session. There were sizeable rebellions over six contentious Bills: the Mental

Capacity Bill, the Identity Cards Bill, the Gambling Bill, the Railways Bill, the Serious Organised Crime and Police Bill and the Prevention of Terrorism Bill. Such Bills are not the usual fare of an immediate pre-election session.

By the end of the Parliament, rebellion had grown so frequent, and so widespread, on the Labour benches that fairly large rebellions were going almost entirely unreported in the press. In January 2005, for example, there was a revolt by 29 Labour MPs on the Railways Bill, which was almost completely ignored by the media. A month later there were five separate backbench Labour rebellions against various aspects of the wide-ranging Serious Organised Crime and Police Bill, which again went almost entirely unreported – neither *The Times* nor the *Daily Telegraph* mentioned them at all – yet they involved a total of 47 Labour MPs, the same number as rebelled over lone parent benefit at the beginning of the Blair premiership in what was then considered to be such a earth-shattering revolt.

The frequency of revolt was also causing problems for the whips, proving the accuracy of Harold Macmillan's observation that an MP should never rebel on more than one thing at a time – because 'it only confuses the whips.' 'We have been stretched as an office,' one whip admitted towards the end of the Parliament. With so many rebellions, across different issues, it was not possible to gather the proper intelligence needed to work out potential trouble spots in legislation. The whips – and ministers – had been taken by surprise by two revolts the previous session during the Housing Bill, the largest involving 26 MPs, on the subject of the government's energy efficiency targets. 'We should have seen it coming,' said one whip – but they didn't. More straightforward for the whips was the Identity Cards Bill, although this did attract more widespread media coverage, not least because the issue also caused divisions within Conservative ranks (see pp. 278–279). The Labour splits were relatively minor. Just nineteen Labour MPs voted against the Bill's second reading; likewise nineteen (largely though not entirely the same people) voted against its third reading.[5] The Bill then fell when the election was called and had to be reintroduced in the 2005 Parliament.

More serious difficulties came with the Gambling Bill (which had had its second reading the previous session and then been carried over into the fourth session) and the Mental Capacity Bill. In addition to updating much of Britain's outdated gambling law, the Gambling Bill allowed for the establishment of 40 so-called super-casinos in Britain. The Mental Capacity Bill gave legal status to 'living wills' – documents outlining an individual's wish to withhold medical treatment if they become severely incapacitated – and gave power of attorney to a third party or 'advocate' to tell doctors to withdraw treatment. Both issues were the subject of whipped votes, despite there being plenty on the Labour benches who thought that the whips should have left them well alone, allowing free votes. This, for example, is Sir Gerald Kaufman, during the Mental Capacity Bill:

Never have I known a government to handle a Bill of this sort in this way. To begin with, no Bill that I have been involved in, dealing with issues of this kind, has been whipped. It has been a tradition of my party – I am not interested in how the other parties conduct themselves – that on issues of conscience such as capital punishment, gay rights or abortion, we are not whipped. I pleaded with the government, both at meetings of the Parliamentary Labour Party and at private meetings with the Chief Whip, not to whip this Bill. It is beyond my understanding why were are being whipped. It is totally beyond me.

Yet although Kaufman claims that he had 'never' known a government deal with an issue 'of this sort in this way', in fact that way was exactly how the government had frequently dealt with issues of that sort. Rather than being breaks in precedent, the Gambling Bill and the Mental Capacity Bill were merely the latest in a line of issues where the government whips had not allowed free votes, despite there being a good prima facie case for so doing. Although the government had granted free votes on some issues – such as gay adoption and hunting – they had also been quite ready to whip in other cases, including the Civil Partnership Bill, the Gender Recognition Bill, the Children Bill, the Human Reproductive Cloning Bill and the Human Tissue Bill.[6]

In many ways issuing a whip is the more logical and consistent position to take. It is difficult logically to justify dealing with these sorts of issue – so-called issues of conscience – as a breed apart from other issues.[7] Why should the government whip on, say, the Iraq war but then give a free vote on, say, smacking? Does anyone really think that the latter is more of a moral issue than the former? In principle, therefore, there is much to recommend the government's stance. Yet in practice, the tactic has serious drawbacks. For one thing, it draws attention to the divisions within the PLP. Moreover, applying the whip in this way can create resentment within parliamentary parties, especially unfortunate when those alienated are normally very loyal to the government. The rebellion over the Human Tissue Bill in the previous session – over 'presumed consent' for organ donation – had alienated otherwise totally loyal MPs such as Steve Pound, the MP for Ealing North, who described himself as 'so loyal I'd donate a live organ of mine to the PM . . . well, it depends which bit he was asking for, I suppose.' The rebellion over the Mental Capacity Bill was similarly a rebellion of the 'unusual suspects', mainly MPs who did not rebel easily but felt deeply offended by the legislation – and even more so by the fact that the government was whipping. The whips were fairly generous with authorised absences for those who wanted to avoid the vote, but this just limits rather than negates the unhappiness caused. When the whip is required in order to win the vote, it may be seen as an unfortunate necessity. But when the government would have almost certainly got its way regardless, it might have been better politics to have granted a free vote.

Both the Gambling and the Mental Capacity rebellions were also interesting because of the pressures that were at work on MPs. 'Representing the constituency' frequently comes top in surveys which ask voters what they want from their MPs – although most issues don't have clear-cut constituency interests to represent. But over the Gambling Bill there was evidence of MPs representing seaside resorts being particularly involved, alongside what one whip called 'hardcore Methodists' who objected to the Bill in principle. And over the Mental Capacity Bill, there was strong lobbying by the Catholic Church – 'massive hardline dig-deep pressure put on by the Catholic Church', in the words of one whip – increasing the pressure on those MPs who had large Catholic populations or were Catholic themselves. A whip therefore described the rebellion as '90 per cent Catholic mafia' (the allocation of the remaining 10 per cent is revealed below).

Many of those with doubts about the Gambling Bill had given the government the benefit of the doubt at the second reading, but had made it clear that they expected to see concessions and were prepared to rebel at the third reading if they didn't get sufficient changes. Concessions duly arrived – most obviously in the form of a sharply reduced number of super-casinos. 'If we hadn't done what we'd done, it would have got a lot bigger,' said one whip; instead the rebellion at the third reading (which consisted of 24 MPs) was smaller than that at the second reading (30). There had, however, been a conscious decision taken within the government not to give any concessions prior to the Bill's second reading – on the grounds that more would then have been demanded later. 'People pocket early concessions,' said one whip. 'A concession given at the last minute is worth two or three times the switchers.'

It was this belief that was responsible for David Lammy's problems during the report stage of the Mental Capacity Bill. Knowing that it was going to face difficulties getting the Bill through the Lords, the government had already begun private negotiations about concessions that could be introduced once the Bill reached the upper chamber. But when it became known that the government was planning to introduce changes to the measure, MPs wanted to know what they were going to be – and questioned why they should vote in support of a Bill which they knew would be changed as soon as it left the Commons. Kaufman tore into what he saw as Lammy's refusal to take the House into his confidence by his persistence not to make known the nature of the concessions that he was proposing. When Lammy attempted a reply, Kaufman's response was stinging: 'May I suggest that if that is the calibre of the Minister's interventions today, he would do better to remain seated?' Lammy's discomfiture intensified when he was asked by the Deputy Speaker, Sir Michael Lord, to reveal to the House the contents of a letter from the Lord Chancellor, Lord Falconer, to the Catholic Archbishop of Cardiff. In the letter, Falconer had indicated that he would try to make explicit in the Bill that it did not authorise any decision aimed at killing, rather than relieving suffering or ending treatment where the patient was in an irreversible coma. This was precisely what many in the Commons were demanding. It took fully six minutes before Lammy was eventually handed a copy of the letter to read out to the House. The largest rebellion that day consisted of 34 Labour MPs voting against their whip – but large numbers abstained, angry about the way they were being treated by the front bench. The whips were not pleased. 'Simply terrible,' one said. 'They completely fucked up.' One Cabinet minister blamed the problem on the Prime Minister's habit of rapidly promoting those MPs, like Lammy, that he thought had talent: 'They've not done enough time in the trenches,' he said. The full description of the motivations of those rebelling over the Mental Capacity Bill, according to one whip, was '90 per cent Catholic Mafia; 10 per cent "David Lammy is not widely liked" ' – although the whip put it in somewhat stronger terms than that, using language thought unsuitable by the publishers.

Lammy's difficulties, though, were just evidence of a more widespread problem afflicting the government. On some legislation, it was now facing significant difficulties in both the Commons and the Lords. Both chambers were putting the boot in. Both were demanding concessions. And the government was well aware that if it gave concessions in the Commons, more would be demanded in the Lords. Because of the lack of a government majority, the Lords was usually seen as the more serious hurdle and so the government frequently aimed to keep major concessions for the upper chamber, even if this meant suffering larger rebellions in the Commons.[8] Some ministers felt uneasy about denying concessions to elected Labour MPs in the Commons but then giving them to unelected opposition peers in the Lords. Others just accepted the slightly unpleasant political realities from the beginning. If they were anticipating difficulties in the Lords, they would refuse to give any major concession in the Commons, and suffer a revolt in the process. The Bill would then go to the Lords, where the government would give precisely the concession that had been requested by MPs, and which they had always intended to give. The problem was that MPs don't like being treated in this way. The trick therefore was not to get caught doing it.

★ ★ ★

Yet no less a figure than the new Home Secretary, Charles Clarke, was to be caught trying a similar wheeze during the issue that provoked most dissent during the session: the Prevention of Terrorism Bill. The Bill resulted from the collapse of central parts of the legislation contained in the Anti-Terrorism, Crime and Security Bill, introduced by David Blunkett amidst so much hoo-ha in 2001 (pp. 87–96). All those debates about sunset clauses in 2001 had proved irrelevant. The Law Lords had made the sun set on the legislation earlier than expected, by declaring imprisonment without trial for foreign nationals illegal.

The Prevention of Terrorism Bill was the government's

response. It allowed suspected terrorists, including British citizens, to be subjected to a range of control orders, such as curfews, electronic tagging and restrictions on movement, extending right up to house arrest. It was clear that there was widespread discontent on the Labour benches about the measure – far greater than there had been when Blunkett had been piloting the original measure onto the statute book. The rebellions at the Bill's second reading halved the government's majority – 32 Labour MPs voting against, along with a significant number of abstentions – but a larger rebellion was prevented only when Clarke made a series of conciliatory remarks in reply to questions from Labour doubters, promising to look again at different aspects of the Bill. Indeed, much of the Bill's passage through the Commons fitted a pattern very familiar by this stage of the Parliament. The government brought forward legislation with which many Labour backbenchers were very unhappy. The government gave a series of concessions in order to try to placate the rebels. The government then won, albeit narrowly. And, another commonality, if those who voted against the Bill at some stage had all done so at the same time, the Bill would have been defeated.[9]

The largest Commons rebellion on the Bill came during the committee stage – which was being taken on the floor of the House, in order to speed the Bill's passage – when 62 Labour MPs backed a cross-party amendment which would have insisted upon a judge determining the restriction of liberty ('non-derogatory orders') of terrorist suspects as well as those cases involving the deprivation of liberty (such as house arrest, which involves a derogation from Article 5.1 of the Human Rights Act). The latter had been agreed by Clarke in a major concession to his backbench critics, but many MPs still felt that a judge should be involved in all cases involving restriction of liberty, including freedom of movement and association as well as house arrest. The rebellion cut the government's majority to fourteen, the second lowest since Tony Blair became Prime Minister. It was the largest rebellion on a civil liberties issue since 1997; you have to go back to July 1977 to see a larger rebellion on an issue related to terrorism.[10] On that occasion, the government had lost by three votes. The rebellion in 2005 consisted of six fewer Labour MPs, a difference of seventeen votes in the majority, and – most crucially of all – a government victory rather than defeat. But it was a close-run thing.

It was at this point that Clarke suffered his little bout of Lammyitis. Knowing that he faced a significant rebellion over control orders, and in order to try to placate the rebels, he let it be known that he was planning to amend the Bill once it reached the Lords. He outlined these proposed changes in a letter to the party leaders, and to his Conservative shadow, David Davis, but he still expected the Commons to vote through the Bill as it currently stood, despite not being able to see the reforms he was planning in detail. Rather than ameliorating the situation, this just further angered MPs, who objected to being asked to vote through a piece of legislation that they knew would be radically altered in the Lords.

By the time the Bill had returned from the Lords the first time a series of concessions from Clarke had managed to calm things down in the Commons. The Home Secretary had held a series of one-to-one meetings with the leading rebels, including Win Griffiths, whose amendment at the report stage had been the subject of the rebellion by 62 Labour backbenchers. By now, the Home Secretary had accepted the need for judicial control of almost all control orders.[11] Clive Betts, another rebel, commented after a private meeting with the Home Secretary:

> Charles Clarke has gone most of the way to addressing most of the issues. The fundamental one was that the order should be made by judges rather than politicians and he addressed that. Generally when a minister moves to address 90 per cent of the issues you have to give them credit.

As a result, any substantial problem in the Commons had been removed – although a hard core of rebels kept rebelling right until the end. Problems remained, though, in the Lords – and it was at this point that things got very difficult for the government. It was used by now to the Lords proving to be difficult; but it had not experienced anything like the opposition it had to endure over the Prevention of Terrorism Bill. On Thursday, 10 March 2005, the Lords dug their heels in over three aspects of the government's proposed legislation. Peers wanted a sunset clause allowing the Bill to expire, they demanded a higher standard of proof on control orders, and they insisted that a group of Privy Counsellors review the legislation. Clarke did not want to concede any of the three. The result was the longest day of parliamentary business since Labour came to power in 1997, with the Bill passing between Lords and Commons for a mammoth 28 hours. Because of this extended parliamentary ping-pong, many of the hardcore rebels notched up a large number of dissenting votes on the same issues over and over again, as the Bill zipped back and forth between Commons and Lords – with the Commons canteen running out of supplies of toast for weary MPs as dawn broke.

According to Hansard, that Friday, 11 March 2005, never took place. In parliamentary terms, it was forever Thursday. Eventually, as exhaustion set in the government conceded that although no formal sunset clause would be introduced, Parliament would have the opportunity to review or repeal the current legislation when a fresh Bill on tackling terrorism was introduced early in the next session. As one opponent of the Bill, Mark Fisher, commented wryly, there was now 'a sunset clause that smells and sounds as sweet by any other name'. In total, the Bill saw 27 separate Labour rebellions, the largest number of rebellions on any government Bill since Labour came to power in 1997. Indeed, it was the largest on any Bill since the passage of the European Communities (Amendment) Bill (more commonly known as the Maastricht Bill) in the 1992/3 session. All but the very last division on the Bill saw a backbench rebellion in the Commons.

★ ★ ★

The last revolts of the 2001 Parliament came during the final stages of the Mental Capacity Bill, after the Bill had returned from the Lords, on 5 April 2005. Even on the day that the Prime Minister announced the date of the general election, Labour MPs were *still* voting against their government. The rebellions were small (the government having given yet further ground on the Bill), but given the circumstances – just like Dr Johnson and the dog walking on its hind legs – remarkable for happening at all.

# Peter Mandelson and Tommy McAvoy

Perhaps the most curious of Peter Oborne's criticisms of the Labour whips was his belief that the Prime Minister was not using the Whips' Office to blood new talent. 'Previous governments,' wrote Oborne, 'used the office as a training ground for rising stars. David Miliband, for example, would have been forced to serve two years' hard labour with the whips rather than be plunged straight into a minister's job. It would have done him good.' Instead 'New Labour fills up the Whips' Office with the dullards and plodders.'[12]

Here, Oborne was revealing his own bias, as a right-of-centre columnist writing for a right-of-centre magazine. Previous *Conservative* governments certainly used to use the Whips' Office for training rising stars. This, however, had never been the tradition in the Labour Party. Indeed, it always used to be one of the differences between the parties. The Conservatives put into the Whips' Office those who they thought were destined for higher things; Labour recruited as whips those who would make good whips – which frequently meant former trade unionists – but not those who were thought of as future ministerial material. Donald Searing's study of the 1970s, for example, found that just 32 per cent of Labour whips went on to a ministerial position after they left the Whips' Office. For the Tories, the figure was 75 per cent.[13] For the Conservatives, the Whips' Office was where the future officer class received their blooding. With Labour, it was where the NCOs did their stuff.

Yet the irony of Oborne's criticism was that when Tony Blair became leader in 1994, his initial aim was to adopt Conservative practice. Witness Peter Mandelson's short apprenticeship in the then opposition Whips' Office between 1994 and 1995, when 'Bobby' was forced to do bench duty along with the most humble whip. Mandelson had no desire to be a whip (his reaction when told by Blair that he was intending to place him in the Whips' Office was 'I should cocoa') and this was a view shared by many of the whips, who didn't particularly want him around either. But Blair insisted and (according to one of Mandelson's biographers) 'strongly defended the practice, started by the Tories, of putting all upwardly mobile frontbenchers through the whips office'.[14]

And the evidence since 1997 provides plenty of examples of former whips moving onwards and upwards. Most of those who have served Blair as a whip have gone on to serve as a minister. Of the 26 MPs who served in the Whips' Office during the 1997 Parliament, five were still there at the end of the parliament. Seven returned straight to the back benches, and another fourteen went on to serve in other posts after they'd done their time. In other words, of those who had ceased to whip, two-thirds went on to another position in government rather than to the back benches.[15]

The trend was even more pronounced in the 2001 parliament under Hilary Armstrong. Of the 28 MPs who served as whips (listed in the table below) almost three-quarters went on to further ministerial office after they'd done their time as a whip. Eight were still in the Whips' Office after the election, and of the remaining 20, one had retired at the election and five went straight onto the back benches. That left fourteen who went onto ministerial posts after being a whip. These were mostly at parliamentary under-secretary level (at least initially), although three of the fourteen had made minister of state, either before or just after the 2005 election. The percentage of whips going on to other ministerial posts is therefore more than double that of the Labour Whips' Office in the 1970s.

Oborne may, though, be partially right. It is striking, for

example, how none of the members of the 1997 or 2001 intake to make it into the Cabinet did time in the Whips' Office. Similarly, of the 24 MPs to serve as minister of state in 2005 just five had served as a government whip. All roads to high office have yet to lead through the Whips' Office. But it is clearly still being used under Labour as much more of a training ground than it ever used to be. The Labour Whips' Office under Armstrong resembles the Conservative Whips' Office far more than it does the Whips' Office of Bob Mellish. For their part, the whips like to see their alumni enter government. In part this is pride, in part self-interest. But it is also that they believe that ex-whips make good ministers. 'They understand how committees work. They understand the need to talk to backbenchers. They stay political,' said one.

## Future careers of Labour whips, 2001–05

| Still whipping | Back benches | Other ministerial office |
|---|---|---|
| Bob Ainsworth | Paul Clark | Nick Ainger |
| Hilary Armstrong | Fraser Kemp | Charlotte Atkins |
| Vernon Coaker | Margaret Moran | Jim Fitzpatrick |
| John Heppell | Dan Norris | Keith Hill |
| Tommy McAvoy | Graham Stringer | Anne McGuire |
| Gillian Merron | | Tony McNulty |
| Joan Ryan | | Jim Murphy |
| Tom Watson | | Ian Pearson |
| | | Bridget Prentice |
| | | James Purnell |
| | | Angela Smith |
| | | Gerry Sutcliffe |
| | | Derek Twigg |
| | | Phil Woolas |

Note: In addition, Ivor Caplin served as a whip from 2001–05, before retiring at the 2005 election. Atkins was a minister after her spell as a whip, before returning to the back benches in May 2005.

That said, as well as future ministerial material, there was also still a place for those who were seen as 'just good whips'. Every Whips' Office has them; every Whips' Office needs them. The epitome of this in the current regime is probably Tommy McAvoy, the MP for Rutherglen and Hamilton West, and the pairing whip – more formally known as the Comptroller of Her Majesty's Household – since 1997. By 2005 McAvoy was one of just four members of the Blair government to have held the same post since 1997: the others being the Prime Minister, the Chancellor, and the somewhat less well-known Baroness Farrington of Ribbleton, a baroness in waiting and government whip in the House of Lords.[16] McAvoy's time in the government Whips' Office makes him the longest continuously serving Labour government whip in the Commons, even closing fast on some of those who enjoyed longer but broken periods of service.[17] He is not destined for higher office, and was not put in – or kept in – the Whips' Office in order to train him up for a career as parliamentary under-secretary in the Department of Transport. He was put in there to whip. A former shop steward for the Amalgamated Engineering Union (now merged into Amicus), he would have been quite at home in the Whips' Office in the 1940s or 1960s. 'He is', said one MP who had crossed him, 'like an elephant. He never forgets.' McAvoy once objected to a description of him as a 'Glaswegian Catholic Stalinist thug'.[18] 'It's a disgraceful thing to say,' he retorted. 'I'm from Rutherglen.'

# 9

# Office without power?

*The records of 2001 – Where we are now – Retirements – Governing with a smaller majority – Signs of dissent already*

> I can't believe the press still talk about Tony's cronies. It's fucking bullshit. It's the biggest pack of lies. This is even worse than the 1970s. – Long-serving Labour MP, 2004

The Keith Flett Prize for the stupidest letter written to a newspaper during the 2005 election campaign was won by a late entrant. The prize – a book of first-class stamps, a cardigan and some crayons – went to an election day letter in *The Times*, which complained about the government's destruction of the British constitution and the behaviour of a 'supine House of Commons'. Its author was someone who believes in a golden age that never existed – and who fails to recognise what is going on in front of his eyes.

As has been made clear throughout this book, the 2001 Parliament was remarkable not for the servility of government MPs but for both the frequency and size of the backbench rebellions that took place. Between 2001 and 2005 the PLP set a series of records which the whips would much rather they had left well alone:

- a higher rate of rebellion than in any other post-war Parliament, and more rebellions than in all but the (longer) 1974–79 Parliament;
- more rebellions in the first session than in the first session of any previous Labour government;
- more rebellions in the final session than in the final session of any postwar Parliament;
- the largest rebellion by Labour MPs over a Labour government's health policy;
- the largest rebellion by Labour MPs over a Labour government's education policy;
- the (joint) largest rebellion at second reading since 1945; and
- the two largest rebellions against the whip by MPs of any party for over 150 years.

It is therefore difficult to take seriously the argument that the Commons had been supine for the previous four years. As one long-serving Labour MP, one of the handful left at Westminster who had served in the 1974–79 Parliament, put it, 'I can't believe the press still talk about Tony's cronies. It's fucking bullshit. It's the biggest pack of lies. This is even worse than the 1970s.' The combination of the rise in backbench rebellion – on a scale that would have been beyond the wildest fears of whips 50 years ago – together with the rise in the assertiveness of the House of Lords (as a consequence of the 'destruction' of the constitution so deplored by the author of that letter in *The Times*), which is now also behaving in a way that would have been unimaginable 50 years ago, have created a Parliament that is far more assertive and much more of an irritant to government than the doomsayers realise.

It is, of course, important not to overstate the case. Cohesion on the back benches weakened during the 2001 Parliament, but it did not collapse. Most votes still saw complete cohesion. When that cohesion weakened, it usually did so only at the margins. And even the most rebellious of MPs voted with their party more often than not. But this is hardly new: it has been true of every Parliament for over 150 years. All the evidence is that MPs today are less supine, more independent, less willing to be told what to do, more willing to break away from the party line and to tell the whips where to go.

There was, of course, one other record set during the Parliament – and this time, by the whips. Despite everything, despite all the huffing and puffing, the government survived the entire parliament undefeated on a whipped vote in the Commons. Excluding the debacle over Donald Anderson and Gwyneth Dunwoody at the beginning of the Parliament (which, as explained in Chapter 4, was explicitly not whipped), Tony Blair's whips won every single vote. By the election in 2005, the Blair government had lasted eight years without suffering a single defeat. No other government since Harold Wilson's elected in 1966 had managed to survive a single term unscathed. It is pretty clear from the events of the Parliament that one of the reasons for this is that there were MPs on the Labour benches who, however much they might rail against things, could not bring themselves to defeat the government. There were Labour MPs who would bark as loudly as they can, but who would never bite.

Again, it is worth not overstating this. With the exception of the period from 1974 to 1979, government defeats in the Commons have always been rare. Margaret Thatcher suffered just one defeat in each of her three Parliaments as Prime Minister. Even the Major government after 1992 only suffered four defeats on whipped votes, despite having a slim majority or no majority at all. Given the size of the Blair government's majorities in the Commons after 1997 – larger than that enjoyed by any of the governments that were defeated from 1970 onwards – it is perhaps not that surprising that it wasn't defeated. The lack of defeats in the Commons can hardly be seen as evidence of parliamentary impotence, especially when combined with the regular string of defeats to occur in the Lords and the regular retreats seen in the Commons. From the very beginning, the

2001 Parliament saw the government give ground to its back-bench critics on measure after measure, including on almost all major policy initiatives, giving way completely on several issues, from House of Lords reform to company pension schemes to fox-hunting. They gave even greater concessions in the face of opposition from the Lords.

That the government usually got its way eventually was not because of the servility of its MPs – but because it enjoyed a quite enormous majority, and was prepared to do deals with its backbenchers in order to get any rebellion down to a manageable size. Which was, of course, the reason why the letter to *The Times* was not just ill informed, it was also spectacularly ill timed. Because as dawn broke the next morning, that enormous three-figure majority was no more – and the prospect for some really intriguing struggles lay ahead.

★ ★ ★

One of the curiosities of modern British politics is that all those jolly sensible people who joined the SDP in the 1980s because the Labour Party was too left wing and full of people like Brian Sedgemore now find themselves in the same party as Brian Sedgemore. On 26 April 2005 Sedgemore, who had already announced that he was retiring from the Commons, defected to the Liberal Democrats, urging other Labour supporters to do the same, and to give Blair a 'bloody nose'. Wheeled out to discuss Sedgemore on the morning of his defection, the education secretary, Ruth Kelly, claimed that Sedgemore had been 'completely ill at ease with New Labour for a very long time'. He had indeed. In his last speech in the Commons he had described the anti-terrorism Bill as 'new Labour's descent into hell', and there were almost a hundred items of hard evidence of him being ill at ease in the 98 occasions when he rebelled against the whip between 2001 and 2005. The whips shed few tears over his departure from the Commons.

Also standing down were another eight of the 30 most

rebellious Labour MPs, those listed on page 53, including Harry Barnes, Denzil Davies, Alice Mahon and the Father of the House, Tam Dalyell. Together with Jim Marshall, who had died in May 2004, it meant that ten of Labour's 30 biggest rebels would not be in the Commons after the 2005 election, no matter what the result. This was a much higher retirement rate than among other members of the PLP; a full third of the most rebellious 30 would not be present post-election, compared to an overall retirement rate by Labour MPs of 14 per cent. The most rebellious, in other words, were standing down at approximately three times the rate of other Labour MPs. On the other hand, very few of the most rebellious MPs sat for marginal seats. Just one of the 30 most rebellious sat for a seat with a majority of below 10 per cent. So both the whips and the rebels knew almost exactly how many of the most rebellious MPs would still be there come 6 May.

When all the dust had settled, the government was left with a majority of 66. It may have survived undefeated since 1997, but it had struggled mightily to enact key pieces of legislation while enjoying a majority of over 160. How would it possibly manage with a majority of almost a hundred fewer? Echoing Norman Lamont's famous verdict on the Major years, one Labour insider had already described the possibility as 'office without power'. The line from Labour HQ on election night, and since, has been that this smaller majority will 'concentrate the mind'. The bloated majorities enjoyed since 1997 had allowed Labour MPs to rebel without giving much thought to the consequences. With a smaller majority, so the argument goes, Labour MPs will have to exercise more self-discipline.

Possibly. There's no doubt that the smaller majority will make *some* MPs more careful about how they will behave. Rebellions can no longer be entered into without a real risk of defeating the government. Some Labour MPs have already made it clear to their whips that they intend to behave differently given the size of the majority. But it's worth remembering the last time a government lost a hundred-plus majority and found itself re-elected with a much smaller one. Immediately after the 1992 election most commentators declared that John Major's 21-seat majority was a perfectly workable state of affairs. But they had reckoned without the extent to which the habit of revolt had been widespread within the Conservative parliamentary party during the Thatcher years, years when (just like those between 1997 and 2005) MPs were able to rebel relatively freely given the size of the majority. Ask Major whether he feels that having such a small majority 'concentrated the minds' of Bill Cash, Teddy Taylor, Teresa Gorman *et al*. Do you think he'd get the joke? Or go back and look at how the Labour government of 1974–79 managed with a small, and sometimes non-existent, majority. Self-immolation rather than self-control were the order of the day then.

Similarly, does anyone seriously believe that Jeremy Corbyn got out of bed the morning after the 2005 election, and decided over his muesli and carrot juice that whilst he'd tried this rebellion malarkey for the last eight years it was now time for him to knuckle down and toe the party line? Does anyone think that John McDonnell immediately reached for the phone to contact his regional whip to ask for the latest instructions? Or that Lynne Jones spent the morning boning up on the standing orders of the PLP? Ditto for Bob Marshall-Andrews (whose mind appears to have been concentrated almost entirely on the removal of Blair ever since he arrived in the Commons), or Bob Wareing or Alan Simpson or Kelvin Hopkins or Dennis Skinner or Kate Hoey or Diane Abbott or Glenda Jackson or Mark Fisher or Neil Gerrard or Mike Wood or Peter Kilfoyle or David Taylor? And that's before you think about Clare Short or Gwyneth Dunwoody or Ian Gibson or Jim Cousins or Frank Field or Gordon Prentice or David Drew or Frank Dobson or Michael Connarty or Harry Cohen or John Austin or Jim Dobbin or Ronnie Campbell or Paul Flynn or Michael Clapham or Roger Berry or Andrew Mackinlay or John Grogan.

Some of these names may not be all that well known outside

Westminster, but they are very well known indeed in the government Whips' Office. The 34 MPs listed above have all rebelled on key votes against the Blair government before, and there can be little doubt that they will do so again at some point during the 2005 Parliament. And to their ranks will, on occasions, be added people such as George Mudie, Ann Cryer, Ian Davidson, Rudi Vis, Geraldine Smith, Bill Etherington, Chris McCafferty, Austin Mitchell, Julie Morgan, Betty Williams and many others far too obscure to mention, even in a book like this.

For the whips the arithmetic is fairly simple – and fairly depressing. Its nominal majority is 66. Its effective majority – once you allow for the non-voting Sinn Fein MPs – is 71. There were 87 Labour MPs with regular 'form', who had voted against the whips on ten or more occasions during the last Parliament. Of these, 27 are no longer in the Commons and/or in receipt of the Labour whip.[1] But this still leaves 60 MPs who rebelled on ten or more occasions between 2001 and 2005. That's more than enough to defeat the government. Still sitting on the back benches, for example, are 56 of those who voted against the Prevention of Terrorism Bill prior to the 2005 election, easily enough to defeat the government should it mishandle similar legislation now, even after the terrorist attacks in July 2005.

Of course, a majority of 66 could still be sufficient. It's hardly wafer thin. If the PLP is treated with a bit of TLC then there shouldn't be too many problems. Blair's immediate post-election speech – in which he promised to listen – certainly sounded as if he might take such an approach. But the Prime Minister always sounds like this. After every bloody nose he gets, Blair *sounds* conciliatory. The problem is that he then struggles to *be* conciliatory. It's not in his political DNA. It's like expecting Graham Norton suddenly to become butch. It just won't happen. And the result will be trouble. Minds may well be concentrated, but if the government continues to govern as it governed in the 2001 parliament, minds will be concentrated on how to defeat it.

The real problem for the government will come when (or if)

it suffers its first defeat. Once it has gone down to its first defeat, and it becomes clear to all and sundry that the sky does not fall in, that no votes of confidence are called and that the government does not collapse as a result, then defeats will become more regular. Once they've been defeated once, the whips will no longer be able to threaten rebels with victory – and defeat could well follow defeat.

★ ★ ★

It is worrying what voting against the party line can do to you. The first Labour MP to rebel in the 1997 Parliament, Jamie Cann, is now dead. The first Labour MP to rebel in the 2001 parliament, Sir Ray Powell, is also now dead. Who would dare to be the first rebel of the 2005 Parliament? Four Labour MPs – Corbyn, Marshall-Andrews, McDonnell and Wareing – were the first to break ranks, supporting a reasoned amendment at the second reading of the Racial and Religious Hatred Bill; Corbyn and McDonnell both went on to oppose the second reading as well.

More attention focused on the second reading of the Identity Cards Bill on 28 June 2005, widely heralded as the first real test of the government's ability to manage its much smaller majority. The largest rebellion comprised 20 backbenchers (with just under ten abstentions), the government's majority falling to 27 at one point. This did not cause too many sleepless nights in the government Whips' Office. There were relatively few surprises in the list of those voting against. The only new rebels from the previous intakes were Frank Cook and John Smith. Cook had abstained over aspects of the legislation in the last Parliament, and had rebelled relatively regularly in the past. But Smith was casting his first-ever vote against the Labour government, having supported the Bill at both second and third readings in the last Parliament. There were also two new MPs among the rebels, Katy Clark and Linda Riordan. Both Clark and Riordan rebelled on other issues as well before the summer recess in 2005, marking themselves out as future trouble for the whips. And there were several others in the 2005 intake that the whips have already identified as potential problems in the future. 'All those London barristers,' muttered one whip, 'are always trouble. They need to get knocked about a bit before they realise they're not hot shots.'

The relatively small size of the rebellion over ID cards led some to doubt whether the government really faced a more difficult time with its new majority. But the measures so far were a relatively poor test of their new status. As was clear in Chapter 8, the issue of ID cards was not one to cause deep division within the PLP. There were just nineteen Labour MPs left in the Commons who had voted against the Bill introduced before the 2005 election. And this time round, the policy was also an explicit manifesto commitment (which it had not been prior to 2005). The whips were relatively pleased that the ID card rebellion had been contained. They viewed most of the 20 ID card rebels as a diehard core with whom they were unable to have much meaningful dialogue – but they felt they were more able to negotiate and discuss with the broader stratum of the 40 or so next most rebellious above this group. More importantly, they know that they have to now. They were well aware that ID cards was just the phoney war; the real trouble is still to come.

Below the surface, however, there were other signs of the new reality. By the summer recess there had been seven separate rebellions, involving 30 different Labour MPs (Corbyn and McDonnell topped the lists, unsurprisingly). The elections to the Parliamentary Committee – the body that liaises between the leadership and the backbenchers – presented the leadership with a fairly bolshie group of backbenchers (Cryer, Angela Eagle, Kevan Jones, Tony Lloyd, Joan Ruddock and Martin Salter), with all those seen as the favoured candidates of the leadership being given the bum's rush. There was talk amongst Labour MPs of trying to establish a backbench committee, akin to the Conservatives' 1922 Committee, to better represent the views of the backbenchers. And there was a revealing dispute over select committee nominations. As a result of the post-2001 dispute, the PLP had agreed a two-term limit on the length of time someone could chair a select committee. The whips therefore expected Gwyneth Dunwoody to relinquish the chair of the Transport Select Committee come 2005. But Dunwoody refused to budge, arguing that since she had begun her period as chair when it was merely a subcommittee rather than a full-blown select committee, she should be allowed to serve another four years. There were plenty of whips who thought this was a spurious, self-serving argument, but rather than precipitate another row, they backed down.[2] They then backed down further when it came to allocating the chairs for the other select committees. Ex-ministers had been lined up for several important committees. The elected members of the Parliamentary Committee said no – and insisted on a series of long-standing backbenchers instead. Again, the whips backed down. Four years before, the whips would have fought. Eight years before, they wouldn't even have been challenged. The signs of power shifting are there for those that want to see them.

# The PLP and A. N. Other

If recent history is any guide, then when Tony Blair stands down as Prime Minister, his replacement – whoever he or she is – should enjoy a honeymoon with the PLP. The Thatcher defenestration produced a definite short-term soothing of the feelings of the parliamentary party, which had been becoming increasingly rebellious until then. By the time of Margaret Thatcher's downfall, Tim Renton, Chief Whip between 1989 and 1990, was said to carry around a list of about 70 Tory MPs who had 'stopped supporting the government on certain matters'.[3] By April 1990, Alan Clark was to note in his diary that 'Party discipline was breaking up.'[4] Yet John Major's initial period as Prime Minister from November 1990 through to the election in 1992 led to a distinct improvement between leader and led, seeing just limited and sporadic backbench revolts, with the parliamentary party in this period being more cohesive in the division lobbies than at any other point during the thirteen years of Conservative government from 1979 to 1992.[5] There was a similar effect when James Callaghan took over from Harold Wilson. Callaghan was elected Labour leader on 5 April 1976, and did not suffer a Commons defeat as a result of Labour backbench dissent for ten months, despite the perilous state of his majority.

But both examples also indicate that any honeymoon effect can be short lived. Major's honeymoon with his backbenchers ended with the Maastricht Bill in 1992, which saw the most serious and sustained campaign of intra-party dissent in the Conservative Party's postwar history. Callaghan's ended on 22 February 1977 when Michael Foot, then Leader of the House, tried to move a guillotine motion in order to make some progress with the Scotland and Wales Bill, which had by then become impossibly bogged down in committee. Twenty-two Labour MPs combined with the opposition to defeat Foot's motion, and with it the Bill. Callaghan's government then went down to a further seventeen defeats as a result of backbench dissent – twelve of them also over devolution, defeats that reshaped the legislation as a result and ultimately led to the government losing a vote of confidence in 1979.[6]

Short-term honeymoons aside, the effect of a change in leader will depend on several imponderables about their style and approach. The first is the ideological direction of the government. Although the real record of the Blair government is far more sophisticated than its frequent caricature as right wing and neo-Thatcherite – in policy terms, if not often in tone, it has been far more redistributive, far more social democratic, than many of its left-of-centre critics allow – it has still frequently asked Labour MPs to back policies with which many of its members were unhappy. A new leader who shifted the focus or tone of the government back to the left would at least dampen down some of the unhappiness within the parliamentary party. A new leader who is 'unremittingly New Labour' – to borrow a phrase used provocatively elsewhere – will just stir things up further.

Assume for a minute that A. N. Other turns out to be Gordon Brown. One of the problems with assessing how a Brown government will turn out is that the longer he is the King over the Water, the greater become the expectations as to what he can deliver. Those – and they do exist, both within and without the PLP – who think that a Brown premiership will usher in some sort of socialist nirvana are surely heading for a fall. Whilst it may see some policy shifts from the status quo, these are unlikely to be sizeable enough to placate many of those on the left. The view of one left-wing MP that 'there's not a gnat's whisker between them' is probably taking it too far, but in some policy areas – especially control of public expenditure and dealings with the public sector trade unions – a Brown government looks possibly even more likely to enrage the left than anything done by Blair.

One of the lessons of the last four years, however, is that it is not just the policy itself that matters; it is also the way the policy is sold, the tone with which it is launched, the narrative that accompanies it. Here Brown will suit the PLP better. Policy may not change that much, but the language accompanying policy, how it is justified and argued for, will be different. Brown is able to talk a Labour narrative, and will be able to connect with the hearts of his backbenchers, in a way that Blair frequently has not. They may well end up voting for exactly the same sort of policy – but they'll probably be happier doing it.

But another lesson – also writ large in this book – is that the process by which policy is developed is also important. A PLP that feels involved in policy-making, that feels that its views have been listened to and taken into account – a PLP in other words, that feels a bit wanted, perhaps even a bit loved – is a less troublesome one. Top-up fees and foundation hospitals would have caused rebellions at the best of times. What made them so much more damaging was the way they were dropped out of the blue onto MPs, without any consultation, any discussion. And so, the next imponderable is the Brown style of governing. Perhaps it will be a consensual, inclusive style, in which the new Prime Minister realises that he and his staff do not have all the answers and listens to the views of those whose votes he will rely on. Perhaps Downing Street will start to listen fully to the views of its backbenchers. Perhaps. But there are plenty of observers who see the likelihood of this as marginal. Those who take the view that Brown is even more controlling and autocratic than Blair – 'the control freak's control freak', to use Andrew Rawnsley's phrase – might expect a less harmonious time between the general and his troops.[7]

Particularly disgruntled will be those MPs who hope for a bright future which then does not materialise, especially all those on the backbenches awaiting the preferment that they deserve but which has been so cruelly denied to them under Blair. Brown is famous for the loyalty he shows to those who are close to him, and there will doubtless be some promotions amongst the ranks of previously overlooked or dismissed Brownites. But in party management terms these will simply be countered by a group of disgruntled Blairites who are equally likely to find themselves newly encamped on the back benches. A handful of non-aligned backbenchers may enter government having had it denied under Blair, but it is unlikely to be more than a handful. 'I mean,' said one whip, 'some of them are just unappointable.' A Whips' Office answering to Brown is likely to reach the same conclusion.

More importantly, all such discussions exaggerate the extent to which the Brownite/Blairite divide extends within the PLP. Whilst there are such MPs, they are relatively few in number.[8] The majority of the PLP is neither Brownite nor Blairite. The myth of the two camps, however, suits both sides. It allows those around Brown to pretend that they control huge swathes of troops, which they order to attack or retreat at will. It is therefore 'Gordon' who decides whether the government wins or loses key votes and who thus decides the fate of the Prime Minister. The myth similarly suits the Blairites, because it allows them to deflect attention away from the real reason that they get into difficulties with their backbenchers, enabling them to place the blame on the Brownites and their devious scheming.

The truth is more prosaic. When Blair has got himself into difficulties with the PLP, it has not been because of 'Gordon' and his Brownites. It has been because he has managed to alienate the broad non-aligned mainstream on his back benches. When Brown runs into trouble with the PLP, it'll be for exactly the same reason.

# Appendix 1

## Glossary of key terms

Parliamentary language is frequently criticised for being confusing and archaic. Some of it undoubtedly is, although much of it is in fact relatively easy to understand. This appendix provides a short glossary of key parliamentary terms used at various points in the book. The following all refer to practice in the Commons, although most of the terms also apply, *mutatis mutandis*, in the Lords. For those who want it, more detail can be found in any of these three excellent introductory texts: Philip Norton, *Parliament in British Politics* (Palgrave, Basingstoke, 2005), Robert Rogers and Rhodri Walters, *How Parliament Works* (5th ed.) (Pearson Longman, Harlow, 2004), and Michael Rush, *Parliament Today* (Manchester University Press, Manchester, 2005). A more detailed work of reference is Robert Blackburn and Andrew Kennon with Sir Michael Wheeler-Booth, *Griffith and Ryle Parliament: Functions, Practice and Procedures* (2nd ed.) (Sweet and Maxwell, London, 2003).

**Act (of Parliament)**. A **Bill** that has been approved by both the House of Commons and the House of Lords and which has then been given **Royal Assent**. An Act becomes part of United Kingdom law.

**Adjournment (debate)**. The House adjourns at the end of a sitting (usually a day), at which point there is a short debate (formally on the motion 'That this House do now adjourn', although in practice on a topic of interest to an MP). More substantial debates occasionally take place on the adjournment, followed sometimes by a vote.

**All-party group**. Groups formed by MPs and peers who share an interest in a subject, regardless of their party affiliations.

**Back benches**. Literally, the rows of benches in the Commons behind those at the front – on which sit members of the parliamentary parties who do not hold ministerial or shadow ministerial positions. These MPs are therefore known as backbenchers.

**Bill**. A proposed piece of legislation put forward for consideration in Parliament. Successful Bills become **Acts**.

**Carry-over**. A procedure by which a **Bill** is introduced in one **session** and then continues its passage in the next session (being 'carried over' from one session to the next).

**Collective responsibility**. The requirement for all members of a government to take responsibility for its actions and to support it publicly, even if they may disagree privately. Open disagreement – especially failure to vote in support of the government in the Commons – leads either to dismissal or resignation.

**Committee (stage)**. Once a **Bill** has received its **second reading** it goes through the committee stage, where its clauses are discussed in detail. This is normally held in a **standing committee**, but it can sometimes take place in the main Commons chamber, with all MPs able to participate (what is known as a Committee of the Whole House).

**Constituency**. The geographical area represented by an MP.

**Division**. A vote, so called because MPs divide, walking through one of two lobbies ('aye' or 'no') to record their votes.

**Early day motions (EDM)**. A motion tabled for debate for 'an early day' but which in reality are not debated. Because they are published, and MPs can add their names in support, they are used to test opinion and to make political points. Thousands are tabled each year, on a vast range of topics.

**Father of the House**. The MP with the longest continuous service.

**Floor of the House**. The main Commons chamber. A matter

being discussed on the floor of the House is being debated in the Commons chamber, rather than in a committee.

**First reading**. The formal first stage of a **Bill**'s passage, taken without debate. The Bill is then ordered to be printed.

**Free votes**. Votes where the party managers (the whips) have not issued instructions to their MPs on how to vote.

**Front benches**. Literally, the rows of benches in the Commons at the front on either side of the despatch box – on which sit members of the parliamentary parties who hold ministerial or shadow ministerial positions. These MPs are therefore known as frontbenchers.

**Hansard**. The record of proceedings in the Commons. Includes debates, votes and questions. Available online (via www.parliament.uk).

**Leader of the House (of Commons)**. The Cabinet minister who deals with Commons affairs and with the organisation of its business.

**Lords amendments**. Amendments made by the House of Lords to a **Bill** which has passed through the Commons. The Commons then debates and votes on these amendments, either accepting or rejecting them. If the latter, the Bill then returns to the Lords.

**Motion**. A proposal that forms the basis for debate. Used for legislation – that a **Bill** be read a second time – but also for motions for the **adjournment** and more **substantive motions**.

**Opposition**. Those MPs not in the government party. The largest opposition party is Her Majesty's Opposition – sometimes called the Official Opposition.

**Opposition days**. Time allocated for the **opposition** parties to raise issues of concern (currently 20 days per session). A debate is followed by a vote on a **substantive motion** (known as an opposition day motion).

**Parliamentary private secretary (PPS)**. An MP who is an aide to a secretary of state or a minister of state. An unpaid position, but one which means that the MP is obliged to follow **collective responsibility**.

**Payroll vote**. MPs who are in the government (broadly defined) and who are therefore expected to vote with the government or resign. Therefore the most reliable supporters of the government in any vote. Somewhat of a misnomer, since it includes **parliamentary private secretaries** and unpaid ministers, none of whom receive a ministerial salary but who are still expected to abide by the convention of **collective responsibility**.

**Ping-pong**. The passage of a **Bill** back and forth between the Commons and the Lords, when the two chambers are in dispute. At its most rapid towards the end of a parliamentary session, with the government desperate to get Bills ready for **Royal Assent** before **prorogation**. Bills ping if the Lords think they pong.

**PLP**. The Parliamentary Labour Party, consisting of all Labour MPs and peers. Has its own elected officers, committees, rules and meetings.

**Prime Minister's Questions (PMQs)**. An opportunity for MPs to question the Prime Minister. Lasts half an hour, every Wednesday when the House is sitting. Parliament at its most tribal and confrontational – and hence the media highlight of the week.

**Private member's Bill**. A **Bill** introduced by a 'private member' rather than by the government.

**Programming**. The timetabling of a **Bill** immediately after the second reading, which allocates specific amounts of time to the different parts of its passage.

**Prorogation**. The formal end of a parliamentary **session**.

**Queen's Speech**. Sometimes called the 'Gracious Speech'. Written by the government and read out by the Queen, it outlines legislation for the coming **session** of the Parliament.

**Reasoned amendment**. An amendment tabled for the second or **third reading**, which sets out why a **Bill** should not proceed. If the reasoned amendment is passed, the Bill falls.

**Report (stage)**. Held on the floor of the House, once a **Bill** has been through the **committee stage**. Technically the committee reporting what they have done to the Bill, it also allows for MPs other than committee members to propose amendments.

**Royal Assent**. The sovereign's agreement to a **Bill** passed by Parliament. Now merely formal.

**Second reading**. The first substantive stage in a **Bill**'s passage through the Commons. A debate and vote on the principle of a piece of legislation rather than on individual clauses.

**Select committee**. A non-legislative committee of MPs (cf. **standing committee**) to investigate particular issues or subjects. Most obviously, the departmental select committees, which monitor the activities of government departments.

**Session**. The period from the State Opening of Parliament (the ceremonial start to a session, which includes the Queen's Speech) to prorogation – usually about a year, from early November to late October.

**Speaker**. The presiding officer of the Commons.

**Standing committee**. A committee set up to consider the details of a particular Bill, and which ceases to exist once its deliberations have concluded.

**Substantive motion**. A motion expressing an opinion or taking a decision (cf. the motion for the **adjournment**).

**Tellers**. Two MPs from each side who count the votes during a **division**.

**Third reading**. The final stage of a **Bill**'s passage through the Commons – the vote on the Bill as it is finally constituted. Like the **second reading**, a debate and vote on the whole of the Bill, rather than on particular clauses.

**Whips**. The MPs responsible for parliamentary party organisation and discipline.

**Whipped votes**. A vote where the party managers (the **whips**) have issued instructions to their MPs on how to vote.

# Appendix 2

## What does and doesn't count

The data used in this book are derived from Hansard, the official record of parliamentary debates. They are based on the number of occasions when a Labour MP voted against his or her whip. This is a deceptively simple statement – but there are a handful of caveats which need to be understood if the data are to make sense.

The first is that this figure excludes all 'free votes'. All reported figures are therefore *not* the number of occasions when an MP deviated from the rest of his or her party; they are rather the number of occasions when an MP defied the whip to do so. This differentiates them from figures available from some of the (otherwise excellent) web-based search engines that are available (such as www.publicwhip.org.uk or www.theyworkforyou.com), which record all occasions when a party's MPs are not 100 per cent united. The focus here is on matters of dissent, on those occasions where MPs defy their party leadership. For one thing, there is a qualitative difference between voting against your party when the whip is on, and doing so when it is not. In addition, not differentiating whipped from unwhipped votes can lead to strange conclusions about an MP's behaviour – such as the belief that the Chief Whip, Hilary Armstrong, 'rebelled' on six occasions between 2001 and 2005. She did not. In six free votes – three of them to do with hunting, the others to do with reforming Parliament – she voted in a way distinct from the majority of voting Labour MPs.[1] It is similarly not really very sensible to talk of Tony Blair rebelling on two occasions.[2] It is sometimes difficult to distinguish definitively between whipped and genuinely free votes – hence the problem that the websites have – and there is a tricky middle ground, where the vote may not be officially whipped but it is quite clear what the party hierarchy want their MPs to do. But based on contacts both with MPs and with whips, it has been possible to identify all those occasions when Labour MPs defied the official instructions of their whips.

It is also important to understand that data gleaned from Hansard are not without their limitations. For one thing, Hansard is not entirely accurate. Take for example, division 133 on 15 January 2002: George Howarth, the Labour MP for Knowsley North and Sefton East was recorded as having voted against the third reading of the NHS Reform and Health Care Professions Bill. But one of the clerks who record MPs' names as they file past had simply crossed off the wrong MP, confusing him with Gerald Howarth, the Conservative MP for Aldershot, and a very different political creature indeed. Similarly, during the 2001 Parliament, Frank Field (Labour) was confused with Mark Field (Conservative), Andy Reed (Labour) with Alan Reid (Liberal Democrat), Phil Woolas (Labour) with Phil Willis (Liberal Democrat), Linda Gilroy (Labour) with Sandra Gidley (Liberal Democrat), and Valerie Davey (Labour) with Ed Davey (Liberal Democrat). This list is indicative, not exhaustive.

Sometimes, though, the mistake is the MPs, not Hansard's, with the member going through the wrong lobby. Voting can be a particular problem on free votes (when MP's lack the whips to advise them), and for Liberal Democrats and those from minor parties because they don't benefit from the sight of masses of their colleagues flooding into one lobby to guide them. It can, though, happen to MPs of all parties. In October 2004, for example, the newly elected Iain Wright, the winner of the Hartlepool by-election, accidentally voted in favour of a Conservative amendment to a European Union document on justice and home affairs. A few months before Wright's mistake, in March 2004, the long-serving MP Gerry Steinberg had walked into the wrong lobby during voting on the Asylum and Immigration Bill – the first and only time he did so in his eighteen years as an MP.

Again, these examples are merely illustrative rather than exhaustive, but in neither case was the MP 'dissenting' from the party line; he had merely made a mistake. Or as another Labour MP who cast a mistaken vote put it, 'I got my geography all wrong.' When this happens, MPs are usually advised to follow the advice given by a parliamentary old hand to the newly elected Joseph Pilgrim, in Andy McSmith's political novel *Innocent in the House*:

> It's very ill-advised to admit a mistake in this place. I did that in my first year: went through the wrong lobby by mistake, owned up; they made me look a terrible fool: the man who rebelled because he got lost in the lobby. With hindsight, I should have said I was driven by my conscience. Rather be a troublemaker than a chump.[3]

Some do own up. In 2004, a very well-concerted campaign by Greenpeace and Friends of the Earth persuaded just over 30 Labour MPs to vote against their government over the energy efficiency targets contained in the Housing Bill. Greenpeace then took out full-page adverts in the press, naming and shaming all those Labour MPs who had previously indicated their support for Greenpeace's stance but who had not then rebelled on the issue in the Commons. A slightly shamefaced letter then appeared in the *Guardian* from Kelvin Hopkins, the MP for Luton North and one of the more rebellious Labour MPs, in which he admitted that he had meant to support the amendment, but had got confused and supported the government by mistake. He said that his 'not-very-good excuse' was that 'I had been away and was out of touch on the day in question.' Hopkins was merely being more honest than many others.

★ ★ ★

MPs sometimes vote in both lobbies as a way of correcting an initial vote cast in error, rushing back through the other lobby once they realise their mistake. For example, in November 2001, two Labour MPs, Martyn Jones and Mark Tami, turned up early to vote on the issue of religious hatred offences during the committee stage of the Anti-Terrorism, Crime and Security Bill. One of the whips indicated to them that the government line was to vote no, and so the MPs did as instructed. Only after voting did they realise that the whip had made a mistake, and that the party line was to vote aye. So back through the aye lobby they went, to cancel out the whip's mistake.

But MPs also vote twice in order to register an abstention. The procedures of the House of Commons give MPs just two formal options: to vote aye or no on whatever question is before them. MPs occasionally get around this by voting in both lobbies. This practice – which has been deprecated by the Speaker[4] – is known by some Labour MPs as a 'Skinner abstention', after the veteran Labour MP Dennis Skinner. It is a curious nomenclature. Skinner is by inclination not the abstaining type – and (as far as I am aware) has never voted in both lobbies to register an abstention. It would be much more sensible to call them 'Taylor abstentions' after the Labour MP for North West Leicestershire, David Taylor, who began to engage in the practice fairly regularly during the 2001 Parliament as a way of casting what he called a 'positive abstention'. 'Otherwise, there is no way of recording that you have mixed feelings about a Bill.'

Because the Commons does not allow MPs to register abstentions – other than by voting twice – it is not possible to read anything into absences from the division lobbies. The whips may have formally sanctioned an absence from a vote; it may be accidental; or it may be deliberate. There is no information on the record that allows us to establish, at least not systematically at any rate, the causes of absences. As a result, all the figures referred to in this book are to dissenting votes; such figures should therefore be taken as the minimum number of occasions on which an MP has defied the whip.

# Appendix 3

## Major parliamentary rebellions, 2001–05

**First session, 6 June 2001–7 November 2002**
**16 July 2001**. Forty Labour MPs opposed the curtailment of debate on the nominations to select committees (Division 25).
**21 November 2001**. Fifteen Labour MPs voted against an order opting out of Article 5 of the European Convention on Human Rights, preventing detention without trial. The debate was held on 19 November, with the House voting two days later using a deferred division (Division 70).

Fifteen Labour MPs voted against a timetable motion that brought debate on the committee stage of the Anti-Terrorism, Crime and Security Bill to a conclusion at 11 p.m. on the second allotted day (Division 71), and 32 Labour MPs then voted against preventing judicial review of the Home Secretary's decisions to detain terrorist suspects without trial (Division 77).
**26 November 2001**. Twenty-one Labour MPs voted against clause 38 of the Anti-Terrorism, Crime and Security Bill, creating a new offence of incitement to religious hatred (Division 80).
**12 December 2001**. During the Lords amendment stage of the Anti-Terrorism, Crime and Security Bill, 21 Labour backbenchers voted against government amendments that failed to meet the Lords' demand for judicial review of the Home Secretary's power to detain terrorist suspects indefinitely without trial (Division 108); and 27 Labour MPs voted against the government's decision to overturn the Lords' attempt to remove the new offence of incitement to religious hatred (Division 109).
**15 January 2002**. During the report stage of the National Health Service Reform and Health Care Professions Bill, 26

Labour MPs supported a new clause in the name of David Hinchliffe, the chairman of the Health Select Committee, that sought to establish patients' councils to oversee the government's new forums (Division 131).

**6 February 2002**. During the report stage of the Education Bill, 46 Labour MPs supported a new clause in the name of Frank Dobson, the former health secretary, that would have obliged all faith schools to admit 25 per cent of their pupils from families of other faiths or no faiths, and would have made it illegal for new faith schools to require children or parents to attend religious services as part of their admissions procedures (Division 157). Forty-one Labour MPs then supported a Liberal Democrat clause that required all new religious schools to admit 25 per cent of their pupils from families of other faiths or no faiths (Division 158). Nineteen Labour backbenchers then supported a Liberal Democrat attempt to abolish selection by aptitude as introduced by the government in the School Standards and Framework Act 1998 (Division 159).

**23 April 2002**. In the largest Liberal Democrat rebellion of the 2001 parliament, fifteen Liberal Democrat MPs voted against the introduction of an aggregates levy (Division 218).

**11 June 2002**. During the report stage of the Nationality, Immigration and Asylum Bill, sixteen Labour MPs opposed a clause which dealt with appeals from within the UK for claimants with unfounded human rights or asylum claims (Division 264); eighteen Labour backbenchers then opposed a clause which removed the right of appeal for unsuccessful asylum claimants in certain circumstances and set out the procedures for their removal from the United Kingdom (Division 265).

**13 June 2002**. During the report stage of the Enterprise Bill, 24 Labour MPs supported an amendment in the name of Harry Barnes that would have required the Office of Fair Trading to take into consideration potentially 'damaging effects to the public interest', such as job losses, before agreeing to mergers and takeovers between private companies (Division 273).

**24 September 2002**. Following the recall of Parliament 56 Labour MPs voted against the adjournment of the House on the issue of possible British military action against Iraq (Division 319).

**30 October 2002**. Fifteen Labour backbenchers supported a second attempt by Harry Barnes, this time after the Enterprise Bill had come back from the Lords, to insert into the Bill a requirement on the Office of Fair Trading to take into account 'the legitimate interests of the balance of distribution of industry and employment' when considering whether mergers and acquisitions were in the public interest (Division 344).

**4 November 2002**. Eight Conservative backbenchers defied their whip to vote in favour of an amendment to the Lords amendment stage of the Adoption and Children Bill that would have allowed unmarried couples to adopt (Division 345).

**5 November 2002**. Forty-two Labour MPs supported a House of Lords amendment to the Nationality, Immigration and Asylum Bill which would have ensured that children of asylum-seekers were not educated in accommodation centres if a place was available in an appropriate mainstream school (Division 347).

**Second session, 13 November 2002–20 November 2003**
**25 November 2002**. In the first government backbench rebellion of the new session, 30 Labour backbenchers voted for a Liberal Democrat amendment which would have required both a UN mandate for military action and a vote in the House of Commons on whether or not to go to war in Iraq (Division 6).

**22 January 2003**. Forty-four Labour backbenchers used an adjournment debate on 'Defence in the World' to express their opposition to the government's policy on Iraq (Division 59).

**26 February 2003**. One hundred and twenty-one Labour MPs voted in favour of an amendment moved by the former culture secretary, Chris Smith, arguing that the case for military action against Iraq was 'as yet unproven' (Division 96). Fourteen Conservative MPs also defied their whip to vote for Smith's amendment. Sixty Labour backbenchers also opposed the government's motion, which backed United Nations efforts to disarm Saddam Hussein, but which did not even mention the possibility of war (Division 97).

**10 March 2003**. During the report stage of the Local Government Bill, seventeen Labour MPs objected to the Bain review's linkage between reform of the fire service and the ongoing negotiations on fire-fighters' pay (Division 110).

**18 March 2003**. In the largest government backbench rebellion since the Corn Laws, 139 Labour MPs supported an amendment moved by Chris Smith which argued that 'the case for war against Iraq has not yet been established, especially given the absence of specific United Nations authorisation,' but nonetheless pledged 'total support for the British forces engaged in the Middle East' (Division 117). Sixteen Conservative backbenchers also voted for the amendment. Eighty-four Labour backbenchers then also opposed the government's motion, which offered support to troops in the Gulf, blamed the French government for blocking moves to a new UN resolution and cited legal advice authorising war, and stated that the government should 'use all means necessary' to disarm Saddam Hussein (Division 118).

**2 April 2003**. During the report stage of the Criminal Justice Bill, fifteen Labour backbenchers supported a Liberal Democrat amendment that would have excised a clause allowing a defendant's previous bad character being admissible in court (Division 158). Thirty Labour MPs then voted in favour of an amendment in the name of Vera Baird that sought to prevent a defendant's bad character being admissible if the evidence was for an offence of the same description or the same category as the one with which he or she was charged (Division 159).

**7 May 2003**. Sixty-five Labour MPs voted in favour of a Labour backbench reasoned amendment in the name of David Hinchliffe declining to give the Health and Social Care (Community and Health Standards) Bill a second reading because of their opposition to the introduction of foundation hospitals (Division 177); 31 Labour MPs then voted against the second reading of the Bill (Division 178).

**8 May 2003**. Twenty-seven Labour MPs voted against the second reading of the Fire Services Bill, which sought to impose a settlement on the long-running fire-fighters' dispute (Division 180).

**19 May 2003**. During the report stage of the Criminal Justice Bill, 33 Labour MPs supported a Conservative frontbench amendment to remove Clause 37, which would have removed trial by jury in certain serious fraud cases (Division 205); 33 Labour MPs then backed another Conservative frontbench amendment to remove Clause 38, another clause relating to the removal of trial by jury (Division 206).

**3 June 2003**. Twenty-seven Labour backbenchers voted against the third reading of the Fire Services Bill (Division 216).

**8 July 2003**. Sixty-two Labour MPs supported a report stage amendment to the Health and Social Care (Community Health and Standards) Bill, removing the foundation hospital clauses from the Bill (Division 280). The government's majority fell to just 35.

**9 July 2003**. Fifteen Labour MPs opposed a government motion welcoming the draft constitution treaty produced by the Convention on the Future of Europe (Division 286).

**12 November 2003**. During the Lords amendment stage of the Fire Services Bill, 41 Labour backbenchers supported an amendment in the name of John McDonnell that would have ensured that the Fire Brigades' Union was permitted in law to take industrial action if it objected to a direction given to the fire service by the government (Division 360).

**18 November 2003**. During the Lords amendment stage of the Criminal Justice Bill, 26 Labour MPs supported the Lords in their attempt to strike out a clause abandoning trial by jury in certain complex or lengthy trials (Division 371). Twenty-eight Labour MPs then supported the Lords in their efforts to strike out another clause from the Bill, removing the right to trial by jury in certain cases (Division 372). And nineteen Labour back-benchers supported a Lords amendment to the Bill limiting applications by the prosecution for a trial to be conducted without a jury to cases where there was an 'overwhelming risk' that a fair trial could not take place because of the danger of jury-tampering (Division 373).

**19 November 2003**. Sixty-one Labour backbenchers voted to remove the foundation hospital clauses from the Health and Social Care (Community Health and Standards) Bill, this time reducing the government's majority to just seventeen (Division 381); seventeen Labour MPs voted against the government over the duties of the regulator (Division 382); and nineteen Labour backbenchers supported the Lords' second attempt to strike out a clause removing trial by jury during the final stages of the Criminal Justice Bill (Division 385).

## Third session, 26 November 2003–18 November 2004

**17 December 2003**. Twenty-five Labour MPs supported a reasoned amendment in the name of Neil Gerrard opposing the Asylum and Immigration (Treatment of Claimants etc.) Bill 'because it contains provisions that would make children destitute' (Division 16); and nineteen Labour backbenchers then voted against its second reading (Division 17).

**27 January 2004**. Seventy-two Labour backbenchers opposed the second reading of the Higher Education Bill, which introduced top-up fees. The government's majority was reduced to just five, the lowest since Labour came to power in 1997 (Division 38).

**1 March 2004**. During the report stage of the Asylum and Immigration (Treatment of Claimants etc.) Bill, 28 Labour MPs supported a new clause in the name of Neil Gerrard calling for the repeal of Section 55 of the Nationality, Immigration and Asylum Act 2002, relating to the refusal of financial support for parents of destitute children taken into care (Division 62).

Thirty-four Labour backbenchers then supported a Liberal Democrat amendment that sought to leave out Clause 11, which removed any judicial oversight of the asylum appeals process (Division 63), and 27 Labour backbenchers supported another amendment in the name of Neil Gerrard that would have had the same effect as his earlier amendment, to repeal Section 55 of the Nationality, Immigration and Asylum Act 2002 (Division 65).

**31 March 2004**. During the report stage of the Higher Education Bill, 54 Labour MPs supported an amendment in the name of Ian Gibson that would have removed the clauses relating to variability of top-up fees from the Bill (Division 123); and eighteen Labour backbenchers then opposed the Bill's third reading (Division 125).

**28 June 2004**. During the report stage of the Human Tissue Bill, nineteen Labour MPs supported a new clause in the name of Liberal Democrat MP Evan Harris that would have made organ donation automatic unless someone had previously registered their objections, a practice known as 'presumed consent' (Division 208).

**20 July 2004**. Thirty-two Labour backbenchers unsuccessfully moved a closure motion after a debate on the Butler report into British intelligence failings in relation to weapons of mass destruction in Iraq (Division 234).

**1 November 2004**. Thirty Labour MPs opposed the second reading of the Gambling Bill (Division 297).

**2 November 2004**. Forty-nine Labour MPs supported an amendment to the report stage of the Children Bill in the name of David Hinchliffe, the chairman of the Health Select Committee, that would have outlawed the physical chastisement of a child on the grounds that it constituted reasonable punishment (Division 305).

**8 November 2004**. Twenty-six Labour MPs supported a Lords amendment to the Housing Bill that would have placed an obligation on the secretary of state in charge of housing to take reasonable steps to ensure an increase of at least 20 per cent in residential energy efficiency by 2010 (Division 311); sixteen Labour backbenchers backed a clause inserted by the Lords that would have required the secretary of state to ensure that all existing social housing stock should achieve an energy efficiency rating according to the government's standard assessment procedure by 2016 (Division 313).

### Fourth Session, 23 November 2004–7 April 2005

**14 December 2004**. During the report stage of the Mental Capacity Bill, 34 Labour backbenchers supported a cross-party amendment in the name of Iain Duncan Smith, the former Tory leader, that would have prevented doctors taking any action that would hasten the end to a person's life (Division 11); 33 Labour backbenchers then supported an amendment in the name of Ann Widdecombe that would have insisted that nothing in the Act authorised the withdrawal of palliative care (Division 12). Eighteen Labour backbenchers then opposed the Bill's third reading (Division 17).

**20 December 2004**. Eighteen Labour MPs supported a back-bench reasoned amendment in the name of the Conservative MP Douglas Hogg declining to support the second reading of the Identity Cards Bill (Division 23). Ten Conservative MPs also backed the amendment – and one supported the government – while the Conservative front bench abstained. Nineteen Labour MPs and ten Conservative MPs then opposed the Bill's second reading (Division 24).

**24 January 2005**. Twenty-four Labour MPs opposed the third reading of the Gambling Bill (Division 43).

**27 January 2005**. During the report stage of the Railways Bill, 29 Labour MPs supported a amendment in the name of John McDonnell that proposed that when a franchise came up for renewal, there should be a public sector comparator to enable an independent assessment to be made of whether the public or the private sector could run the better system, and that the contract should be awarded as a result of that assessment (Division 54).

**7 February 2005**. During the report stage of the Serious Organised Crime and Police Bill, 26 Labour backbenchers supported a Liberal Democrat clause that would have offered a degree of extra statutory protection for those affected when people sought to use religion to incite hatred against racial groups (Division 69). Thirty-four Labour backbenchers then supported a Liberal Democrat amendment that would have abolished the offences of blasphemy and blasphemous libel (Division 70); and 22 Labour backbenchers voted against a government clause that would have required all demonstrations due to take place in a designated area around Westminster to be notified to the Metropolitan Police Commission six days in advance (Division 74).

**10 February 2005**. Nineteen Labour MPs opposed the third reading of the Identity Cards Bill (Division 85).

**23 February 2005**. Thirty-two Labour MPs opposed the second reading of the Prevention of Terrorism Bill (Division 94).

**28 February 2005**. Twenty-six Labour MPs opposed a programme motion to the Prevention of Terrorism Bill, which ensured that both the committee and report stages of the Bill would be carried through the Commons in just one day (Division 100). During the Bill's committee stage 62 Labour MPs then supported an amendment that would have insisted upon a judge determining the restriction of liberty (non-derogatory orders) of terrorist suspects as well as those orders involving the deprivation of liberty (including house arrest) (Division 101). The rebellion saw the government's majority reduced to fourteen, the second lowest since Labour came to power in 1997. Thirty Labour MPs then voted against the Bill's third reading (Division 104).

**9 March 2005**. Seventeen Labour MPs opposed the Prevention of Terrorism Bill's third programme motion (Division 121). When the Bill returned from the Lords, 25 Labour MPs opposed a government amendment which permitted control orders to be issued if 'urgent action' was required, subject to judicial oversight within seven days (Division 122); 37 Labour backbenchers supported a Lords amendment that would have involved the Director of Public Prosecutions before control orders were made by the Home Secretary (Division 123); and 29 Labour MPs backed the Lords' insistence on 'reasonable suspicion' as opposed to the Home Secretary's preference for the 'balance of probabilities' concerning the burden of proof before control orders could be made (Division 124).

Twenty-two Labour backbenchers supported a Lords amendment calling for a review into the Bill's provisions by a committee of Privy Counsellors (Division 125); 22 Labour MPs supported a Lords amendment that would have introduced a sunset clause, ensuring that the Bill would be replaced by November 2005 (Division 126); 21 Labour MPs supported a Lords amendment that would have seen the Lord Chief Justice set the rules for control orders (Division 127); and 23 Labour backbenchers supported a Lords amendment that would have made the procedure for control orders compatible with the European Convention on Human Rights, specifically the right to a fair hearing (Division 128).

**10 March 2005**. At the beginning of a marathon sitting of Parliament to discuss the Prevention of Terrorism Bill, 28 Labour MPs backed the Lords in their insistence that 'reasonable suspicion' be required rather than the 'balance of probabilities' as the standard of proof before non-derogatory control orders could be applied (Division 131); and seventeen Labour backbenchers then supported the Lords in their insistence that a committee of Privy Counsellors review the Bill, rather than the government's preference for an independent annual review (Division 132).

Twenty-four Labour MPs supported Baroness Hayman's amendment to the Bill that introduced a sunset clause after one year (rather than the original Lords' preference of eight months) (Division 133); 23 Labour backbenchers supported the Lords' insistence that the Lord Chief Justice set the rules for control orders (Division 134); and 23 Labour MPs again backed the Lords in their insistence that 'reasonable suspicion' be required rather than the 'balance of probabilities' as the standard of proof before non-derogatory control orders could be applied (Division 135).

When the Bill returned (yet again) from the Lords, fifteen Labour backbenchers once more supported the Lords over having a committee of Privy Counsellors review the legislation (Division 136); 20 Labour MPs again supported the Lords in their insistence that a sunset clause be introduced one year after the Bill's passage (Division 137); and seventeen Labour MPs once more supported the Lords in their insistence that 'reasonable suspicion' be required rather than the 'balance of probabilities' (Division 138).

And with the Bill once more returned from the Lords, nineteen Labour MPs backed the Lords over the sunset clause (Division 140); and, for a final time, fifteen Labour MPs supported the Lords over requiring a 'reasonable suspicion' rather than the 'balance of probabilities' as the standard of proof (Division 141).

# Appendix 4

## The Conservatives

It was once famously said that the Conservative Party's secret weapon was loyalty – although when it was last in government, between 1992 and 1997, its secret weapon appeared to have deserted it. By 1993, a mere 19 per cent of the electorate saw the party as united; the percentage fell to single figures for parts of 1996. 'Not since the polls asked the question in the early 1970s has the party been so widely regarded as split,' wrote Ivor Crewe in 1996.[1] The blame for this was laid largely, though not exclusively, at the feet of the party's MPs. When the Conservatives gathered for their first party conference following defeat in the 1997 general election, speaker after speaker was cheered whenever they criticised the parliamentary party and its behaviour. It was a view with which the outgoing Prime Minister was in agreement: 'I love my party in the country,' he told his biographer, 'but I do not love my parliamentary party.'

Between 2001 and 2005, at a time when Tony Blair was having almost identical thoughts about *his* parliamentary party, with the PLP splitting frequently and deeply over almost all areas of policy, what had become of the Conservative parliamentary party? Under first Iain Duncan Smith (a former Maastricht rebel, and one of those for whom John Major definitely had little love) and then Michael Howard (a party loyalist *par excellence*),[2] how were Conservative MPs behaving?

The 2001–05 period saw some significant splits over free votes – most obviously over Lords reform (under Duncan Smith) and over moral issues (under Howard), but relatively few rebellions on whipped votes. During the 2001 Parliament, there were 1,061 occasions when the Conservative parliamentary party was whipped by its leadership. Out of these, Conservative MPs voted against their party whips on just 102 occasions (9.6 per cent): 41 times in the first session, 33 in the second session, 17 in the third and 11 in the fourth. Conservative rebellions therefore occurred at a rate of roughly one in every twelve divisions, compared to one in five for Labour. The majority of these rebellions occurred under Duncan Smith's leadership: 70 of the rebellions occurred whilst he was Conservative Party leader, during which rebellion was running at approximately one every ten votes.[3] Following Duncan Smith's defenestration, however, there were just 30 revolts, approximately one rebellion every 20 votes. Most of the rebellions were fairly small, involving a mean average of just three Conservative MPs per rebellion (the median figure is just two). Yet there were three issues that caused more significant problems; Duncan Smith's came over the Adoption and Children Bill and over Iraq; Howard's came over identity cards.

★ ★ ★

The Adoption and Children Bill began life as a fairly uncontentious piece of legislation. But during its committee stage it was amended by backbench Labour MPs to include clauses allowing adoption by unmarried couples. Although the Bill made no distinction between heterosexual or homosexual unmarried couples (and although single gay people were already able to adopt), the issue was thereafter nearly always referred to as one of 'gay adoption'. The government granted its MPs a free vote on the issue. After much discussion in shadow Cabinet the Conservatives, by contrast, decided to issue a whip, telling the party's MPs and peers to vote against the legislation. But, faced with opposition from a vocal minority of Conservative MPs, the leadership let it be known that they would allow MPs to be absent from the Commons if the issue caused them difficulties (what became known, somewhat oxymoronically, as a 'soft three-line whip').

The issue reached the floor of the Commons in May 2002 and four Conservative MPs defied their party's whip and voted in favour of the legislation. Several others, including four shadow Cabinet members, found convenient reasons to be absent from the Commons. After amendment in the Lords the Bill then returned to the Commons in November, with more damaging consequences. At the second time of asking, the numbers voting against the whip climbed to eight. A further number of Tory MPs also abstained.[4] In quantitative terms, this was not especially damaging: eight MPs constituted just 5 per cent of the parliamentary party. An equivalent rebellion from amongst the ranks of the PLP would have seen 20 Labour MPs defying their whip, and rebellions of that size were by then rarely reported. But there was an important qualitative dimension to the Conservative rebels. They included John Bercow, absent from the vote in May but who now resigned from the shadow Cabinet in order to vote and speak against the party's line. Michael Portillo and Kenneth Clarke – both of whom had stood against Duncan Smith when he won the leadership – also voted against their party whip. The other five – David Curry, Julie Kirkbride, Andrew Lansley, Andrew Mackay and Francis Maude – included four former members of the shadow Cabinet.

The following day, the newspaper headlines were, in Portillo's words, 'truly terrible'. The rebellion resulted in a renewed focus on the issue of the Conservative leadership, made even more intense when Duncan Smith held a press conference at Conservative Central Office, during which he claimed that 'for a few, last night's vote was not about adoption but an attempt to challenge my mandate to lead this party.' He then told his party that it had to 'unite or die'. Yet the split – and the subsequent crisis – was almost entirely self-inflicted and eminently avoidable. It is quite common to see occasions when one major party allows a free vote, but the other enforces a whip. But it is almost always the other way round from the Adoption and Children Bill: governments, who need to get their legislation through, often enforce a whip, even if this reveals division, whilst the opposition can allow a free vote, thus disguising any division. This is one – indeed, perhaps the only – luxury of opposition.

Writing in *The Times* (5 November 2002), Peter Riddell called Duncan Smith's decision 'both wrong and tactically inept'. It is not obvious that the first part of Riddell's complaint is valid. In many ways issuing a whip was the more logical and consistent position to take. It is difficult logically to justify dealing with these sorts of issue – so-called 'issues of conscience' – as a breed apart from other issues.[5] That is why the Liberal Democrats had (largely unnoticed) imposed a whip, believing the subject to be a human rights issue, and having included it in their 2001 manifesto. But the Liberal Democrats could do this safe in the knowledge that they were not split on the issue. The second part of Riddell's complaint was more valid. For the Conservatives, this clearly was tactically inept. To impose a three-line whip, when there was no pressing need to do so, and when it was clear that there were serious divisions within the party, was crass in the extreme. No one noticed the nineteen Labour MPs who voted with the Conservatives over adoption, nor, because of the furore, did the following day's much larger rebellion of 42 Labour MPs over asylum legislation attract much attention. All the focus was on the Tories and their internal divisions instead.

★ ★ ★

In the run-up to the war in Iraq, the Conservative front bench was extremely supportive of the government, and Conservative anti-war sentiment was confined to a minority of MPs (during the 2002/3 parliamentary session, a total of 21 Conservative MPs rebelled over the issue), but it was a vocal minority, and, just as over the Adoption and Children Bill, there was a qualitative dimension to the rebellion. The former Chancellor of the Exchequer, Kenneth Clarke, was particularly vociferous in his opposition to war, arguing during the 26 February debate that the 'revolting nature of the Iraqi regime' was not a sufficient legal basis for war. He was joined by Douglas Hogg, another former Cabinet minister, who co-sponsored the cross-party anti-war amendments, around which opposition to the war was to coalesce. The largest Conservative rebellion on Iraq came on 18 March 2003, when sixteen Conservatives joined 139 Labour MPs (and an assortment of MPs from the minor parties) in voting in favour of the anti-war amendment. Three Conservative junior frontbench spokesmen – Jonathan Sayeed (environment), Humfrey Malins (home affairs) and John Baron (health) – resigned from their frontbench positions, as John Randall had earlier resigned as a Conservative whip, in order to speak out against the war.[6]

★ ★ ★

Michael Howard's most significant backbench rebellion came over the issue of identity cards. It had been clear for a long time that there was a significant group within the Conservative parliamentary party who were opposed to ID cards. They included several MPs serving in Howard's frontbench team. Howard's shadow Home Secretary, David Davis, was also known to be an opponent. But Howard was personally in favour, having tried to introduce a similar scheme when Home Secretary, and also believed that it was important for the Conservatives not to be 'out-flanked' on law and order issues by Labour. This ruled out the party voting against the ID card Bill at its second reading.

The Conservative front bench therefore abstained in December 2004 when a reasoned amendment against the second reading of the Identity Cards Bill was moved by Hogg – but ten Conservative MPs supported Hogg's amendment. Twenty minutes later, the very same ten Conservative backbenchers voted against the Bill's second reading. Of far greater concern for the Conservative leader, however, was the fact that only 82 Conservative MPs – around half the parliamentary party – joined Howard in the aye lobby with the government. In part, a low

Conservative attendance was understandable on such votes. When the Conservative front bench elects to vote with Labour in the division lobbies, far fewer Conservative backbenchers tend to join in: Labour is already assured of victory; why help the other side to win by even bigger margin? But around 130 Conservatives would normally vote on a Bill's second reading, leaving around 50 Conservative MPs unaccounted for. Some may genuinely have had pressing engagements elsewhere, but others were deliberately absenting themselves, an action that was encouraged by the Conservative whips for those known to have difficulties with the issue.

These difficulties resurfaced at the Bill's report stage. In the largest Conservative rebellion since Iraq (and the largest under Howard's leadership), fourteen Tory backbenchers supported a Liberal Democrat amendment that would have broken the link between applications for passports and ID cards. Twelve then voted against the Bill's third reading. In total, 21 Conservatives voted against their frontbench advice during the passage of the Identity Cards Bill.[7] These figures were an under-estimation of the strength of opposition amongst the party's backbenchers. With the election so close, many opponents of ID cards were quite happy to absent themselves from the vote, especially as many doubted the Bill would have time to make it onto the statute book before the election. They were proved right – with the Bill falling when Parliament was dissolved.

★ ★ ★

A total of 74 Conservative MPs (about 45 per cent of the party) rebelled at some point between 2001 and 2005, although only ten Conservative backbenchers cast ten or more rebellious votes against the party line.

The most rebellious Conservative MP during the parliament was Douglas Hogg, who voted against the party line 38 times. Hogg, who once declared that 'every vote is a free vote,' would probably have been even more clearly out in front of the rest of the pack were it not for his boycott of deferred divisions. But it is a sign of the difference between the behaviour of Conservative and Labour MPs that even the most rebellious Conservative MP would not make it into a league table of the most rebellious Labour MPs. There were 26 Labour MPs who rebelled more often than Hogg during the same period, and Jeremy Corbyn rebelled almost four times as often. Richard Shepherd was the Conservatives' second most rebellious MP on 33 votes, with Bob Spink a clear third on 23. The top ten includes one husband-and-wife pairing (Andrew Mackay and Julie Kirkbride), and one member of the 2001 intake, Andrew Turner (along with Spink, who returned in 2001, having been first elected in 1992).

Below the top ten, there are another ten Conservative MPs who rebelled on between five and nine occasions, four who did so on four occasions and thirteen who did so on three occasions. This last group includes Andrew Hunter (but counting only those occasions before he resigned the party whip on 2 October 2002) and Robert Jackson (similarly only counting votes before he crossed the floor on 15 January 2005).[8] And below them are nineteen Tory MPs who rebelled twice and a further eighteen who did so once.

★ ★ ★

The Conservative parliamentary party was therefore not in an especially rebellious mood between 2001 and 2005. There were relatively few rebellions – fewer, for example, than there had been under William Hague[9] – and rebellion decreased after Howard took over the leadership midway through the Parliament. But this was in part because Howard was more willing to allow leeway within the parliamentary party, offering it free votes on issues where he knew it was divided and where he thought it was safe to do so. Howard's MPs were just as divided on issues relating to sexuality as Iain Duncan Smith's – but those divisions did not become anywhere near as problematic because Howard did not try to whip the parliamentary party when there was no need to do so. Even on ID cards, where Howard judged a free vote was not appropriate, the whips were willing to allow widespread absence in order to keep the level of overt rebellion to a minimum. The days when the Conservative parliamentary party's behaviour drove party leaders to distraction have gone – but they can still give them a few headaches from time to time.

# Appendix 5

## The Liberal Democrats

Studies of backbench behaviour used largely to ignore the third party – on the not entirely unreasonable grounds that there wasn't all that much to study. When you could fit the entire Liberal parliamentary party into a taxi cab, it was a little difficult to have a sensible discussion about its cohesion. If only one of them voted, was he (and it was almost always a he) rebelling – or was he just the only one who'd turned up that night? Even at the height of the SDP–Liberal Alliance – at the end of the 1979 parliament, when their ranks were bolstered by more than 30 defections from Labour – Alliance MPs accounted for just 6 per cent of the House of Commons. But then, first in 1997 when 46 were elected, and then in even greater numbers in 2001, when the Liberal Democrats won 52 seats (rising to 55 as a result of a defection from Labour and by-elections), the party became big enough both to warrant, and to facilitate, study.[1]

That said, there's not all that much to report. Liberal Democrat cohesion on whipped votes is astonishing. During the whole of the 2001 Parliament, there were 1,072 occasions when the Liberal Democrat parliamentary party was whipped. Out of these, Liberal Democrat MPs voted against their party whips on just 45 (4 per cent): twelve in the first session, seventeen in the second session, eleven in the third and just five in the fourth. That meant that fewer than one in 25 divisions saw a Liberal Democrat rebellion – however small – compared with around one in twelve for the Conservatives and one in five for Labour. Or put another way, there were more rebellions by Labour MPs in every single session of the 2001 Parliament than there were by Liberal Democrat MPs in the entire Parliament.

Moreover, most of the revolts were fairly small. They involved a mean average of just two Liberal Democrat MPs per rebellion (the median figure is just one). The largest revolt occurred during the Budget resolutions in April 2002, when fifteen Liberal Democrat MPs voted against the aggregates levy. Those fifteen MPs constituted 28 per cent of the parliamentary party, as it then was. It was the largest parliamentary rebellion in the history of the Liberal Democrats – although this isn't saying very much.

Sixty per cent of Liberal Democrat MPs (or 33 out of 55) defied the party line between 2001 and 2005, but around half of these MPs (sixteen) rebelled against the party line only once, while a further nine did so only twice. Five Liberal Democrats – Vincent Cable, Sue Doughty, Paul Marsden, Lembit Opik, and Bob Russell – rebelled on three occasions.[2] Colin Breed was the third most rebellious Liberal Democrat MP, having dissented on five occasions. His colleague John Burnett was in second place with eight rebellious votes. But far and away the most rebellious Liberal Democrat MP was Mike Hancock, the MP for Portsmouth South, who voted against his party line on no fewer than 22 occasions between 2001 and 2005. Hancock's behaviour accounts for one-quarter of his party's dissenting votes in the whole parliament (which total just 84). Hancock preferred to vote either for or against the government when the Liberal Democrat line was to abstain, behaviour which was responsible for eight of his rebellious votes. He was the nearest thing that the Liberal Democrats had to a persistent rebel – the first since Nick Harvey, who rebelled repeatedly during the 1992 Parliament, but Harvey's differences with his party were essentially single issue (Europe), whereas Hancock's have ranged more widely. But even Hancock, rebellious as he is compared with the rest of his colleagues, wouldn't get anywhere near a list of the most rebellious Labour rebels. There are 44 Labour MPs who rebelled more often during the Parliament.

★ ★ ★

There were much more obvious divisions on free votes, most notably during the long-running saga to ban hunting with dogs. The various hunting bills introduced during the Parliament were the origins of no fewer than 31 Liberal Democrat free votes, all but one of which saw a split. At times, the splits could be astonishingly deep. On 16 November 2004, for example, during the vote on the possibility of allowing hunting to continue under a licensing system, the Liberal Democrats split right down the middle: 22 voted for the compromise amendment, 22 against.[3] (Most of those to vote for the compromise represented rural seats; most of those to vote for the all-out ban represented urban seats.) A vote on Clause 56 of the Children Bill – allowing reasonable chastisement of a child if it did not result in actual bodily harm – saw a similarly stark division, with 22 supporting its removal, 23 supporting its introduction. The Liberal Democrats also split on issues as diverse as sitting hours and gender recognition disclosure for members of the clergy.

This is hardly a new phenomenon. It has long been the case that some 'moral' issues have the potential to split the Liberal Democrats (and their precursor parties) in a way that they rarely do with the other parties.[4] In the 1997 Parliament, for example, the Liberal Democrats had split deeply on free votes over, for example, gun control, hunting (again), euthanasia, and sitting hours (again).[5] Pointing it out did, however, lead the Liberal Democrat Chief Whip to write to the *Guardian*, calling the complaint that Liberal Democrats 'sometimes' vote in different directions on free votes 'most odd'. 'Isn't that just what's supposed to happen when it's a free vote?' he asked.[6] Indeed it is – although the difference is that whereas free votes tend to cause the other parties to splinter, they can cause the Liberal Democrats to split.

# Appendix 6

## Government defeats in the House of Commons

There are three types of government defeat in the House of Commons:

1. Defeats on votes of confidence. These are motions that explicitly declare confidence in the government or motions to which the government declares confidence attaches. If defeated, the convention is that the government resigns or requests a dissolution of Parliament. The last government to be defeated on a vote of confidence was the Callaghan government on 28 March 1979.

2. Defeats on major issues of government policy. The government may then decide to resign or request a dissolution, or seek a vote of confidence from the House. The more recent historical practice has been to seek a vote of confidence from the House – as the Major government did following its defeat over the 'social protocol' of the Maastricht treaty in 1993.

3. Defeats on issues that are not deemed to be major. In these cases (the majority of government defeats in the twentieth century), the government need only decide whether to accept the defeat or to seek its de facto reversal at a later stage. No wider constitutional questions arise.

To a large extent, it is a matter for government to determine in which category a defeat falls (although the opposition can always table a motion of no confidence).

★ ★ ★

Defeats on the second reading of government Bills are extremely rare. The twentieth century saw just three – the Rent Restrictions Bill in 1924, the Reduction of Redundancy Rebates Bill in 1977 and the Shops Bill in 1986 – and none of these triggered a vote of confidence.

There would therefore have been no need for a motion of (no) confidence in the government if it had lost the second reading of the Higher Education Bill. The government could have chosen to table such a motion itself if it wished (in order to present a united front) as could have the Conservatives (in order to draw attention to the government's divisions). The government would have won any such vote easily – with Labour MPs rallying behind their leadership – but it might have been an opportunity for the leader of the opposition to emphasise the divisions within the government. That, though, would have been for the government and/or the opposition to decide. There was nothing automatic about any vote of confidence.

As explained in the text (pp. 197–198), it has been claimed that the Prime Minister planned to call a vote of confidence if the second reading vote had been lost, and that the vote would have included a sentence endorsing the government's proposals to reform higher education, forcing Labour MPs to have chosen between their opposition to variable fees and a general election. Yet passing a motion endorsing the policy would not have ensured the passage of the Higher Education Bill. That would have required a vote on the Bill itself, once the government had reintroduced it (as they would have been fully entitled to do). The tactic of attaching a vote of confidence to a motion had worked for the Major government in 1993 over the social protocol only because the social protocol vote was not part of the Maastricht Bill per se, but was instead an associated motion.

There would therefore have been nothing to stop a Labour MP voting for the vote of confidence (and giving generalised support for the government's higher education policy) but then against the reintroduced Bill. Any apparent inconsistency would be easily defensible on the grounds that the MP had been effectively blackmailed into voting for the motion. In order to ensure the passage of the Bill, therefore, the government would have needed to make the second reading of the reintroduced Bill itself a vote of confidence. Such a tactic is more risky than a generalised motion on confidence in Her Majesty's Government, as previous experience (both under John Major in 1994 and Edward Heath in 1972) is that dissident MPs will not always back the government on votes of confidence that are explicitly linked to Bills. It was this tactic in November 1994 that had led to the creation of the 'whipless' nine Conservative MPs. It was not clear that this was a happy precedent to be following.

# Notes

### Fings ain't wot they used t'be

1 Peter Osborne, 'Blair downgraded the Labour whips – and now he is paying the price', *Spectator*, 17 January 2004.

2 See, for example, the essay by John E. Owens, 'Explaining Party Cohesion and Discipline in Democratic Legislatures: Purposiveness and Contexts', *Journal of Legislative Studies*, 2003, or the articles in the rest of that special issue of the journal, 'Cohesion and Discipline in Legislatures'.

3 Hugh Berrington, 'Partisanship and Dissidence in the Nineteenth-century House of Commons', *Parliamentary Affairs*, 1967-8.

4 See A. L. Lowell, *The Government of England* (rev. ed.) (Macmillan, New York, 1926), vol. 2.

5 Published by Constable, 1967.

6 The unusual circumstances of the 2005 election – the South Staffordshire election being delayed due to the death of one of the candidates and the almost immediate by-election in Cheadle as a result of the death shortly after the general election of the incumbent MP – meant that this figure varied immediately after the election. But by the summer recess in 2005 it had settled at 66.

7 Anorak alert! The government's nominal majority (at the time of writing) was 66, which requires a minimum of 34 Labour MPs to vote with the other side to defeat it; but because the five Sinn Fein MPs do not take their seat, its effective majority is 71, which requires 36 Labour rebels. And because it is rare to see a full turnout by all opposition parties, the government's effective majority is probably slightly higher still.

8 Measured as a percentage of the parliamentary party, this rebellion remains the largest by members of the PLP when in government, larger, as a proportion of Labour's MPs, even than the Iraq rebellions of 2003.

9 The largest revolt of the parliament came when 64 Labour MPs voted against their party over the appointment of Lord Hunsdon, a prominent opponent of the General Strike, as the first Public Works Loan Commissioner.

10 This remains the highest number of consecutive rebellions by Labour MPs in one day.

11 Philip Norton, *Dissension in the House of Commons 1974–1979* (Clarendon Press, Oxford, 1980), p. 439.

12 E. Ozbudun, *Party Cohesion in Western Democracies: A Causal Analysis* (Sage, Beverly Hills, CA, 1970), p. 316.

**It's bit more complicated than that**

1 Peter Jones, 'Members of Parliament and Issues of Conscience', in Peter Jones (ed.), *Party, Parliament and Personality*, (Routledge, London, 1995), p. 141.

2 Most of the media attention concentrated on the unusual (though not unique) fact that the three party leaders had all voted on the losing side. But the truly remarkable feature of the vote was the Prime Minister's isolation from the rest of his party. Answers on a postcard: when was the last time a party leader of one of the major parties, let alone a Prime Minister, was so detached from the majority of his or her party? This author cannot think of an occasion in the postwar period when a PM has been so isolated.

3 See especially Appendix 5 on the Liberal Democrats.

4 Sidney Low, *The Governance of England*, (T. Fisher Unwin, London, 1927), p. 119.

5 J. Richard Piper, 'Backbench Rebellion, Party Government, and Consensus Politics: The Case of the Parliamentary Labour Party 1966–70', *Parliamentary Affairs*, 1974.

6 There is a second category of vote, deferred divisions, which are conducted through the collection of ballot papers on Wednesday afternoons. Introduced as part of Labour's 'modernisation' of the Commons, they are now rarely used.

7 The overall number of divisions in any postwar Parliament has varied from that of February 1974, which saw just 109 divisions to that of 1987 (the postwar record) with 1,597.

8 Hugh Berrington, 'Partisanship and Dissidence in the Nineteenth-century House of Commons', *Parliamentary Affairs*, 1967–8.

9 Paul Flynn, *Commons Knowledge*, (Seren, Bridgend, 1997), p. 16.

10 Iain Maclean, Arthur Spirling and Meg Russell, 'None of the Above: The UK House of Commons Votes on Reforming the House of Lords', *Political Quarterly*, 2003.

11 Jeremy Paxman, *The Political Animal*, (Penguin, London, 2003), p. 165.

12 'The "attack poodle" bites back', thisisthenortheast.co.uk, 15 February 2002.

13 Donald D. Searing, *Westminster's World: Understanding Political Roles*, (Harvard University Press, Cambridge, MA, 1994).

14 Tim Renton, *Chief Whip: People, Power and Patronage in Westminster* (Politico's, London, 2004), p. 324.

15 Philip Norton, *Conservative Dissidents* (Temple Smith, London, 1978), p. 168.

16 Renton, *Chief Whip*, pp. 20–21.

17 'It's just good people management,' said a whip wryly. 'If someone needs to be away somewhere, and you can help him, it'd be silly not to let him.'

18 Searing, *Westminster's World*, p. 256.

19 Philip Ziegler, *Wilson: The Authorised Life* (Weidenfeld and Nicolson, London, 1993), p. 248.

20 Teresa Gorman, *No, Prime Minister!* (Blake Publishing, London, 2001), pp. 3–6.

21 See for example, Philip Norton and David M. Wood, *Back From Westminster: British Members of Parliament and Their Constituents* (University of Kentucky Press, Lexington, 1993).

22 See for example, Greg Power, *Representatives of the People?: The Constituency Role of MPs* (Fabian Society, London, 1998).

23 The third of the city's MPs being a whip at the time.

24 For the record, he held his seat in 2005.

25 An over-estimate by 11 percentage points – but who's counting?

26 Woodrow Wyatt, *Turn Again, Westminster* (Andre Deutsch, London, 1973), p. 100.

## Of sheep and men

1 Philip Cowley and Philip Norton with Mark Stuart and Matthew Bailey, *Blair's Bastards* (Centre for Legislative Studies, Hull, 1996).

2 Steve Richards, 'In search of cracks on tax', *New Statesman*, 26 July 1996.

3 Tony Blair, speech to the PLP, Church House, London, 7 May 1997.

4 'If control freakery means strong leadership, then I plead guilty', *Independent*, 20 November 1998.

5 S. H. Beer, *Modern British Politics* (Faber and Faber, London, 1969), pp. 350–1.

6 This chapter summarises material from Philip Cowley, *Revolts and Rebellions: Parliamentary Voting under Blair* (Politico's, London, 2002).

7 Andrew Rawnsley, *Servants of the People* (Hamish Hamilton, London, 2000), p. 114.

8 One junior minister, plus three PPSs.

9 Rawnsley, *Servants of the People*, p. 113.

10 Hugh Berrington, 'Partisanship and Dissidence in the Nineteenth Century House of Commons', *Parliamentary Affairs*, 1967–8.

11 *Guardian*, 3 November 2000.

12 Abstainers numbered between 14 and 20 Labour MPs.

13 *Observer*, 2 May 1999.

14 When we control for the size of the respective parliamentary parties, the 1997 Parliament comes fourth, sharing that position with the Parliament of 1950.

15 See Sarah Childs, *New Labour's Women MPs: Women Representing Women*, (Routledge, London, 2004), esp. Ch. 1.

16 Anne Perkins, 'Women: so far, so what?', *Guardian*, 29 April 1999.

17 A handful of others abstained.

18 *Sunday Times*, 4 October 1998.

19 See, for example, Philip Cowley and Sarah Childs, 'Too Spineless to Rebel? New Labour's Women MPs', *British Journal of Political Science*, 2003.

20 Most of these dissenting votes were cast on one Bill, the Prevention of Terrorism Bill in the final session of the Parliament. But she had also voted against the government twice over the Housing Bill in the previous session; her rebellion therefore was not something unique to the one issue.

21 There is some evidence that their lower rates of rebellion helped them achieve slightly higher rates of promotion. See Philip Cowley, 'The well-behaved get office', *New Statesman*, 14 June 2004.

## Saint Gwyneth and the Grand Old Duke of York

1 Gwyneth Dunwoody, 'The government's abuse of Parliament must now end', *Independent*, 18 July 2001.

2 Robin Cook noted in his diary that 'all hell had broken loose'. Robin Cook, *The Point of Departure* (Simon and Schuster, London, 2003), p. 20.

3 In the words of one whip, the outcome of the votes 'was not a failure of whipping but a consequence of not whipping'.

4 In the event, there does appear to have been an informal payroll vote in operation; only one member of the payroll voted against the proposals (Colin Pickthall, Jack Straw's PPS). But Pickthall's presence indicates that that was not enforced, and several other ministers – including the Leader of the House – abstained.

5 Cook, *Point of Departure*, pp. 20–1.

6 All figures include tellers. Hansard records Oona King as having voted in both lobbies.

7 Although it was to be Anderson's committee which interviewed the MoD scientist Dr David Kelly and concluded, entirely erroneously as it turned out, that he was not the source for Andrew Gilligan's claims about the 'sexing up' of the government's Iraq dossier.

8 The Prime Minister's questioners included several MPs not normally known for their rebelliousness. Peter Pike, for example, made it clear that he expected to see improvements in his local council estates; Debra Shipley made a similar point about her local hospitals. Neither Pike nor Shipley had voted against the government between 1997 and 2001, but both were to do so between 2001 and 2005.

9 The only rebellion comprising more than ten MPs came immediately prior to the votes on select committee membership, when there was a whipped vote against the government's plan to curtail the debate; some 40 Labour MPs defied their whip to vote for the debate to continue.

10 Stephen Pollard, *David Blunkett* (Hodder and Stoughton, London, 2005), p. 276.

11 Frank Johnson, 'Muesli-eaters fail to have Blunkett for breakfast', *Daily Telegraph*, 20 November 2001.

12 The final vote on derogation was taken two days after the debate, in a deferred division.

13 Pollard, *David Blunkett*, p. 276.

14 Just nine Labour MPs went on to back a new Conservative clause that would have applied sunset clauses to other parts of the Bill.

15 This was widely reported as 23, but this was because two Labour MPs voted in the wrong lobby by mistake and then, to cancel out their mistake, both voted in the other lobby as well (see p. 262).

16 The 2002/3 session alone saw 88 defeats, more than there had been in any one session since 1975/6.

17 Philip Norton, 'Cohesion without Discipline: Party Voting in the House of Lords', *Journal of Legislative Studies*, 2003. Direct comparison is problematic – since peers are able to absent themselves from votes where they have a disagreement far more easily than MPs – but, however you slice the data,

there is absolutely no evidence that the parliamentary parties in the Lords are less cohesive than those in the Commons.

18 In effect the SIAC was turned into a part of the High Court, with all the powers that would otherwise pertain to a High Court, but with security procedures in place so that sensitive information provided by the security services could not be disclosed.

19 Pollard, *David Blunkett*, p. 276.

20 Pollard, *David Blunkett*, pp. 277–8.

21 Cm. 5291.

22 The original proposal had been for a mere 11 per cent, but the figure had been raised to 20 per cent during discussions in Cabinet committee.

23 See her article 'Second thoughts on the second chamber', *The Times*, 1 November 2001.

24 Cook, *Point of Departure*, p. 77. Although he attributes the idea to Russell in his diary entry of 9 January, on 14 November 2001 Cook's diary also records him as having the idea in a conversation with Jean Corston, the chair of the PLP (ibid., p. 54).

25 Cook, *Point of Departure*, p. 78.

26 In a note circulated with the findings, the MPs said, 'While we should not pretend under any circumstances that this is the precise "centre of gravity" that Robin Cook referred to in the parliamentary debate – we can honestly claim that it is the first serious attempt to locate it and gives a reasonable steer to those trying to find a percentage which could command a consensus . . . If a figure in this area [58 per cent] is proposed by the Prime Minister, is properly campaigned and supported by the payroll vote I believe the vast bulk of the PLP would unify behind it.'

27 Both letters from 23 October 2003.

28 Again, in the *Mail on Sunday*. 'He had his arm across my throat . . . he'd lost it', *Mail on Sunday*, 9 December 2001.

29 Catherine Bennett, *Guardian*, 27 November 2003.

### The Mother of All Rebellions

1 Robin Cook, *The Point of Departure* (Simon and Schuster, London, 2003), p. 203.

2 Fifty-three voted no, along with two tellers for the noes, and – in order to ensure a vote – one acted as a teller for the ayes.

3 The government would dispute almost every part of this sentence, arguing both that there was a UN resolution authorising war (which is what it argued Resolution 1441 was) and that there was widespread international support for military action, with the 'coalition of the willing' numbering 50 countries, including Australia, Italy and Spain. Opponents retorted that 1441 wasn't sufficient in their view, and that the coalition wasn't broad enough.

4 Philip Cowley, *Revolts and Rebellions: Parliamentary Voting under Blair* (Politico's, London, 2002), pp. 44–6.

5 For example, just after the first mammoth Iraq revolt in February 2003, the 'comedian' Mark Thomas wrote in the *New Statesman* that he 'didn't realise that there were 122 spines in the PLP'. But the rebellions in the previous

session, 2001/2, had involved a total of 122 Labour MPs, exactly the same number as were to back the rebel amendment in February 2003.

6 For what it's worth, one cynical MP argued that 'MPs always lie about their post . . . No one ever knows. It's just standard practice. If you want to discredit something, then you say, "Well, I've not had a single letter about this." Although it's better to say you've just had one, because otherwise you can get caught out. And if you want to build something up, then you say, "I'm getting inundated with post over this."' 'So,' I said, 'have you been lying to me?' 'Oh no,' he said, 'I'm different.'

7 Roy Hattersley, 'The days of unquestioning obedience are over', *Observer*, 2 March 2003.

8 Joe Ashton, 'Why so many Labour MPs rebelled', letter to the editor, *The Times*, 1 March 2003.

9 Cook, *Point of Departure*, p. 252.

10 Although Straw did not promise that such a vote would necessarily occur *before* military engagement, on the grounds that there might be circumstances where the safety of British forces required the element of surprise.

11 Two Labour MPs were recorded as having voted twice.

12 Forty-two Labour MPs voted in the aye lobby, with a further two Labour backbenchers acting as tellers for the noes, in order to ensure a division.

13 Sixty Labour MPs also supported Tony Wright's EDM 733, demanding 'an unequivocal confirmation' that any British military action would require the prior approval by a vote in the House of Commons. All but eight of the 60 had also already rebelled and/or signed another anti-war EDM. With these eight included, therefore, 156 Labour MPs had expressed publicly some anti-war sentiment even before the votes in February and March.

14 John Kampfner claims that Blair's party fixer, Sally Morgan, had been expecting the revolt to be 'a little higher' than the one in September 2002, 'perhaps up to eighty or ninety at most', and that Blair himself thought he could reduce the rebellion to around 50 (John Kampfner, *Blair's Wars* (Free Press, London, 2003), p. 277). Those closer to the pulse of the PLP were not quite so confident – nor as wrong.

15 For a fuller exposition of Smith's case against war, see Chris Smith, 'No, it's not right to invade', *Independent*, 6 March 2003.

16 Reed was a PPS, and was therefore tied into the notion of collective responsibility, expected to back the government in the division lobbies. Normally he would have been sacked immediately. It was sign of the difficulties that the government were in that he was allowed to remain in post for a few days, before he resigned. 'It was an exceptional circumstance,' one whip admitted.

17 Chris Buckland, 'Order! Order!: Why PM's so calm before desert storm', *News of the World*, 2 March 2003.

18 *Sunday Times*, 9 March 2003.

19 Peter Stothard, *30 Days: A Month at the Heart of Blair's War* (HarperCollins, London, 2003), p. 88, also pp. 93–5.

20 Kampfner, *Blair's Wars*, p. 307.

21 Philip Norton, 'The Organization of Parliamentary Parties', in S. A.

Walkland (ed.), *The House of Commons in the Twentieth Century* (Clarendon Press, Oxford, 1979), p. 21.

22 The Campaign Group became so disgruntled with PLP meetings that it organised a rota of its members to attend, so that only one person would have to suffer but they could at least find out what was going on; one group member described it as 'the victims' rota'.

23 Robin Cook, 'Why I had to leave the Cabinet', *Guardian*, 18 March 2003.

24 They included Anne Begg, who had abstained over the amendment, but who voted against the government's motion – the only Labour MP to vote in this way.

25 When he was writing his disgruntled Labour supporter's critique of the Blair government, *So Now Who Do We Vote For?*, the author John Harris contacted Skinner to find out why he had not taken part in the Iraq revolt. Skinner replied that he has been 'lying in the Brompton Hospital having heart surgery', adding for good measure, 'I voted against bombing Iraq when Mr Almighty Bloody Pure Virgin Robin Cook was the Foreign Secretary.' John Harris, *So Now Who Do We Vote For?* (Faber and Faber, London, 2005), p. 170.

26 The MP replied, 'It's about the issue.'

27 From a piece from his website (www.austinmitchell.org) entitled 'War diary – Pvt Austin Mitchell (Grimsby Sappers)' and subtitled 'Written at an undisclosed location behind the lines. Subject to military censorship by Brigadier Lazarus Mandelson (Cashiered), recalled to national service from editing the *Hartlepool Sycophant*'.

28 Paul Waugh, '40 Labour MPs call for Blair to resign', *Independent*, 12 March 2003.

29 Randeep Ramesh (ed.), *The War We Could Not Stop* (Faber and Faber, London, 2003), p. 50.

30 Mary Ann Sieghart, 'How Chirac and the Left saved the PM's skin', *The Times*, 14 March 2003.

31 It was almost responsible for adding more new rebels than any other issue in Blair's premiership – although the rebellion over lone parent benefit in December 1997 just tops it. Being the first major rebellion of the government gives it a bit of an advantage.

32 Tam Dalyell, 'Blair, the war criminal', *Guardian*, 27 March 2003. Although less vociferous, anti-war Labour MPs were not entirely silent on the conduct of the war. Sixty-two Labour MPs signed an EDM calling for a ban on the use of cluster bombs; 65 signed another EDM calling on the government to publish all the available evidence to prove that Parliament had not been misled over claims about Iraq's 'alleged possession of, and intention to use, weapons of mass destruction'.

33 On 4 June 2003, a Liberal Democrat opposition day motion calling for an independent inquiry into the handling of intelligence on weapons of mass destruction attracted eleven Labour rebels; a Conservative opposition day motion on 16 July, also demanding a full independent inquiry, yielded eight. On 10 September 2003, another Liberal Democrat motion – this time

dealing with the role of the United Nations in Iraq – was supported by only one Labour MP; on 9 March 2004, four Labour MPs supported an opposition day motion, co-sponsored by Plaid Cymru and the SNP, that all advice prepared by the Attorney General on the legality of the war in Iraq should be published, and eight backed another Liberal Democrat opposition day motion in May 2004.

### Sedgefield privatisers and Darlington money-changers

1 Anthony King et al, 'Modes of Executive–Legislative Relations', *Legislative Studies Quarterly*, 1976. The over-the-shoulder quote is from his 'Implications of One-Party Government', in Anthony King et al, *Britain at the Polls 1992* (Chatham House, Chatham, NJ, 1993).

2 Douglas Hurd, 'The Present Usefulness of the House of Commons', *Journal of Legislative Studies*, 1997.

3 See Alan Milburn, 'We have to give the voters more than this', *The Times*, 7 August 2002.

4 A subject that is discussed in more detail in Philip Cowley, *Revolts and Rebellions: Parliamentary Voting under Blair* (Politico's, London, 2002), ch. 8, and especially Philip Norton, 'The Organization of Parliamentary Parties', in S. A. Walkland (ed.), *The House of Commons in the Twentieth Century* (Clarendon Press, Oxford, 1979).

5 See Christopher Garner and Natalia Letki, 'Party Structure and Backbench Dissent in the Canadian and British Parliaments', *Canadian Journal of Political Science*, 2005, which explains the difference between the levels of cohesion displayed by the Canadian Liberals and British Labour MPs largely on the basis of the much better involvement in policy formation enjoyed by the former. Canadian MPs feel involved and thus don't rebel. British MPs don't – and therefore do.

6 The Brownite version of events is well explained in Robert Peston, *Brown's Britain* (Short Books, London, 2005), esp. pp. 295–308.

7 He also repeated his earlier insistence that 'to borrow off balance sheet would eventually become a request on the Treasury, because it would not be possible for us to allow that hospital to go bankrupt.'

8 The only saving grace for the government was that the committee rejected earlier claims that foundation hospitals would create a two-tier NHS: 'We believe the two-tier claims originate from an overly simplistic argument which fails to recognise that, despite the best of efforts, the NHS is a multiple-tier service.'

9 The figure includes two rebel tellers.

10 'Pym's Law', editorial, *The Times*, 8 May 2003.

11 Peter Oborne, *The Rise of Political Lying* (Free Press, London, 2005), pp. 140–8.

12 It's not that Milburn didn't try – just that identical arguments had less impact when they came from him than from Reid. Ian McCartney's article in December 2002 was a good example of a pre-Reid attempt to sell the legislation: 'Keep your nerve: this is the rebirth of popular socialism', *Guardian*, 2 December 2002.

**The Rebels**

13 Jackie Storer, 'Citizen Reid tries to woo popular front', BBC News Online, 1 October 2003.

14 *Guardian*, 17 November 2003.

15 John Reid, 'It's Labour's rebels who block choice', *Guardian*, 19 November 2003.

16 This was widely reported as the lowest majority the government had endured since 1997, although the government's majority had previously fallen to just 25 in February 1999, albeit not as a result of a rebellion (see p. 59).

17 Frank Dobson, 'Health is now Blair's second front', *Guardian*, 14 March 2003.

18 Polly Toynbee, 'The rebels have won', *Guardian*, 2 May 2003.

19 In the event, 156 out of the 165 Conservative MPs voted in the no lobby, up from the 130 Conservatives who had voted in the July rebellion on foundation hospitals.

20 Letter and accompanying briefing paper from John Reid MP to Labour MPs, 17 November 2003.

21 William Miller, 'The Periphery and its Paradoxes', in Hugh Berrington (ed.), *Britain in the Nineties: The Politics of Paradox* (Frank Cass, London, 1998), p. 170.

22 It was widely reported to have happened after July's vote – when the government had sneaked in with a majority of 35 but with 41 Scottish Labour MPs voting in the government lobby. But on that occasion there were also three Scottish Labour, nine Scottish Liberal Democrat and five SNP MPs in the other lobby. The logic that argues that it is wrong for Scottish MPs to vote with the government also precludes them from opposing it. If *all* Scottish MPs had been removed from the vote in July, the government would still have won, with a majority of eight. As the Liberal Democrat Chief Whip, Andrew Stunell, pointed out, it 'was not the Scottish jackboot that forced foundation hospitals on us. It was New Labour' (*Daily Telegraph*, 12 July 2003). Nevertheless, had the vote been confined solely to English MPs (that is, not including Welsh MPs), then the government would have lost.

23 Simon Carr, 'Labour rebels without claws snatch defeat from the jaws of victory', *Independent*, 20 November 2003.

24 J. Richard Piper, 'Backbench Rebellion, Party Government, and Consensus Politics: The Case of the Parliamentary Labour Party 1966–70', *Parliamentary Affairs*, 1974, p. 385.

25 The largest of all rebellions during the Parliament, however, came over an amendment to the Justices of the Peace Bill in October 1968, when 75 Labour backbenchers rebelled.

26 There were also later rebellions on the same issue in 1969 and 1970, which saw 49 and 61 Labour MPs respectively vote against their whips.

27 Parliament First, *Parliament's Last Chance*, 2003, esp. pp. 6, 26.

28 See for example, Eric Shaw, 'New Labour: New Pathways to Parliament', *Parliamentary Affairs*, 2001.

29 This excludes by-election winners after 2001, and also Shaun Woodward, elected for the first time as a Labour MP in 2001 but who had first been

elected to the Commons in 1997 as a Conservative.

30 The figure would have been 25, since Paul Daisley, then terminally ill with cancer, was opposed to the Iraq war, but was too ill to vote.

31 See for example, Alexandra Kelso, '"Where were the massed ranks of parliamentary reformers?" – "attitudinal" and "contextual" approaches to parliamentary reform', *Journal of Legislative Studies*, 2003.

32 I am grateful to Ruth Greenwood, formerly of Hull University, for her work on the 2001 intake for this quotation.

33 Statistically significant at $p < 0.01$. The reported correlation is for just those MPs who rebelled at least once; the correlation with all the newly elected MPs is even stronger at 0.61 ($p < 0.01$).

34 $p < 0.01$. The figure for all of the 1997 intake is 0.74 ($p < 0.01$).

35 $p < 0.01$. The figure for all of the 1997 intake is 0.92 ($p < 0.01$).

36 In the very last session of the 2001 Parliament, he shared first place with Bob Marshall-Andrews.

**Not Mission Impossible but Mission Bloody Difficult**

1 Just sixteen out of the 103 MPs said that they supported the government, with seventeen saying that they were undecided.

2 Statements like this can give the impression that there were neat and precise categories of opponents. In reality, people's objections are imprecise and amorphous, sometimes overlapping, and frequently illogical. There are also MPs who fit into none of the categories. For example, the objections raised by the former Downing Street adviser Jon Cruddas, the newly elected MP for Dagenham (that there was no economic benefit to such an increase in the university population), were almost *sui generis* amongst the PLP (see, for example, his 'Cementing the class divide', *Tribune*, 7 November 2003). When Cruddas met the Chief Whip to discuss his objections, he was told, somewhat bemusedly, 'No one else has that view.' The Prime Minister's response was, 'But that's a ridiculous position.' It wasn't; it was just different.

3 Thirty-five signed an anti-fees amendment, and although that amendment was never voted on, 34 Labour backbenchers voted for a related amendment to retain maintenance grants for low-income families, along with around 15 abstentions. Of the 34, 22 were left in the Commons by the time of the top-up fees issue, the majority of whom also opposed top-up fees, seeing it, as one of them put it, as 'a matter of principle and consistency'.

4 This view was reinforced by a critical report from the Commons Education Select Committee in July 2003, claiming that capping fees at £3,000 a year would not work because too many universities would levy the maximum amount. The committee concluded that a wider range of charges, up to £5,000, would be required to create a market in higher education.

5 Robin Cook, 'Top-up fees are a gamble which can only harm the party and the Prime Minister', *Independent*, 9 January 2004.

6 Their joint paper was entitled *Excellence, Equity and Access: Squaring the Circle of Higher Education Funding*.

7 Steve Richards, 'Now Mr Blair must start to win back the support of his neglected backbenchers', *Independent*, 28 January 2004.

8 *Ambitions for Britain*, Labour Party, 2001, p. 20.

9 Martin Kettle, 'This isn't a revolt on tuition fees, it's a revolt against Blair', *Guardian*, 20 January 2004.

10 Rachel Sylvester, interview with Alan Johnson, 'We need to get rid of the rope ladder and build a staircase', *Daily Telegraph*, 6 December 2003.

11 The VCs probably controlled more votes than the whips thought. MPs with universities in their constituencies reported extensive lobbying from their vice-chancellors.

12 Despite being blindingly obvious to anyone working in the university sector, this argument was not widely appreciated on the left – although the *New Statesman* did run a series of leaders pointing out the extent to which the status quo was a quite astonishing system of working-class subsidy for middle-class kids.

13 Paul Routledge, 'Profile: Alan Johnson', *New Statesman*, 29 November 2004.

14 'Marathon charm offensive wins over rebel', *The Times*, 27 January 2004.

15 Peter Riddell, 'Top-up row puts Clarke at odds with his party', *The Times*, 9 January 2004.

16 Of the 20 Labour MPs who were absent or abstaining, all but two had signed Ian Gibson's EDM, and were known to be opposed. The other two were James Wray (who was seriously ill, but was believed to be an opponent of the legislation) and Jeff Ennis (who sat in the chamber throughout the vote, in order to abstain publicly). Three Labour women MPs – Ann Cryer, Valerie Davey and Helen Jones – also deliberately sat out the vote in the chamber. Others of the 19 have since confirmed their abstention.

17 After the vote, there were claims that some of the SDLP had backed the government in return for a deal. There was an attempt at a deal: Clarke even slipped out of the chamber to have a pint with Seamus Mallon and John Hume of the SDLP in an attempt to persuade the SDLP to vote with the government. But it failed, and all three SDLP MPs voted against the government.

18 Paul Routledge, *New Statesman*, 23 January 2004. As one of the Conservative MPs listed by Routledge said, 'in the end, I swallowed pretty hard, held my nose, and did all the other things you do when you vote with your party thinking they are doing something pretty stupid.'

19 Five days before the second reading vote, for example, the BBC published a survey of those Labour MPs who signed Ian Gibson's anti-top-up fee EDM. Excluding the 43 who refused to participate, 62 said that they would vote against the government along with three who said that they would abstain. Another eight said they would vote with the government and 16 admitted to being undecided. The day before the vote the *Guardian* listed 81 Labour backbenchers said to be voting against, and a further 11 still in doubt or probably abstaining. The *Financial Times* suggested that 78 Labour MPs were planning to vote against the Bill, with six abstaining. But these ratios of cross-votes to abstentions (20:1 in the case of the BBC, 13:1 for the *FT*, or the *Guardian*'s 7:1) were just not realistic (as this author – rather smugly – pointed out at the time). Other large Labour rebellions since 1997 had seen a ratio somewhere around the 2:1 or 3:1 mark. This made it likely that many of

those saying that they would vote against would end up abstaining.

20 Along with three Labour MPs who did not sign the EDM.

21 Cook, 'Top-up fees are a gamble'.

22 Anthony Seldon, *Blair* (Free Press, London, 2005), p. 648.

23 Moreover, if Nick Brown hadn't defected – and if the government had still been heading for a defeat by 6.30 p.m. (or 6.40 or 6.50 or whenever), then perhaps other MPs would have buckled under the pressure in order to avoid a government defeat. Who knows?

24 In part this was because the defeat was overshadowed by the fact that the same evening US aircraft bombed Libya, but even without the Libyan bombing there is no evidence that Labour intended to call for, or move, a vote of confidence.

25 Of course, opponents of the legislation would argue that removing a potentially unpopular piece of legislation would prove advantageous in electoral terms and thus helpful to the government in the long run, something which would more than compensate for any short-term cost.

26 Robert Peston, *Brown's Britain* (Short Books, London, 2005), p. 317.

27 Gibson denied that, claiming that the existing legislation (Section 26 of the Teaching and Higher Education Act 1998) would have prevented fees being raised above their present level of £1,125.

28 By the time the Bill returned from the Lords in June, the appetite for rebellion had gone; just ten Labour MPs voted to retain an amendment made by the Lords that would have abolished top-up fees after the third year of study at university, and only one – Jim Cousins – supported a second Lords amendment that would have hypothecated any income from top-up fees.

29 He is considered more quotable than just three other postwar Prime Ministers: Heath (six quotations), Douglas-Home (five) and Eden (three). Not surprisingly, Churchill tops the list with 95 separate entries.

30 One, slightly unfortunate, consequence of Major's categorisation is that those in government become known as the 'possessed'.

31 Three rebelled on exactly the same number of occasions; the rest did so less often.

32 There were, for example, 26 MPs who had rebelled during the 1997 Parliament but on fewer than ten occasions, and who went on to rebel on more than ten occasions after 2001.

33 He went on to back another seven amendments in various Bills that would have strengthened the rights of workers.

34 Gerald Kaufman, 'The genial statesman with a lethal sting', *Sunday Telegraph*, 7 August 2005.

### Pig-sticking, Lammytitis and the odour of dissolution

1 Peter Oborne, 'Blair downgraded the Labour whips – and now he is paying the price', *Spectator*, 17 January 2004.

2 The only rebellions to take place were tiny: Frank Field was the only Labour backbencher to support a Liberal Democrat amendment at the report stage; when the Bill returned from the Lords, three Labour backbenchers rebelled over the separate issue of pension annuities.

3 It is equally difficult to argue that the Hunting Bill was any or more any less urgent an issue than, say, the Sexual Offences Amendment Act.

4 The analysis of the election results by John Curtice *et al.* contained in the definitive Nuffield study (Dennis Kavanagh and David Butler, *The British General Election of 2005* (Palgrave, Basingstoke, 2005)) found that an MP's position on the Iraq war, foundation hospitals, and the Prevention of Terrorism Bill made no difference to an MP's electoral performance. Controlling for everything else that might affect an MP's electoral performance, those who voted against top-up fees appeared to have done slightly better (by about three-quarters of a percentage point) than those who didn't. Similar research by this author found something very similar – and identified just six MPs who it could be said had their electoral fortunes decided by the rebellions: three survived but might have lost had they rebelled, three lost but might have survived if they had rebelled. Geraldine Smith wasn't one of them.

5 There were six Labour revolts in all during the Bill's passage, involving a total of 26 MPs.

6 For example, in November 2004, 49 Labour MPs defied their whips to vote for an amendment that would have outlawed the physical chastisement of a child on the grounds that it constituted reasonable punishment. Labour MPs were, however, granted a free vote on a different clause, permitting reasonable chastisement of a child that did not result in actual bodily harm, referred widely in the media as allowing parents to administer 'a light tap' to their children. The government's argument was that the rebel amendment would have been unworkable – and hence the government had a duty to vote it down – whereas the second clause was a matter of preference and thus suitable for a free vote.

7 See, for example, Peter Jones, 'Members of Parliament and Issues of Conscience', in Peter Jones (ed.), *Party, Parliament and Personality*, (Routledge, London, 1995), or Philip Cowley (ed.), *Conscience and Parliament* (Frank Cass, London, 1998).

8 As one whip put it, 'you've got to give something to the Lords – they're wankers.' You won't read *that* in any constitutional law textbook.

9 The largest rebellion saw 62 Labour MPs vote against their whip, but the total number to rebel at any point in the Bill's passage was 15 greater.

10 Then, 68 Labour MPs had supported an amendment to the Criminal Law Bill that would have allowed a person held under the Prevention of Terrorism Act 1976 to inform a third party of his or her choosing of their arrest and place of detention.

11 Except in cases where a suspect was at risk of disappearing and 'urgent action' was required: such orders would, however, still be subject to judicial oversight within seven days.

12 Osborne, 'Blair downgraded the Labour whips'.

13 See Donald D. Searing, *Westminster's World: Understanding Political Roles*, (Harvard University Press, Cambridge, MA, 1994), p. 278. Also see F. M. G. Willson, 'Some Career Patterns in British Politics: Whips in the House of Commons 1906–1966', *Parliamentary Affairs*, 1970–71; Donald Searing and

Chris Game, 'Horses for Courses: The Recruitment of Whips in the British House of Commons', *British Journal of Political Science*, 1977.

14 Donald Macintyre, *Mandelson and the Making of New Labour* (HarperCollins, London, 1999), p.133. He writes it as 'koko', but it is surely 'cocoa'?

15 This includes two MPs who went on to serve as PPSs after their time in the Whips' Office, which would normally be seen as a demotion. Similarly, Nick Brown's move from Chief Whip to minister of state was also widely seen as a demotion. But even with these three excluded, more whips went on to other posts within government than went straight onto the back benches.

16 Three others who come close are Elliot Morley, who has stayed in the same department since 1997, but doing a slightly different job and at a different level; Dawn Primarolo (for whom the same applies); and John Prescott, who has kept the titles of Deputy Prime Minister and First Secretary of State since 1997, but whose departmental responsibilities have changed on several occasions.

17 For example, Joe Harper was a whip for nearly ten years in total from 1964–70 and 1974–78 (he died in office), and the legendary Walter Harrison was a whip for 9½ years from 1966–70 and 1974–79. There's also William Whiteley, a government whip for 8½ years from 1929–31 and 1945–51, a figure that rises to 13½ if you also include his service in the wartime coalition.

18 In fact, the description – in Philip Cowley, *Revolts and Rebellions: Parliamentary Voting under Blair* (Politico's, London, 2002), p. 151 – did not identify him as its target, and merely reported other MPs saying that there was 'a whip' who was a 'Catholic Stalinist thug' (presumably a dictatorial bully who felt guilty about it afterwards). It didn't take people too long to work out who was being referred to.

### Office without power?

1 Sixteen retired, nine were defeated in the election, one has died, and one – George Galloway – left the party.

2 'She would have made herself so fucking difficult,' said one grudgingly.

3 Kenneth Baker, *The Turbulent Years: My Life in Politics* (Faber and Faber, London, 1993), p. 330.

4 Alan Clark, *Diaries* (Phoenix, 1994), p. 295.

5 There were just 35 backbench revolts in total.

6 On Burns Night in 1978, the government went down to defeat over an amendment which insisted that if less than 40 per cent of the those entitled to vote in a devolution referendum voted yes, then the Scotland Act would be repealed – and devolution scrapped – even if the majority of those voting in the referendum had backed devolution. Various attempts to reverse that decision were made by the government but the Labour rebels stood firm, rebuffing all attempts to repeal or amend the 40 per cent rule and causing a string of government defeats in the process. Arcane as it may sound, the 40 per cent rule was a matter of real importance. A narrow majority of Scots to vote in 1979 supported devolution and the establishment of a Scottish Assembly. But because the turnout was relatively low, those voting in favour constituted just 32.9 per cent of the Scottish electorate. As a result of the 40

per cent clause, the Scotland Act was therefore repealed, and Scottish devolution was postponed by two decades. In response, the Scottish Nationalists withdrew their support for the government – support which Callaghan needed to continue – and the government fell later the same year.

7 Andrew Rawnsley, 'Duelling monarchs of Downing Street', *Observer*, 18 May 2003.

8 Given how vague the labels are, it's difficult to do this exercise with any certainty – but a pre-election analysis by the BBC's Research and Analysis Unit estimated around 50 Brownites and just under 50 Blairites. That left around 300 MPs (around three-quarters of the PLP) who were members of neither faction. Other estimates might put the figures slightly higher or lower – but not by much.

## Appendix 2

1 There is one other problem with the various web-based sources on MPs' voting. When a party's official line is to abstain, they fail to detect MPs who are breaking their whip to vote on an issue (either for or against). This is usually less of a problem for the government – since it is extremely rare for the government to be neutral on an issue – but it can be a much more serious problem when analysing the behaviour of MPs from opposition parties. And it can prove a problem with government MPs too. It means, for example, that those MPs who participated in the largest revolt of the first session of the 2001 Parliament on Iraq, when the government line was to abstain, are overlooked by such searches.

2 Once on hunting, once on Lords reform.

3 Verso, London, 2001, p. 12.

4 HC Deb, 19 December 2000, cols 207–9.

## Appendix 4

1 Ivor Crewe, '1979–1996', in Anthony Seldon (ed.), *How Tory Governments Fall: The Tory Party in Power since 1783* (Fontana, London, 1996), p. 432.

2 Whilst a backbencher, Howard voted against the party whip on two occasions, both under William Hague's leadership, and both over Northern Ireland, an issue which frequently caused disquiet amongst Conservative MPs during the 1997–2001 Parliament.

3 There were an additional two rebellions between the 2001 election and Duncan Smith becoming leader.

4 A total of 35 Conservatives were absent from the vote. Many newspapers therefore talked of 35 abstentions, even though it was clear that many of these 35 were simply away from the Commons on other business.

5 See, for example, Peter Jones, 'Members of Parliament and Issues of Conscience', in Peter Jones (ed.), *Party, Parliament and Personality*, (Routledge, London, 1995).

6 After hostilities ended, the Conservative leadership appeared to backtrack on their initial support for the government, calling for a public inquiry into the circumstances in which the government chose to go to war – a decision that provoked one Conservative MP to defy his party by voting in a pro-

government direction. Sir Patrick Cormack argued that the Conservative position undermined the integrity of Parliament by suggesting that the Intelligence and Security Committee could not conduct 'a rigorous, honest and open inquiry' into the handling of intelligence on weapons of mass destruction. There were two further, very small, Conservative revolts on Iraq. On 17 May 2004 Douglas Hogg and Tony Baldry were the only two Conservatives to support a Liberal Democrat opposition day motion noting with concern the mistreatment of Iraqi detainees, and on 20 July 2004 David Heathcoat-Amory and Richard Shepherd were the only two Conservatives to support a closure motion at the end of an adjournment debate on the Butler report into British intelligence failings in relation to weapons of mass destruction in Iraq.

7 Two of them, Henry Bellingham and Ann Widdecombe, doing so in a pro-government direction, with the others voting against when the Conservative front bench was abstaining.

8 The last group also includes Ann Winterton; her three dissenting votes do not, however, include the two occasions when she voted against the Conservatives while not in receipt of the party whip. Winterton had the Conservative whip withdrawn on 26 February 2004 for making an inappropriate joke relating to the deaths of Chinese cockle-pickers in Morecambe Bay. While she was not in receipt of the whip, her turnout was 75 per cent, and she voted with the Conservatives on 47 occasions, and against on only two occasions. Winterton had the whip restored on 31 March 2004 after a belated apology for her remarks.

9 See Philip Cowley, *Revolts and Rebellions: Parliamentary Voting under Blair* (Politico's, London, 2002), pp. 204–5. Conservative backbench rebellions between 2001 and 2005 were also smaller on average – by roughly half – than those between 1997 and 2001.

**Appendix 5**

1 Paul Marsden's defection back to Labour, during the Parliament's dying days, shrank the party back to 54 MPs.

2 The raw figures would put Cable higher than this, as he seems to wander into the wrong lobby by mistake occasionally (presumably whilst thinking deep thoughts about fiscal drag or something) – or else is the victim of higher-than-usual Hansard errors.

3 The previous vote on the issue (on 18 March 2002) had seen them split 17/26 against a licensing system.

4 See for example, Philip Cowley and Mark Stuart, 'Sodomy, Slaughter, Sunday Shopping and Seatbelts: Free Votes in the House of Commons 1979–1996', *Party Politics*, 1997.

5 See Philip Cowley, Darren Darcy, Colin Mellors, Jon Neal and Mark Stuart, 'Mr Blair's Loyal Opposition?: The Liberal Democrats in Parliament', *British Elections and Parties Review*, 2001.

6 Letter from Andrew Stunell, Liberal Democrat Chief Whip, *Guardian*, 1 January 2005.

# Index